Thilo Stadelmann

Voice Modeling Methods

Thilo Stadelmann

Voice Modeling Methods

for Automatic Speaker Recognition

Südwestdeutscher Verlag für Hochschulschriften

Impressum/Imprint (nur für Deutschland/ only for Germany)
Bibliografische Information der Deutschen Nationalbibliothek: Die Deutsche Nationalbibliothek verzeichnet diese Publikation in der Deutschen Nationalbibliografie; detaillierte bibliografische Daten sind im Internet über http://dnb.d-nb.de abrufbar.

Alle in diesem Buch genannten Marken und Produktnamen unterliegen warenzeichen-, marken- oder patentrechtlichem Schutz bzw. sind Warenzeichen oder eingetragene Warenzeichen der jeweiligen Inhaber. Die Wiedergabe von Marken, Produktnamen, Gebrauchsnamen, Handelsnamen, Warenbezeichnungen u.s.w. in diesem Werk berechtigt auch ohne besondere Kennzeichnung nicht zu der Annahme, dass solche Namen im Sinne der Warenzeichen- und Markenschutzgesetzgebung als frei zu betrachten wären und daher von jedermann benutzt werden dürften.

Verlag: Südwestdeutscher Verlag für Hochschulschriften Aktiengesellschaft & Co. KG
Dudweiler Landstr. 99, 66123 Saarbrücken, Deutschland
Telefon +49 681 37 20 271-1, Telefax +49 681 37 20 271-0
Email: info@svh-verlag.de
Zugl.: Marburg, Uni, Diss., 2010

Herstellung in Deutschland:
Schaltungsdienst Lange o.H.G., Berlin
Books on Demand GmbH, Norderstedt
Reha GmbH, Saarbrücken
Amazon Distribution GmbH, Leipzig
ISBN: 978-3-8381-1632-7

Imprint (only for USA, GB)
Bibliographic information published by the Deutsche Nationalbibliothek: The Deutsche Nationalbibliothek lists this publication in the Deutsche Nationalbibliografie; detailed bibliographic data are available in the Internet at http://dnb.d-nb.de.

Any brand names and product names mentioned in this book are subject to trademark, brand or patent protection and are trademarks or registered trademarks of their respective holders. The use of brand names, product names, common names, trade names, product descriptions etc. even without a particular marking in this works is in no way to be construed to mean that such names may be regarded as unrestricted in respect of trademark and brand protection legislation and could thus be used by anyone.

Publisher: Südwestdeutscher Verlag für Hochschulschriften Aktiengesellschaft & Co. KG
Dudweiler Landstr. 99, 66123 Saarbrücken, Germany
Phone +49 681 37 20 271-1, Fax +49 681 37 20 271-0
Email: info@svh-verlag.de

Printed in the U.S.A.
Printed in the U.K. by (see last page)
ISBN: 978-3-8381-1632-7

Copyright © 2010 by the author and Südwestdeutscher Verlag für Hochschulschriften Aktiengesellschaft & Co. KG and licensors
All rights reserved. Saarbrücken 2010

Abstract

Building a voice model means to capture the characteristics of a speaker's voice in a data structure. This data structure is then used by a computer for further processing, such as comparison with other voices. Voice modeling is a vital step in the process of automatic speaker recognition that itself is the foundation of several applied technologies: (a) biometric authentication, (b) speech recognition and (c) multimedia indexing.

Several challenges arise in the context of automatic speaker recognition. First, there is the problem of data shortage, i.e., the unavailability of sufficiently long utterances for speaker recognition. It stems from the fact that the speech signal conveys different aspects of the sound in a single, one-dimensional time series: linguistic (what is said?), prosodic (how is it said?), individual (who said it?), locational (where is the speaker?) and emotional features of the speech sound itself (to name a few) are contained in the speech signal, as well as acoustic background information. To analyze a specific aspect of the sound regardless of the other aspects, analysis methods have to be applied to a specific time scale (length) of the signal in which this aspect stands out of the rest. For example, linguistic information (i.e., which phone or syllable has been uttered?) is found in very short time spans of only milliseconds of length. On the contrary, speaker-specific information emerges the better the longer the analyzed sound is. Long utterances, however, are not always available for analysis.

Second, the speech signal is easily corrupted by background sound sources (noise, such as music or sound effects). Their characteristics tend to dominate a voice model, if present, such that model comparison might then be mainly due to background features instead of speaker characteristics.

Current automatic speaker recognition works well under relatively constrained circumstances, such as studio recordings, or when prior knowledge on the number and identity of occurring speakers is available. Under more adverse conditions, such as in feature films or amateur material on the web, the achieved speaker recognition scores drop below a rate that is acceptable for an end user or for further processing. For example, the typical speaker turn duration of only one second and the sound effect background in cinematic movies render most current automatic analysis techniques useless.

In this book, methods for voice modeling that are robust with respect to short utterances and background noise are presented. The aim is to facilitate movie analysis with respect to occurring speakers. Therefore, algorithmic improvements are suggested that (a) improve the modeling of very short utterances, (b) facilitate voice model building even in the case of severe background noise and (c) allow for efficient voice model comparison to support the indexing of large multimedia archives. The proposed methods improve the state of the art in terms of recognition rate and computational efficiency.

Going beyond selective algorithmic improvements, subsequent chapters also investigate the question of what is lacking *in principle* in current voice modeling methods. By reporting on a study with human probands, it is shown that the exclusion of time coherence information from a voice model induces an artificial upper bound on the recognition accuracy of automatic analysis methods. A proof-of-concept implementation confirms the usefulness of exploiting this kind of information by halving the error rate. This result questions the general speaker modeling paradigm of the last two decades and presents a promising new way.

The approach taken to arrive at the previous results is based on a novel methodology of algorithm design and development called "eidetic design". It uses a human-in-the-loop technique that analyses existing algorithms in terms of their abstract intermediate results. The aim is to detect flaws or failures in them intuitively and to suggest solutions. The intermediate results often consist of large matrices of numbers whose meaning is not clear to a human observer. Therefore, the core of the approach is to transform them to a suitable domain of perception (such as, e.g., the auditory domain of speech sounds in case of speech feature vectors) where their content, meaning and flaws are intuitively clear to the human designer. This methodology is formalized, and the corresponding workflow is explicated by several use cases.

Finally, the use of the proposed methods in video analysis and retrieval are presented. This shows the applicability of the developed methods and the accompanying software library `sclib` by means of improved results using a multimodal analysis approach. The `sclib`'s source code is available to the public upon request to the author. A summary of the contributions together with an outlook to short- and long-term future work concludes this book.

Acknowledgements

God my father, I am just starting to discover how much you have given me with your love. I am excited to learn to live in this reality. It is so much more than the tangible blessings that I have also received beyond all measure. I am so glad. That this work has ended up well was out of range of what I could do on my own. In the name of your son Jesus—

Soli deo gloria.

When I look back, several people have influenced and supported the way that finally lead here—to this book that constitutes my Ph.D. thesis. Naturally, it starts with thanksgiving to the parents. Dorli and Helge, I love you. To highlight one issue, you endured having a nerdy son and waited patiently until it settled. Thank you for being parents and having become friends. I also thank my friends. If you are reading this just because you know me, I probably mean you. Your friendship formed me during the last 5 and a half years, while this work just earned my living (ok, it also sanded my personality, was immensely interesting and provided the basis for the job I wanted to do).

My dad had one of those first laptop computers in the beginning of the 1990s. My uncle Klaus introduced me to its usage, and when it went out of business, it was Manfred von Torklus who assembled my first PC out of the laptop's single components. This started the fever. Sacht [1988] introduced me to programming. I bought the book for 1 DM in a second-hand book shop and read it during the one week of illness that my oral surgeon provided. Though I even did not understand the concept of a loop then, it had quite an impact. It lead to that nerdy interlude and me studying computer science together with my friends, Daniel and Tobias Webelsiep. Professors Aris Christidis from the Giessen-Friedberg University of Applied Sciences, and Bernhard Seeger of Marburg University encouraged me to pursue a Ph.D. when my hunger for deeper understanding emerged and I was discontent with a future of mere standard software development, yet unsure of my capabilities. What they taught me was that "if you are really curious for [research/a Ph.D./a certain job/fill in your favorite challenge here], then you will make it". Meanwhile I tested this rule of thumb several times on my own and others (students, preferably), and it works reliably.

It was Martin Schwalb who introduced me to the Distributed Systems Group in Marburg and the multimedia analysis project conducted by Dr. Ralph Ewerth and Professor Bernd Freisleben. I wrote my diploma (M.Sc.) thesis in this context and afterwards extended the work to produce this dissertation. Ralph, thank you for supervising my diploma thesis even if it did not earn you a paper directly. Especially, thank you for the last weeks. Bernd, thank you very much for giving me the opportunity to pursue Ph.D. research by supervising my thesis and giving me a job. Thank you for the support with all the formalities, the correction suggestions and the casual talks about how to go on. I profited a lot from them, and I am very thankful for how uncomplicated and fast the finish has been. I also always felt absolutely safe economically in the world of usually unsafe, fast-switching research assistant contracts. Thanks go also to the Deutsche Forschungsgemeinschaft (German Research Foundation) for providing funding in the context of SFB/FK615 "Media Upheavels", Project MT.

Last October, the ACM Multimedia 2009 conference made a deep impression on me. For the first time, I had a sense of belonging to a larger community of researchers in the same area. It substantially changed my view of research. Thank you, ACM-MM organizers, and thanks to the special people who broadened my scope and strengthened my self-confidence there: Gerald Friedland of ICSI, Roeland Ordelman of Twente Unversity, Martha Larson of Amsterdam Unversity and Xavier Anguera Miró of Telefonica.

I am a collaborative person. I cannot develop an idea until I have the opportunity to talk about it, thereby sharpening the thoughts in the course of exchanging arguments. I thank those people without whose help in this direction I would not have developed one usable idea: foremost, thanks go to Anne and Martin Schwalb. Schmärt, no one compares to you as a discussion partner for computer science problems. Christian Schridde and Ralph Ewerth also sacrificed a lot of time listening to my problems and ideas, then patiently helped to get them right. Professors Angelika Braun and Hermann J. Künzel helped me gaining insight into a phonetician's viewpoint. Professors Alfred Ultsch and Eyke Hüllermeier helped in solving the AMU mystery introduced later in Chapter 4. Professor Hüllermeier suggested the "or" variant in the AMU's equations, and Dr. Timothy J. Hazen of MIT (and 3 anonymous reviewers) provided very insightful comments on the way towards solving the MixMax/MFCC puzzle, especially by suggesting a competitive baseline approach. This would not have helped without the support of Wei-Ho "Wesley" Tsai, who provided the source code and data of his singer-recognition experiment and discussed its potential drawbacks with me. Thank you very much!

The study presented in Chapter 6 was only possible because of a group of selfless probands who where willing to invest 1.5 hours of their time in my potential success. Kay, Micha, Mika, Renate, Roland, Tobi, Christian, Ernst, Andrea, Markus, Caro, Ralph, Heidi, Helmut, Dominik, Doro, Rudolph, Anne, Alex and Heiko, I thank you a lot, also for behaving as I expected (though not presumed ;-). The writeup then profited from the shepherding of Zhengyou Zhang from Microsoft Corporation, and the whole idea emerged from a pleasureful telephone call to C. Gregor van den Boogaart of Augsburg University.

I want to give special thanks to some (former) colleagues: Mustafa, Matthew, Dominik, Markus and Steffen, your comradeship meant and means a lot to me. It is one thing to be nice at work, and another thing to invest into a relationship. Thank you for being more than colleagues. Mustafa, you improved my English more than any other teacher (maybe excluding my former teacher, Mrs. Stomps). Matthew, I enjoyed Canne de Combat with you very much! Dominik, I hope our families stay in contact, we met too seldom. Markus, you always helped and supported me, and you looked up all those stuff from my office bookshelf while I worked at home. Steffen, jamming together really was an event. Thank you!

Bernd, Schmärt, Steffen, Markus, Ernst, Dominik and Renate, thank you for proofreading (parts of) this book. Katrin Martin and SVH, thank you for publishing the book and managing everything so efficiently.

Finally, Renate, I want to thank you for the hours, days and weeks you spared me to finish this work. I am looking forward to marry you as soon as possible (which will be very soon) and to be united with you for the rest of our lives. I love you, my dear, and I am excited to be part of this team with you for god.

Contents

1 Introduction   **13**
- 1.1 Prologue 13
- 1.2 Motivation 14
- 1.3 Problem Statement 15
- 1.4 Contributions 16
- 1.5 Publications 18
- 1.6 Organization of this Book 20

2 Fundamentals   **23**
- 2.1 Introduction 23
- 2.2 Automatic Speaker Recognition 24
  - 2.2.1 Goals and Challenges 25
  - 2.2.2 Insights from Forensic Phonetics 26
- 2.3 Speech Production and Perception 27
  - 2.3.1 The Source–Filter Theory of Speech Production 28
  - 2.3.2 The Auditory System 29
  - 2.3.3 Insights from Psychoacoustics 31
    - Phase Locking 31
    - Temporal Processing 31
    - Masking 32
    - The Organization of Perception 32
    - A Special Speech Mode? 33
    - Speech Perception Theory 33
- 2.4 The Speech Signal 33
  - 2.4.1 From Signal to Samples 34
    - The Waveform and Frame-Based Processing 34
    - The Fractal Nature of Speech 35

Contents

	2.4.2	Signal Processing	35
		The Spectrum	36
		The Spectrogram	37
	2.4.3	Nonlinear and Non-Stationary Speech Processing	38
2.5	Pattern Recognition Basics	39
	2.5.1	Statistical Pattern Recognition	40
	2.5.2	The Normal Distribution	40
	2.5.3	Likelihoods	42
	2.5.4	Numerical Stability in Software Implementations	43
	2.5.5	Unsupervised Machine Learning	44
	2.5.6	Supervised Machine Learning	44
	2.5.7	Statistical Tests	46
2.6	The Pattern Recognition Process	46
	2.6.1	Preprocessing	47
	2.6.2	Feature Extraction	48
		Mel Frequency Cepstral Coefficients	48
		Linear Predictive Coding	49
		Time-Domain Features	50
		Pitch and Formants	50
		Phase Features	51
		Human Used Features	52
	2.6.3	Modeling	53
		The Gaussian Mixture Model	53
		Other Voice Models	55
	2.6.4	Recognition	55
		Distance Computation	56
		Decision Making	56
		Figures of Merit	58
2.7	A Complete Speaker Identification System	58
	2.7.1	A Classic System and Setup	59
	2.7.2	The State of the Art	60
2.8	Speaker Change Detection	61
	2.8.1	BIC-Based Segmentation	61
	2.8.2	Promising New Ways	64
2.9	Current Trends in Audio Processing	66
2.10	Summary	66

Contents

3 Short Utterance-Tolerant Voice Models   **69**
- 3.1 Introduction 69
- 3.2 Feature Distributions 70
- 3.3 The Dimension-Decoupled GMM 72
- 3.4 Experimental Results 73
- 3.5 Conclusions 75

4 Noise Robust Modeling   **77**
- 4.1 Introduction 77
- 4.2 The MixMax Idea 78
- 4.3 Definition of the MixMax Model 79
  - 4.3.1 Model Training 80
  - 4.3.2 Model Evaluation 81
- 4.4 MixMax and MFCC Feature Vectors 82
- 4.5 Explaining Good Results Using "MixMax" and MFCCs 82
  - 4.5.1 The Actual Model Used 84
  - 4.5.2 Experimentation 85
    - Databases 85
    - Experiments Confirming the AMU's General Suitability 87
    - Experiments Indicating the AMU's "True" Identity 88
  - 4.5.3 Discussion 90
- 4.6 Proving the MixMax' Ineptness for Cepstral Features 93
- 4.7 Conclusions 95

5 Fast and Robust Model Comparison   **97**
- 5.1 Introduction 97
- 5.2 A New Approach to Speaker Clustering 98
  - 5.2.1 Parameter-Based Comparison 99
  - 5.2.2 The Earth Mover's Distance 100
  - 5.2.3 Using the EMD for Speaker Clustering 101
- 5.3 Experimental Results 102
- 5.4 Conclusions 104

6 Modeling Temporal Aspects of a Voice   **107**
- 6.1 Introduction 107
- 6.2 Analyzing the Process 110
  - 6.2.1 Motivation 110
  - 6.2.2 Design 111

Contents

		6.2.3	Results 113

        6.2.3 Results 113
                Quantitative Results 113
                Quantity as Expressed in Common Figures of Merit 115
                Qualitative Results 117
  6.3 Harnessing the Results 119
        6.3.1 Interpretation 119
        6.3.2 Discussion 121
  6.4 Implementation and Results 122
  6.5 Conclusions 125

7 Perceptually Motivated Algorithm Design   127

  7.1 Introduction 127
  7.2 A Methodology for Speech Research & Development 128
        7.2.1 Problem Refinement 129
        7.2.2 The Proposed Methodology and Workflow 130
        7.2.3 A Case Study 133
  7.3 Tool Support 135
        7.3.1 Resynthesis 135
                Related Work 135
                A New Resynthesis Framework 136
        7.3.2 WebVoice 138
                Service-Oriented Deployment 138
                The Interface 140
        7.3.3 PlotGMM 142
  7.4 Conclusions 144

8 Implementation and Integration   147

  8.1 Introduction 147
  8.2 The sclib Class Library 148
        8.2.1 Content 149
                Signal Analysis 149
                Feature Extraction 149
                Modeling 150
                Classification 151
                Segmentation 151
        8.2.2 Design Principles 152
        8.2.3 Workflows 153

8.3	Integration	153
	8.3.1 Videana and the Grid	154
	8.3.2 Code Wrapping	155
	8.3.3 A Service-Oriented Architecture for Multimedia Analysis	158
8.4	Conclusions	159

9 Application to Video Content Analysis and Retrieval   161

9.1	Introduction	161
9.2	Semantic Video Analysis in Psychological Research	162
	9.2.1 Background	162
	9.2.2 Audio Type Classification	164
	9.2.3 Results	165
9.3	The TRECVid Evaluations	166
	9.3.1 Rushes Summarization and Retrieval	166
	9.3.2 Semantic Concept Detection	168
9.4	Discussion	170
9.5	Conclusions	171

10 Conclusions   173

10.1 Summary	173
10.2 Tactical Prospects	175
10.3 Strategic Prospects	176
10.4 Epilogue	177

A Additional Material for the Human Speaker Grouping Study   181

A.1 Introduction	181
A.2 Experimental Instructions: Speaker Grouping	181
A.3 Assessment Sheet	185
A.4 Individual Participant's Results	189

List of Figures   193

List of Tables   197

List of Listings   198

Bibliography   200

*"Pitch your demands heaven-high and they'll be met.
Ask for the Morning Star and take (thrown in)
Your earthly love."*

Clive Staples Lewis (1898–1963)

1 Introduction

1.1 Prologue

It is said that the first sentence in a work of writing matters the most. However, thinking about a suitable introduction, I am reminded of a conversation I had numerous times in the last $5\frac{1}{2}$ years... it usually starts like this: *oh, nice—what do you work on?*

It's about speaker recognition.

No, not speech recognition. Speaker recognition, the identification of a person based on his or her voice.

Specifically, automatic speaker recognition, using a software system to be created for a standard computer.

More specifically, about what makes up a voice from a technical perspective, and how this essence can be captured by some "model" inside the software.

Even more specifically, about voice models that still work under "real world" conditions as encountered, for example, in movies. For a software system, these conditions are really "adverse

Chapter 1. Introduction

conditions", so they need some special care.

You need it for... imagine you have a fancy, intelligent new video recorder, and load the DVD of *Terminator 2—Judgment Day*. Then you tell'em to jump to the scene where Arnold says *"Hasta la vista, baby!"*. If the recorder recognizes that this sentence has been spoken by Arnold Schwarzenegger, it is probably a technology inside that is related to the methods described in this book.

The topic of this book is quite easy to convey even to laypersons, given that it is anyhow concerned with state-of-the-art basic and applied research in a field not encountered everyday by everybody. It is, however, far more difficult to explain the reasons for such methods to be useful and for their development to be necessary. This is why the motivation of this book got its own section (it is in this next section that the serious text starts, too).

A word of purpose: in large parts, this book resembles my Ph.D. thesis. This means that its primary purpose is to be a concise, precise scientific treatise of a research topic, written in scholarly style. The fundamentals chapter, the introduction of the `sclib` software library or the method of "eidetic design" however can be of considerable interest also in education and practice. The strategic outlook may even be of value to executives. Enjoy!

1.2 Motivation

This work is motivated (and has been launched) by the project *Methods and Tools for Computer-Assisted Scientific Media Research* (MT). It is part of the cultural sciences' research center *Media Upheavals* (SFB/FK 615) colocated at the universities of Siegen and Marburg and funded by the German Research Foundation (DFG). While the research center's goal is to analyze the great media upheavals at the gates of the 20th and the 21st century (marked by the introduction of cinema and the Internet, respectively), MT's aim is to provide a comprehensive video analysis platform for those projects within the research alliance that perform scientific film studies.

The developed video analysis workbench `Videana` supports all aspects of quantitative film analysis that are amenable to automated extraction. One of these aspects is the detection and subsequent recognition of persons in a video. This can also be performed in the visual domain based on, for example, faces [Ewerth et al. 2007a] and in the audio domain based on the voice. The data collection of the research center ranges from early cinematic work to contemporary mixed-reality movies. Only the latter ones are relevant to the task of audio analysis and speaker recognition, because the former ones are usually silent films.

Voice modeling thus is the topic of this book as it is central to the task of automatic speaker recognition. The scope of the sought methods is thereby set by the research center's data collection: speaker recognition on this kind of material is a high goal, by far unmatched by current automatic speaker recognition systems. In this sense it is rather a destination to be approached than an ultimate yardstick of success. It is the primary motivation and one of the areas of application of this book's content.

There are several other areas that benefit from improved voice modeling methods and thus contribute to the motivation. The ever increasing availability of multimedia documents on the Internet and the corresponding need for automatic indexing and retrieval in order to overcome the information overdose has been stressed a lot recently and needs no further comment nor explanation. It, however, creates a market for intelligent search engines on the web or video recorders at home that support users in their professional and leisure activities. At the other end of the application range are tasks of voice biometrics for access control and applications in surveillance and forensics.

1.3 Problem Statement

The ultimate goal of movie analysis mentioned in the previous section demands *robust* voice modeling methods. This is due to data being characterized by the following properties: cinematic works convey conversational speech including emotions and transient exclamations. Additionally, dialogs are often underlaid with highly variable sound effects as well as with music. In contrast to typically analyzed broadcast news and telephone speech (which have their own challenges like channel and handset mismatch), movie soundtracks can best be characterized as being *unconstrained*.

This directly leads to two specific problems for voice modeling for automatic speaker recognition:

1. **Short utterances**. Any speaker recognition system working under the described circumstances needs to take specific care of coping with short utterances in the range of (and below) 1 second of speech. Achieving this goal would be a considerable improvement: typically, 30–100 seconds of speech are regarded as necessary for the characterization of a voice, and the best current systems work with at least 7–10 seconds.

2. **Background noise**. Methods have to be robust against background noise, whether by removing interfering influences prior to modeling or building a model that ignores disturbances. Achieving this goal might require using speech enhancement methods, while typical speaker recognition-related literature primarily focuses on the noises present during telephone transmissions and proposes handset- and channel normalization techniques.

The following problem is a subordinate problem, yet an omnipresent goal in every pattern recognition system aimed to be useful in real applications employed by real users on real

Chapter 1. Introduction

computers:

3. **Computationally efficient software.** Speed of processing is crucial because desktop computers of media scientists have limited resources, and the audio-visual analysis of complete corpora of film quickly becomes very time-consuming due to the sheer number of different analysis algorithms. Additionally, because the proposed methods are directly linked to an application scenario and a customer, stable implementations in carefully designed and maintainable software are sought. Achieving this goal means to optimize certain algorithmic steps for efficiency as well as providing infrastructures for distributed computing. It includes writing reusable code rather than implementing a mere research tool.

The all-embracing question behind the surface is:

4. **Bottlenecks for improvement.** State-of-the-art automatic speaker recognition, especially in the subfield of operating on audio streams without any additional prior knowledge, work considerably less satisfactory from a human point of view than expected. Achieving this goal means to determine the limiting factors and to propose solutions beyond beaten tracks.

1.4 Contributions

This book makes the following contributions to advance the scientific state of the art:

- A novel voice modeling technique is proposed to address the problem of small sets of training- and evaluation data. This is achieved by reducing the number of necessary free parameters in a conventional model with the aim of obtaining more stable statistical estimates of model parameters and likelihoods. The model shows improved recognition accuracy with less data, is computationally more efficient and can easily be combined with other short utterance approaches proposed in the literature. This contribution is presented in Chapter 3.

- An in-depth discussion is given of the suitability of a common noise-robust voice model in a certain environment, inspired by contradicting views expressed in several recent publications. The contradictions are dissolved by experiments, arguments and proofs. This has an impact on the state of the art in automatic singer recognition. Additionally, small errors in the corpus of the model's training equations are corrected. This contribution is presented in Chapter 4.

1.4. Contributions

- A novel approach to speaker clustering is proposed that improves its speed and robustness. The basic idea to achieve speed of processing is to compare parametric speaker models directly based on their estimated parameters using a first-time application of a suitable distance measure from the image retrieval domain to speech data. To achieve robustness in the presence of noise, a method is proposed to use the distance measure in conjunction with the noise cancellation scheme mentioned in the previous paragraph. Experimental results show competitive accuracy, enhanced robustness and an improvement in speed by a factor of 120. This contribution is presented in Chapter 5.

- An experimental setting is proposed to find the bottleneck in the process of current speaker clustering methods. The result implies that improving other parts of the processing chain will probably not show the full potential of that improvement. Then, it is stated explicitly how speaker clustering can be improved qualitatively by exploiting time coherence information. An implementation of a speaker clustering system is presented that experimentally supports these claims by improving existing results by more than 50%. This contribution is presented in Chapter 6.

- A methodology for speech processing research and development is conceptualized that systemizes the search for hypotheses about the reasons of unexpected algorithmic behavior. Based on this methodology, a set of tools is introduced that facilitates the proposed workflow. These tools comprise a novel algorithmic framework for audio resynthesis as well as new service-oriented ways to deploy the software. This contribution is presented in Chapter 7.

- A class library has been developed in the course of this book and is introduced as a novel toolkit for speaker recognition. It fills the void of missing public- and open-source speaker recognition software and contains most of all state-of-the-art algorithms. Using the example of the `sclib`, several software engineering concepts for the integration within service-oriented architectures are introduced. They have been developed in collaboration with researchers from the Distributed Systems Group in Marburg. This contribution is presented in Chapter 8.

- An extended audio type classification algorithm is proposed together with its application to video content analysis, summarization and retrieval. The multimodal analysis approach has been developed in cooperation with other parts of the MT project and shows competitive performance in the annual TRECVid evaluations as well as in interdisciplinary psychological research. This contribution is presented in Chapter 9.

Additionally, the introductory Chapter 2 gives a unique composition of valuable clues for speaker recognition from relevant disciplines. Some of these clues have played a role in the contributions mentioned above, but overall the given survey contains the potential for even more promising research ideas.

1.5 Publications

Several papers have been published in the course of the research leading to this book:

Thilo Stadelmann, Yinghui Wang, Matthew Smith, Ralph Ewerth, and Bernd Freisleben. Rethinking Algorithm Development and Design in Speech Processing. In *Proceedings of the 20th International Conference on Pattern Recognition (ICPR'10)*, accepted for publication, Istanbul, Turkey, August 2010. IAPR.

Thilo Stadelmann and Bernd Freisleben. On the MixMax Model and Cepstral Features for Noise-Robust Voice Recognition. Technical report, University of Marburg, Marburg, Germany, July 2010a.

Thilo Stadelmann and Bernd Freisleben. Dimension-Decoupled Gaussian Mixture Model for Short Utterance Speaker Recognition. In *Proceedings of the 20th International Conference on Pattern Recognition (ICPR'10)*, accepted for publication, Istanbul, Turkey, August 2010b. IAPR.

Markus Mühling, Ralph Ewerth, Thilo Stadelmann, Bing Shi, and Bernd Freisleben. University of Marburg at TRECVID 2009: High-Level Feature Extraction. In *Proceedings of TREC Video Retrieval Evaluation Workshop (TRECVid'09)*. Available online, 2009. URL http://www-nlpir.nist.gov/projects/tvpubs/tv.pubs.org.htm.

Ernst Juhnke, Dominik Seiler, Thilo Stadelmann, Tim Dörnemann, and Bernd Freisleben. LCDL: An Extensible Framework for Wrapping Legacy Code. In *Proceedings of International Workshop on @WAS Emerging Research Projects, Applications and Services (ERPAS'09)*, pages 638–642, Kuala Lumpur, Malaysia, December 2009.

Dominik Seiler, Ralph Ewerth, Steffen Heinzl, Thilo Stadelmann, Markus Mühling, Bernd Freisleben, and Manfred Grauer. Eine Service-Orientierte Grid-Infrastruktur zur Unterstützung Medienwissenschaftlicher Filmanalyse. In *Proceedings of the Workshop on Gemeinschaften in Neuen Medien (GeNeMe'09)*, pages 79–89, Dresden, Germany, September 2009.

Thilo Stadelmann and Bernd Freisleben. Unfolding Speaker Clustering Potential: A Biomimetic Approach. In *Proceedings of the ACM International Conference on Multimedia (ACMMM'09)*, pages 185–194, Beijing, China, October 2009. ACM.

Thilo Stadelmann, Steffen Heinzl, Markus Unterberger, and Bernd Freisleben. WebVoice: A Toolkit for Perceptual Insights into Speech Processing. In *Proceedings of the 2nd International Congress on Image and Signal Processing (CISP'09)*, pages 4358–4362, Tianjin, China, October 2009.

Steffen Heinzl, Markus Mathes, Thilo Stadelmann, Dominik Seiler, Marcel Diegelmann, Helmut Dohmann, and Bernd Freisleben. The Web Service Browser: Automatic Client Generation and Efficient Data Transfer for Web Services. In *Proceedings of the 7th IEEE International Conference on Web Services (ICWS'09)*, pages 743–750, Los Angeles, CA, USA, July 2009a. IEEE Press.

Steffen Heinzl, Dominik Seiler, Ernst Juhnke, Thilo Stadelmann, Ralph Ewerth, Manfred Grauer, and Bernd Freisleben. A Scalable Service-Oriented Architecture for Multimedia Analysis, Synthesis, and Consumption. *International Journal of Web and Grid Services*, 5 (3):219–260, 2009b. Inderscience Publishers.

Markus Mühling, Ralph Ewerth, Thilo Stadelmann, Bing Shi, and Bernd Freisleben. University of Marburg at TRECVID 2008: High-Level Feature Extraction. In *Proceedings of TREC Video Retrieval Evaluation Workshop (TRECVid'08)*. Available online, 2008. URL http://www-nlpir.nist.gov/projects/tvpubs/tv.pubs.org.htm.

Markus Mühling, Ralph Ewerth, Thilo Stadelmann, Bing Shi, Christian Zöfel, and Bernd Freisleben. University of Marburg at TRECVID 2007: Shot Boundary Detection and High-Level Feature Extraction. In *Proceedings of TREC Video Retrieval Evaluation Workshop (TRECVid'07)*. Available online, 2007a. URL http://www-nlpir.nist.gov/projects/tvpubs/tv.pubs.org.htm.

Ralph Ewerth, Markus Mühling, Thilo Stadelmann, Julinda Gllavata, Manfred Grauer, and Bernd Freisleben. Videana: A Software Toolkit for Scientific Film Studies. In *Proceedings of the International Workshop on Digital Tools in Film Studies*, pages 1–16, Siegen, Germany, 2007. Transcript Verlag.

Markus Mühling, Ralph Ewerth, Thilo Stadelmann, Bernd Freisleben, Rene Weber, and Klaus Mathiak. Semantic Video Analysis for Psychological Research on Violence in Computer Games. In *Proceedings of the ACM International Conference on Image and Video Retrieval (CIVR'07)*, pages 611–618, Amsterdam, The Netherlands, July 2007b. ACM.

Ralph Ewerth, Markus Mühling, Thilo Stadelmann, Ermir Qeli, Björn Agel, Dominik Seiler, and Bernd Freisleben. University of Marburg at TRECVID 2006: Shot Boundary Detection and Rushes Task Results. In *Proceedings of TREC Video Retrieval Evaluation Workshop (TRECVid'06)*. Available online, 2006. URL http://www-nlpir.nist.gov/projects/tvpubs/tv.pubs.org.htm.

Thilo Stadelmann and Bernd Freisleben. Fast and Robust Speaker Clustering Using the Earth Mover's Distance and MixMax Models. In *Proceedings of the 31st IEEE International Conference on Acoustics, Speech, and Signal Processing (ICASSP'06)*, volume 1, pages 989–992, Toulouse, France, April 2006. IEEE.

Ralph Ewerth, Christian Behringer, Tobias Kopp, Michael Niebergall, Thilo Stadelmann, and Bernd Freisleben. University of Marburg at TRECVID 2005: Shot Boundary Detection and Camera Motion Estimation Results. In *Proceedings of TREC Video Retrieval Evaluation Workshop (TRECVid'05)*. Available online, 2005. URL http://www-nlpir.nist.gov/projects/tvpubs/tv.pubs.org.htm.

1.6 Organization of this Book

The remainder of this book is organized as follows:

Chapter 2 introduces the fundamental concepts and methods used as building blocks in the following chapters. The focus of this chapter is to foster understanding rather than giving an encyclopedic summary of definitions and equations. Instead, it gives reference to important and valuable works from the literature.

The algorithmic contributions of this book start in Chapter 3:

Chapter 3 introduces a voice model specifically aimed at reliably modeling short speech utterances. This addresses the first part of the problem statement.

Chapter 4 addresses the second part of the problem statement. It discusses an effective method for noise cancellation within the voice model and adjusts its confusing use within the related work.

Chapter 5 proposes a method to compare conventional voice models as well as the previously introduced noise-robust model in a novel, computationally more efficient way. Together with the previous chapter, this addresses part two of the problem statement and additionally part three.

1.6. Organization of this Book

Chapter 6 constitutes the main part of this book by addressing part four of the problem statement. Using an integrated, human-centered approach, the question is answered what the limiting factors in speaker recognition under adverse conditions are. A solution in the form of a novel approach to voice modeling is proposed.

In the following chapters the focus shifts from algorithmic work towards cross-cutting concerns: how can voice models like the proposed ones be conceptualized, implemented and applied?

Chapter 7 reviews the factors leading to initial ideas and final success in the research presented in the previous chapters. Based on this analysis, a methodology for speech processing research, development and education is formulated and supported. This does not address any of the previously given problem statements specifically, but emerged as an unexpected but welcomed by-product.

Chapter 8 presents the implementation of the proposed approaches within the software library `sclib` as well as their integration within service-oriented architectures and the scientific media analysis workbench. This addresses part three of the problem statement.

Chapter 9 reports on the application of the developed methods to multimodal video analysis. This addresses part three of the problem statement.

Chapter 10 concludes this book with a summary of achievements and outlook to promising areas of future work.

Some conventions used throughout this book are noteworthy: abbreviations for common methods are given on first occurrence, which happens most often in the fundamentals chapter, and are then used in the remaining part of this book. Important terms are printed in *italic* font at their first occurrence, and the names of used data sets as well as of research software toolkits are always printed in `typewriter` font. Related work for the specific problems targeted in this book is discussed directly in the context where it arises, and credits for adapted or used pictures are given in conjunction with the list of figures.

Finally, a disclaimer: all company and product names appearing in this book may be the registered trademarks of their respective owners.

*"Do not worry about your problems with mathematics,
I assure you mine are far greater."*

Albert Einstein (1879–1955)

2
Fundamentals

2.1 Introduction

Automatic processing of speech is one of the oldest areas of applied computer science. First works reach back to the 1950's, inspired by the goal of turning computing machinery into general information processing and communication devices, given the weight speech has in human communication and information processing. To study speech has an even longer tradition also in many other scholarly areas. Thus, automatic speech processing is an inherently multidisciplinary field of activity. Many disciplines, areas, fields and niches add to it, and in order to think beyond beaten paths it is important to consider this whole wealth of approaches.

A broad catchment area for ideas fosters interdisciplinary understanding and inspires new research approaches: physiology, psychology, linguistics, phonetics [Ladefoged 2005] and natural language processing play a role by explaining cause and purpose of a voice (here and later in this chapter, references to valuable resources are given whenever appropriate to point to accessible texts for further reading in addition to the necessary quotations). Fundamentals are also contributed by physics (acoustics), signal processing, communication- and information theory as well as mathematics and statistics.

Computer science concentrates these threads in algorithms research, machine learning, pattern recognition and finally speech recognition. Multidisciplinarity thus opens new perspectives—and needs special care. Friedland [2009] recently wrote an article that specifically addresses

Chapter 2. Fundamentals

the issue of communication between speech- and vision researchers within multimodal speech analysis.

This chapter introduces the topics serving as a technical basis for this book as well as being sources of inspiration. It is the aim of this chapter to explain interrelationships and foster a general understanding of the involved methods and their interaction. Detailed algorithmic descriptions and definitions are typically spared due to them being available in the given references.

The introduction of fundamental concepts starts with an overview of the field of (automatic) speaker recognition in Section 2.2: the purpose and direction of all further comments shall be known right from the beginning. Then, the underlying basics are highlighted by first following the way the speech signal takes from its production to perception in humans: the physiological side of speech is presented in Section 2.3 (speech production and perception), and the technical aspects directly related to the corresponding signal are described in Section 2.4 (the speech signal).

Then, details are given on how this signal can be analyzed automatically in order to derive meaning from it: pattern recognition basics are presented in Section 2.5 and the pattern recognition process for speech processing is explained in Section 2.6. Its flow of events is the basic pattern to be recognized in all the algorithms of the remaining chapters, and the main ideas and approaches to voice modeling from the related work are introduced here as well along with their common abbreviations.

The basic concepts introduced so far are then assembled to build a more complete picture: in Section 2.7 (a complete speaker identification system), a use case is given by briefly reviewing a complete system that is referred to in several subsequent chapters. Section 2.8 discusses the important step of speaker change detection and Section 2.9 gives a synopsis of current trends in the audio processing domain before conclusions are drawn in Section 2.10.

2.2 Automatic Speaker Recognition

Speaker recognition, also known as voice recognition, splits into speaker verification, -identification and -clustering. It is the purpose of this section to explain the whys and wherefores of these and other general terms.

Therefore, this section continues as follows: Subsection 2.2.1 presents the goals and challenges in conjunction with automatic speaker recognition. Subsection 2.2.2 then broadens this perspective with insights from manual speaker identification in a law enforcement environment.

2.2.1 Goals and Challenges

Recognizing voices automatically is useful for several applications. For example, it supports biometric authentication [Wu 2006] for security-relevant services like telebanking. This corresponds to the task of *speaker verification* [Reynolds and Rose 1995]: a model is trained for the voice of each authorized person a priori (the *training* phase), and when a speaker demands access to the secured service, his voice is compared with the model corresponding to his additionally given identity claim (the *evaluation-* or *test* phase). Based on the similarity of the current voice to the claimed model, access is granted or the speaker is rejected.

Automatic voice recognition also helps making automatic speech recognition robust [Furui 2005] by adapting learned speech models to a certain speaker. Therefore, all potential speakers are *enrolled* in the system (i.e. models of their voices are trained), and in the evaluation phase the current speaker's voice is compared with all enrolled models. The identity of the model's speaker being most similar to the current voice is returned in this *speaker identification* scenario [Campbell 1997] if the similarity is not below a certain threshold.

Last, automatic voice recognition enables search engines to index spoken documents and thus improves retrieval performance [Makhoul et al. 2000] and surveillance. To this end, first, all speech segments of individual speakers in the audio document have to be identified and segregated from each other and the non-speech content. Then, the number of distinct speakers and their respective segments have to be identified simultaneously through *speaker clustering* [Kotti et al. 2008b], i.e. grouping together the most similar segments until a certain threshold is reached. The complete process of generating this "who spoke when"-index over time of the complete audio document, including the removal of non-speech content, is known as *speaker diarization* [Reynolds and Torres-Carrasquillo 2005].

All three flavors of automatically recognizing a voice are referred to as *speaker recognition*. Historically, speaker recognition is further divided into text dependent and text independent approaches, the former ones playing a role mainly in access control environments within verification and identification scenarios. In this book, speaker recognition is used as the general term, and all presented approaches work text-independently. Sometimes it is referred to speaker identification or -clustering individually if the concrete experimental setting is of importance. Developed models and auxiliary methods are generally applicable to all voice recognition-related tasks, although the details and demands of a specific task make some methods inappropriate in certain contexts (see Chapter 6).

In contrast to *automatic speech recognition* (ASR), that has matured into products of industry strength, automatic speaker recognition is still in its infancy, being an area of basic research. Early work concentrated on analyzing content from broadcast news, where the speech happens in a very controlled environment with long speaker turns, small number of overall speakers and

Chapter 2. Fundamentals

under the absence of interfering noise. In the late 1990's, work in the domain of meeting recordings began, offering additional degrees of freedom with regard to participants' behavior (such as considering cross-talk). The new challenges were met with new technologies like multiple microphones, beam forming and multimodal analysis [Anguera Miró 2006].

Not until recently did the automatic speaker recognition community start analyzing more natural, unconstrained content like movies or general video footage using only such input and sensors that are also available to a human listener. Early results of, for example, Nishida and Kawahara [1999] have not been encouraging. Existing algorithms face two main challenges: limited data, and background noise. Limited data refers to the fact that, for example, in a movie, a typical speech segment has an average length of just 1 second, whereas existing algorithms are designed to work on chunks of data in the range of minimally 3, yet typically 10-30 seconds and more.

Background noise is everything in the acoustic signal that does not belong to a single speech signal. This might be sound effects, accompanying music as well as co-occurring speech, i.e., things that are also omnipresent in amateur videos and in professional, edited material.

2.2.2 Insights from Forensic Phonetics

Forensic phonetics deals with recognizing voices in a law enforcement or law suit environment [Jessen and Jessen 2009]. It relies mainly on the expertise of trained phoneticians who perform the task manually in order to give precise testimonies in the context of often very adverse data conditions but a life-or-death impact of their judgment. This striving for certainty makes insights from this discipline very appealing for new approaches to automatic speaker recognition. A good introduction to the field is given by Rose [2002].

The forensic phonetic process relies very much on the phonetic training of the phonetician, taking into account that an acoustic pattern can only be interpreted if one knows the structure it realizes. Thus, the human analyzer selects comparable acoustic units (e.g., equal vowels) for which a minimum of 30 observations per item is needed for a precise judgment. Then, a semi-automatic process may start that arrives at a final decision via Bayesian inference using *likelihood ratios* with alternative hypothesis [Drygajlo 2007; Rose 2006].

A problem for complete automatic analysis is that the anatomy of the speaker, as the primary carrier of identity, does not correlate with any absolute acoustic values, but only limits their variability. That means there is no simple mapping between acoustic parameters and identity. Additionally, many acoustic parameters (i.e. those features that can be measured automatically) vary more with articulation than with speaker identity.

This uncertainty of acoustic parameters can also be seen in human speaker recognition performance, when only short temporal segments of speech are available: using the single word "hello", probands conducted 26% misjudgments for voices of their inner family circle and 55% error for unfamiliar voices, respectively [Rose 2002, p. 98]. Only by using additional information like language understanding they where able to increase their performance by a factor of 2.

Given these results, a more stable feature for speaker recognition seems to be voice quality, because its features are quasi-permanent within an utterance [p. 280]. Voice quality refers to those components of speech that distinguish voices when pitch and loudness are not regarded, such as harshness, breathiness or nasality [Keating and Esposito 2007]. It can be measured as the deviation from an idealized neutral vocal tract (mouth) configuration [p. 279]. Thereby, the focus should be on individual events in the signal, not on global averages [p. 73].

In forensic phonetic environments, quasi-automatic software solutions like **BATVOX** show optimal behavior with 1 minute of training data and 10 seconds of evaluation data. Results are still usable with 15–30 seconds of training data, whereas 7 seconds define the absolute minimum using technologies and setups based on the ones to be introduced in Section 2.7 [Agnitio S.L. 2008].

A different methodology is proposed by Rahman [2009a,b]: averaged long-term spectra of either 30-40 seconds long speech utterances or just the vowels within are treated like real structures in crystals and are compared using R-factors [Ramsperger 2005]. The method showed some success in German law suits and attracted some attention due to its internals being concealed until lately, but overall it has been reviewed very critically in the community, partly due to several misjudgments in court [Schattauer 2007].

Summarizing the state of the art in automatic processing, Bonastre et al. [2003] conclude with a warning: "at the present time, there is no scientific process that enables one to uniquely characterize a person's voice or to identify with absolute certainty an individual from his or her voice."

2.3 Speech Production and Perception

Up to date, the *source–filter theory* of speech production introduced by Fant [1960] is the unchallenged explanation of how speech comes into existence [Rose 2002, p. 207]. This section gives a brief overview of the technically relevant aspects and related vocabulary of this theory in Section 2.3.1. Then, Section 2.3.2 illustrates the basics of auditory perception, before Section 2.3.3 gives an account of results from the discipline of psychoacoustics with respect to speech perception and voice recognition.

2.3.1 The Source–Filter Theory of Speech Production

According to Fant [1960], the production of speech can be sketched as a two-stage process: in the beginning, a basic signal is produced by the airflow through the vocal cords in the glottis. This is known as the signal *source*. Two distinct types of signal are producible: first, a *voiced* signal that comprises the periodic oscillation of the vocal cords at a certain *fundamental frequency* (F_0). The frequency is determined by anatomy (i.e., the length of vocal cords) as well as will (intended tension). The vibration produces a harmonic signal consisting of multiples of F_0 and corresponding with a periodic tone as in the vowel of the word "wow". Second, an *unvoiced* signal can be produced, where the air is pressed through the (nearly) closed vocal folds, resulting in turbulent airflow and a noise-like signal as in the consonants at the end of the word "hiss".

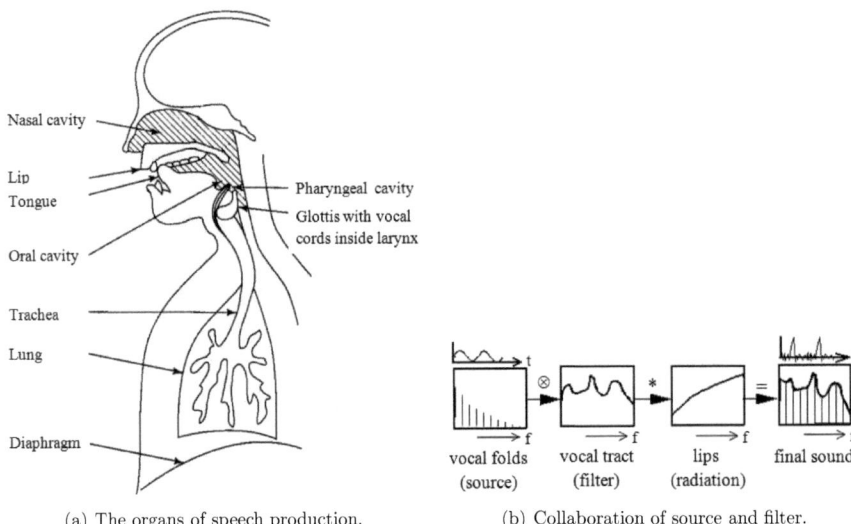

(a) The organs of speech production.   (b) Collaboration of source and filter.

Figure 2.1: Human speech production.

The process and the corresponding organs are depicted in Figure 2.1. Figure 2.1(b) shows the airflow schematically by providing graphs of the spectra and waveforms at each stage (see Section 2.4 for a description of both displays). It can be seen that the source spectrum consists of individual peaks that belong to the fundamental frequency and its *harmonics* (integer multiples). The harmonics are introduced with a spectral slope of 12 dB, i.e., the harmonic at twice the frequency has a 12 dB lower amplitude. The process continues with the glottal source signal proceeding through the *vocal tract*. The vocal tract is the striated area within Figure

2.1(a), i.e., everything above the vocal cords until the end of the lips. It acts like a *filter* with a specific transfer function on the source signal: the (continuous) spectrum of the filter function shapes the (discrete, due to only individual harmonics being present) source's spectrum via *convolution*.

Major peaks in the filter's spectrum are called *formants*: they change with the movement of, for example, the lips and tongue (i.e., with articulatory movements) but are also determined by the anatomy of the throat (e.g., length and width). The formants correspond to the resonance frequencies of the vocal tract. Additional shaping happens to the filtered signal at the lips: via radiation, the high frequencies are amplified as if a first-order difference filter would be applied.

Several hints for speaker recognition can be deduced from this theory: for one, speaker-specific (i.e., anatomy-based) information is found as well in the source- as in the filter information. It can be recovered by measuring both their acoustic correlates. Yet, both sources of information are also controlled in a finite, but wide range by will, so the speaker-specific information can only be extracted by looking at many measurements and observing their statistical distributions.

Another point stemming from speech sounds being anatomy-based is a difference in gender: because men and women have a different physiognomy that results in typical differences, for example, in size, men normally have a lower-pitched voice due to longer vocal cords as well as 20% lower formant center frequencies due to a larger vocal tract.

Finally, it can be noted that speech sounds even from the same speaker inherit a great variability due to the production being based on the smooth (i.e., continuous) movement of organs: first, a single *phoneme* sounds different depending on the previous and next articulatory position, a phenomenon called co-articulation. Here, a phoneme is the smallest unit of a sound that tells two words apart in any given language, in contrast to the *phone*, that is the smallest unit with a difference in sound that does not necessarily result in a difference in meaning. Second, the transition from one phoneme to the next is fluent, without any steady point. Thus, to view speech as a series of distinct patterns that correspond with phonemes is too simplified a model.

Further relevant resources on the speech production process from a technical perspective are provided by Rabiner and Juang [1993] as well as Dellwo et al. [2007].

2.3.2 The Auditory System

Human auditory perception as described by Munkong and Juang [2008] starts with the outer ear (pinna and auditory canal) receiving a sound (called a stimulus) as air pressure variations. The pinna thereby serves in modifying the stimulus such that a sense of direction is made possible. The sound wave then proceeds through the middle ear (composed of the eardrum, the three bones of malleus, stapes and incus and the oval window) that serves as a transducer from the medium of air to a fluid inside the *cochlea*.

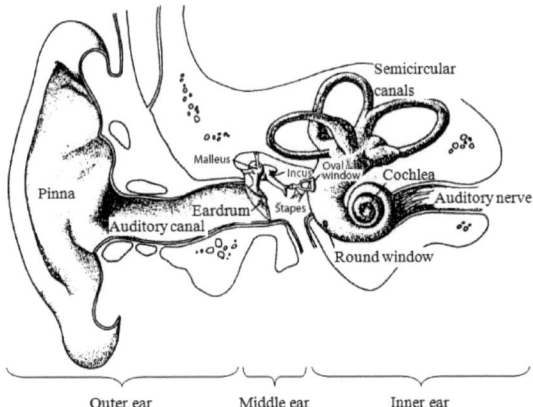

Figure 2.2: The human auditory system.

The cochlea performs some sort of frequency analysis not unlike the wavelet transform: it contains the basilar membrane, and attached to it hair cells that are connected with nerve fibers (neurons) ending in the auditory nerve. Each frequency component of a stimulus (viewed as if composed of pure, sinusoidal tones) passing through the cochlear fluid excites the hair cells at other places along the basilar membrane. Thereby, another transduction takes place from a continuous excitation of the hair cells to bursts of electrical spikes within the neurons, where the information is coded not in the amplitude of the spikes, but in their temporal pattern. Each pure tone stimulus excites not only one hair cell, but a range of them called an "auditory filter", comparable to a filter bank in digital signal processing. Yet, this set of filters is not discrete and seems to assemble just in time such that there is an auditory filter centered at each occurring frequency. The involved organs are depicted in Figure 2.2.

The presented low-level processing makes a very wide range of sensings possible: the frequency range of the auditory system allows for tones between 20–20 000 Hz to be heard. Thereby, differences as small as 3.6 Hz between tones are discernible (even smaller when considering not only frequency- but also phase differences). The dynamic range, i.e., the set of possibly perceivable loudness-values, is also very broad and hence measured in decibel (dB). Decibel is a logarithmic scale of sound pressure ratio to some basic value. Every 10 dB, the perceived loudness doubles as the physical sound power increases tenfold. A normal sound level as in conversations has approximately 65 dB loudness, while a non-impaired ear is able to perceive sounds as quiet as 0 dB (with a regard to some reasonable basic value), but will be impaired if it encounters 120 dB even for a short time.

2.3.3 Insights from Psychoacoustics

Work in the discipline of psychoacoustics suggests that several additional aspects and effects of auditory perception are noteworthy. Many of them help the auditory system to achieve better analysis results as could be expected from the above given low-level processing capabilities via a smart combination and exploitation of the co-occurrence and sequence of sensed events. Further reading is provided by Moore [2004] and excperted in the following paragraphs.

Phase Locking

Phase information about a stimulus up to 4–5 kHz (i.e., information about the current state of the period of the periodic frequency components) is encoded in the temporal pattern of the firing of the neurons: nerve spikes "lock" to a specific part of the cycle. It is argued that phase locking is partly responsible for a perception of relative loudness and of pitch (perceived tone "height") in complex tones. Additionally, it takes part in increased frequency resolution due to a later-on sharpening of the originally more diffuse output of the basilar membrane.

A complex tone, as opposed to a pure tone, here means one that consists of more than one pure sinusoid. Typically, psychoacoustic results are established based on experiments with pure stimuli only. The results are subsequently extrapolated to complex tones on the basis of viewing the auditory system as being linear. This is not totally true, but a reasonable simplification. A system is considered to be a *linear system* if it obeys the two principles of homogeneity (formally written: $f(k \cdot x) = k \cdot f(x)$) and superposition ($f(x)=a \wedge f(y)=b \Rightarrow f(x+y)=a+b$).

Temporal Processing

The human auditory system has a temporal resolution of 1–2 ms, maybe even down to 0.25 ms. Smaller gaps in an otherwise continuous stimulus are not recognizable. In order to have a buffer from which past events can be "loaded" and correlated with current input, there exists a temporal integrator for all measured events. The integrator window has a length of 100 ms, but only a relatively small peak area of 7 ms length gets a high weight. Word recognition, for example, relies on even longer stretches of analyzed sound.

Temporal processing facilitates auditory object recognition, too: this task relies on the periodicity as well as the irregularity of the sound to be detected. The smooth fluctuation with time of all aspects of the sound (timbre, pitch, loudness and location) are important as well as other timed events like synchronicity of harmonics and common onset and offset times. Sounds that are coherent with respect to such changes tend to fuse to one auditory object regardless of their complexity, whereas incoherent ones are segregated. Additionally, preceding- and following sounds play a role. The default mode of the auditory system, however, seems to be that there is only one stream—one auditory object—at a time, and this assumption is changed only on considerable counter evidence.

Masking

A stimulus at one frequency can suppress a stimulus at a neighboring frequency up to its imperceptibility if the relative loudness of the former one as compared to the latter one exceeds a certain threshold. This effect is known as masking. The maximum distance in frequency between the two stimuli at which masking may occur varies with the difference in loudness. Masking may also take place along the temporal dimension, meaning that a loud sound at a certain frequency masks following (and even preceding) sounds in its spectral neighborhood.

Higher level auditory processing (i.e., in the auditory cortex of the brain) uses different cues to nevertheless detect masked tones, such as cross-filter comparisons, temporal patterns and envelope changes. The temporal buffer is also taken into account to fill gaps from memory, an activity known as "closure".

The Organization of Perception

From the very beginning, auditory analysis seems to be partly under the control of higher level functions from the auditory cortex. That is, auditory processing cannot be viewed as a strict one-way process from lower to higher levels. Instead, two-way interaction between sensors, encoders and active analyzers takes place ubiquitously. Compared to this fact the binaural processing (i.e., hearing with both ears) seems to play only a minor role overall. Nevertheless, it is helpful in detecting sounds in noise and locating sources in space.

The auditory system seems to comprise many mid-level detectors that are specialized for concrete events like, e.g., loudness, frequency, on- and offsets, location, periodicity or duration. The detectors exist in special variants for different levels of loudness. They also form combinations of feature detectors, employing non-linear processing. Their outcomes are collectively evaluated in certain multi-range detectors at higher hierarchical levels in the cortex.

If only one feature would be considered, humans could only tell 5–6 different sounds apart. Using the multi-range detectors and hence many more possible feature dimensions, the selectivity increases. This also makes the auditory system a good change detector: it adapts to a steady input, and any change in one of its dimensions stands out perceptually.

A Special Speech Mode?

Good evidence suggests that the auditory system operates in a special speech mode when confronted with speech sounds, although this theory is not unquestioned. In this mode, acoustic components are grouped that would otherwise violate the rules for perceptual grouping within auditory object recognition. Additionally, special areas of the cortex are active in speech hearing, although the same auditory processing as for ordinary sounds might still take place.

Speech, in opposition to non-speech, is perceived categorical: differences within a single phoneme are not perceived, only differences between phonemes play a role. This is remarkable, since the acoustic patterns for a phoneme vary greatly based on the given context. Phonemes are furthermore not perceived as discrete events, but rather as a stream that is grouped together. This raises doubts whether phonemes are really the basic units of speech perception, or just abstract linguistic concepts whereas the auditory system does not segregate speech below the level of syllables or even words at all.

Speech Perception Theory

Different theories of speech perception exist, yet no single one explains all phenomena equally well. The motor theory, for instance, suggests that speech production and perception are inherently linked. The basic units of perception are thus deemed to be the intended phonetic gestures of the speaker, memorized in the brain as specific articulatory movements.

The cue- or invariant feature-based approach states that, first, landmarks are detected in an incoming speech signal by tracking peaks, valleys and discontinuities in the spectrum. Then, motor commands (as above) near the landmarks are sought and combined with other features and the respective context to feature sequences. These sequences are compared with a mental dictionary, given that there exists a relatively invariant mapping of acoustic patterns to perceived speech if the processing is done correctly.

The trace model suggests a 3-layer neural network of highly interconnected nodes, where the layers represent phones, segments and words, respectively. Each node represents one hypothesis about the incoming phone, segment or word, and firing means that this hypothesis might be active in the current stimulus. Activations of individual neurons are passed along layers and time, and higher-level functions extract the most probable hypothesis.

2.4 The Speech Signal

This section introduces the speech signal itself: the result of speech production, uttered at a rate of typically 10–20 different phonemes per second. Subsection 2.4.1 conveys its general properties and technical representation within an automatic analysis system. Subsection 2.4.2

Chapter 2. Fundamentals

enlarges on the necessity of processing this signal prior to further analysis, while Subsection 2.4.3 briefly introduces new trends in nonlinear and non-stationary speech signal processing.

2.4.1 From Signal to Samples

The information conveyed in the speech signal is not bound to any specific frequency range. Yet, most speaker-specific information is contained in the range of 500-5 000 Hz. The original land line-based telephone only transmits the band of 300-3 400 Hz, but in the end 1kHz of bandwidth is enough for intelligible reconstruction of the content. In fact, mobile phones do much greater harm to the signal by heavy processing and compression via an analysis–resynthesis approach [Hasegawa-Johnson and Alwan 2002]. For speech to be useful for accurate communication, a *signal-to-noise ratio* (SNR) of 6 dB should be maintained (i.e., the signal has to be 4 times stronger than the noise).

The Waveform and Frame-Based Processing

Technically, the analog signal resulting from measuring the air pressure variation and expressing it as variations of electrical current is further commuted to a digital signal via sampling [Prandoni and Vetterli 2009]. While music is best sampled at sample rates of 44.1 kHz and above to represent its structure, for speech processing purposes a sample rate of 16 kHz suffices, allowing for a maximum inherent frequency of 8 kHz according to Nyquist's sampling theorem [Nyquist 2002].

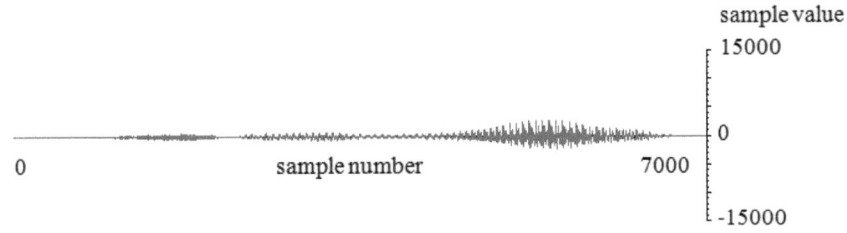

Figure 2.3: Waveform of the phrase "she had", spoken by a female voice.

Figure 2.3 displays the waveform (i.e., plot of time versus samples values) of the short phrase "she had", sampled at 16 kHz. It can be seen that the vowel part of "had" is the loudest part, i.e., it contains a lot of energy. Additionally, the waveform shows some periodic repetitions. Both is typical for voiced sounds. Once in digital form, the signal can be imagined as an array of signed integer values inside a *digital signal processing* (DSP) software system. Hence, the ordinate in the graph is labeled with possible values for signed short integer values.

2.4. The Speech Signal

The audio signal exhibits the property of being quasi-stationary: on the long run it is a truly and highly non-stationary signal, but on relatively short, phoneme-sized chunks, its statistical parameters are relatively stable. This is the reason for dividing the signal into chunks of 20–30 ms size (and typically 30–50% overlap) called *frames* that are used as stationary starting points for further analysis.

The Fractal Nature of Speech

The speech signal is a one-dimensional signal, yet, it contains information on many levels: information about whether it contains non-speech or speech, information about the linguistic content of the speech, information about the speaker, his gender, emotional state, origin, localization, and many more. In order to deconvolve these different types of information, it is on the one hand necessary to transform it to a domain with more dimensions, where some of these different "channels" are explicitly segregated into (or more easily by) different dimensions. This is enlarged in the next subsection with the introduction of the frequency domain.

On the other hand, it is necessary to look at the speech signal on different time scales: linguistic information is contained in it in every millisecond; yet, speaker based information unfolds as longer chunks in the range of typically 10 seconds and more are statistically summed up. This makes certain comparisons of the speech signal with a fractal obvious [Mandelbrot 2000]: regardless of the resolution, useful information is detected that looks similar in structure also at lower- and higher levels. Hence, it can be analyzed using related approaches. For example, speech of individual speakers does not naturally part into segregated clusters for each speaker in the frequency plane, but into clusters of similar phonemes. Yet, inside the phoneme clusters, individual clusters for distinct speakers are found [Wu 2006].

This might be called the *fractal nature* of speech [Al-Akaidi 2004; Pickover and Khorasani 1986]. It is responsible for the close relationship of automatic speech- and speaker recognition methods, or rather speech processing techniques in general: the same signal with the same properties is analyzed, but just (loosely spoken) at different time scales.

Additional material on audio signal acquisition and representation is provided by Camastra and Vinciarelli [2008]. Rabiner and Juang [1993] give additional information regarding the speech signal.

2.4.2 Signal Processing

The great variability offered by the speech production process through the articulatory movement implies that there is no exact period-to-period repetition in the speech waveform, not within the duration of a single phoneme, and not between different realizations of the same phoneme. Uttered speech sounds similar, but does not look similar—at least in the time domain. Additionally, a single sample does not convey any exploitable information, and with only rough loudness- and repetition-information gainable from longer chunks of samples, the time domain is not very feature-rich. This adds to the demand for a transformed domain raised in the previous subsection.

The Spectrum

A suitable domain happens to be the frequency domain: after the signal has been prepared to meet the mathematical demand of stationarity by chopping it into frames and tapering each frame's endings softly to zero using, for example, the Hamming window, each frame can be transformed using, for instance, the *fast Fourier transform* (FFT) algorithm [Cooley and Tukey 1965]. It is hoped that each frame roughly corresponds to a single phoneme. The overlapping of frames thereby compensates for the non-existing explicit alignment of frame borders with phoneme segmentations.

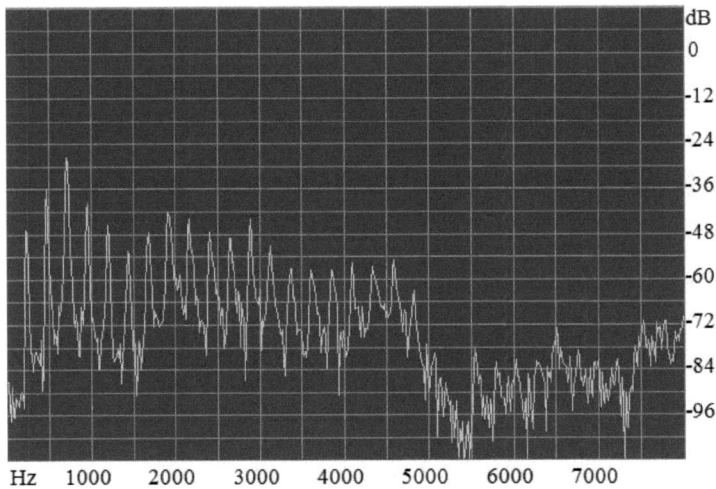

Figure 2.4: Spectrum from the near-end vowel part of the phrase "she had", extracted with a 1024-point FFT using a Hamming window.

Figure 2.4 shows a short-term power spectrum (frequency versus amplitude plot) of the near-end vowel part of the sentence "she had" from the previous subsection. In the frequency domain, time resolution is traded for frequency resolution. Thus, the 1024 samples used for the FFT account for a relatively fine-grained analysis of which frequency components are contained with which respective power. The range of possibly occurring frequencies between 0 Hz and the Nyquist frequency (half the sample rate, i.e., 8 kHz in the example) is divided into 512 bins.

2.4. The Speech Signal

The number 512 stems from the Fourier transform being a linear, invertible transform, hence it contains exactly the same amount of information as the time-domain waveform with its 1024 samples. But the power spectrum's counterpart that contains the other half of the information, namely the *phase spectrum*, has been omitted in the plot because it is typically not considered useful for automatic speech processing (see Section 2.6.2).

The spectrum reveals not only which frequencies carry the biggest part of the signal energy (obviously the first formant lies approximately at 750 Hz). Also, the harmonic structure of the vowel and hence its pitch can be read off when looking at the periodic peaks repeated every 250 Hz. From the position of the formants, it could even be deduced which vowel has been uttered here. Opposed to such a short-term spectrum, a long-term spectrum comprises ≥ 20 s of speech. It is used to characterize the gross spectral shape of a single speaker if enough data is available. Details like individual harmonics are, however, not revealed, because they cancel out each other over the long temporal span of the analysis.

The Spectrogram

The most valuable information is extracted from the speech signal if the time-frequency plane is surveyed simultaneously. This is done using a spectrogram. To create a spectrogram, successive spectra are measured for overlapping short frames and plotted as successive columns of a matrix. Here, time runs from left to right, frequency from bottom to the top and energy is expressed with lighter colors of the single pixels in each column. Figure 2.5 shows an example for the established phrase "she had".

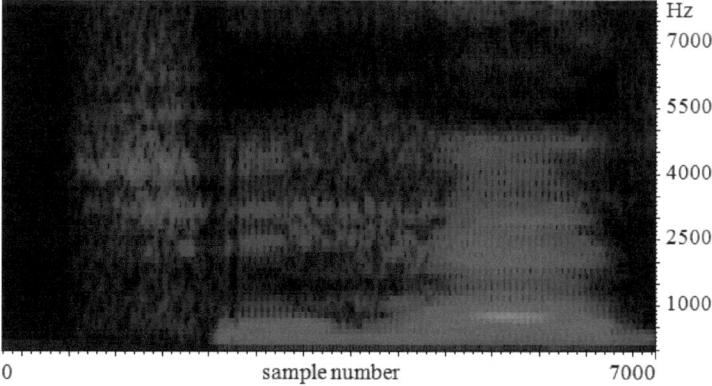

Figure 2.5: Corresponding wideband spectrogram of the phrase "she had". A frame length of 128 samples is used in conjunction with a Blackman window and a logarithmized energy-scale.

Voicing appears in the spectrogram as bright horizontal bands that correspond with formants. Vertical striation indicates the instants of glottal pulses, i.e., the opening of the vocal folds, within voiced speech. Typically, most parts of speech are voiced. This is important, because some automatic speaker recognition methods are actually only applicable to voiced speech from a theoretical point of view.

An expert can see many more details in a spectrogram, like, for example, dialects or speech disorders. Yet, spectrogram analysis is not an analytical process with a defined protocol to be followed. Instead, it is gestalt-based, meaning that the (forensic phonetic) expert perceives the display as a whole [Rose 2002, p. 116] and judges it intuitively.

Depending on the size and overlap of frames, different structures can be made visible in a spectrogram: long frames (ca. 50 ms) create good spectral- but bad time resolution, allowing for events like individual harmonics to be seen. This is called a narrowband spectrogram. A wideband spectrogram uses shorter frames of 15 ms length and 1 ms step, giving high temporal resolution and revealing, for example, individual glottal pulses.

Overall it has to be noted that the spectrogram does not show the *real* time-frequency plane. It gives an approximation to it that has been achieved making certain simplifying assumptions like, e.g., stationarity. This has to be considered when deriving features for automatic speech analysis from the FFT-based spectral domain: they only approximate the truth, hence expectations cannot be to arrive at, e.g., the performance of the human auditory system. Auditory spectrograms [Cooke et al. 1993] come closer to the truth in this respect by showing what humans hear instead of what can be measured by a certain method, but are far more difficult to compute [Chi et al. 2005; Patterson 2000]. This complexity is, however, typically avoided in automatic speaker recognition.

More background on digital signal processing is provided by the following authors: Mallat [2001] introduces the wavelet transform as an alternative to the FFT with improved time-frequency resolution. Smith [2003] gives a very accessible introduction to general DSP, while Rabiner and Schafer [1978] write on DSP especially for the speech signal.

2.4.3 Nonlinear and Non-Stationary Speech Processing

By employing the FFT and related methods in speech processing, it is implicitly assumed that the signal is the result of a linear production process. It has already been mentioned that this is a reasonable simplification. Moreover, to approximate the true interrelationships in the signal has been necessary in the beginning of automatic speech analysis because otherwise the resulting computations would not have been manageable on former computers.

Lately, several researchers explored the possibilities of applying nonlinear analysis techniques to the speech signal [Faúndez-Zanuy et al. 2002]. They raise the question if this technique could finally close the gap between what is observed in human capabilities as opposed to the shortcomings of the automatic counterparts.

Their results have been encouraging, but as Kantz and Schreiber [2004] point out, the field of nonlinear time series analysis is not mature yet. The application of developed methods cannot be done in a block-box manner. Instead, prior knowledge is needed of what precisely is sought in the data in order to select proper algorithms, tune the parameters accordingly and possibly arrive at results that affirm the prior hypothesis.

Besides this warning, two promising nonlinear features have been found: Lyapunov-exponents have been tested for phoneme recognition with good results, yet, they appear very unstable [Kokkino and Maragos 2005]. This corresponds with the analysis of Kantz and Schreiber [2004]. The correlation dimension [Jingqiu et al. 2006] has shown potential as a supplementary feature to standard automatic speech processing parameters (MFCC, see Section 2.6.2 below). It allows to distinguish very similar, otherwise inseparable voices [Seo et al. 2004].

Another direction of research aims at not only disposing the linearity assumption, but also the simplification of (piecewise) stationarity. The *Hilbert Huang transform* (HHT) introduced by Huang et al. [1998] is meant as a replacement of the Fourier transform with less rigorous requirements on the data. HHT employs a two-stage process: first, the signal is decomposed into mono-component modes by the empirical mode decomposition (EMD) algorithm [Kizhner et al. 2004; Rilling et al. 2003]. An iterative process called "sifting" thereby splits the signal into parts that contain only one frequency component at a time. Then, Hilbert transform can be applied to each mode in order to estimate its instantaneous frequency, i.e., the frequency *per sample*.

HHT has been applied to problems of pitch extraction [Huang and Pan 2006], speech detection [Wang et al. 2006b] and *speech enhancement* [Zou et al. 2006], among others. Yet, its overall success is limited, accompanied by severe run-time increases and critical reviews in the community [LASG Forum 2004; Rato et al. 2008].

2.5 Pattern Recognition Basics

Automatic speech processing is an instance of a pattern recognition problem: certain perceptually meaningful events shall be detected and recognized automatically. Yet, they are only implicitly represented in data derived from measurements. To recognize the patterns anyway, abstract representations of the measured events called "features" are sought in which these patterns stand out explicitly.

A prerequisite for the understanding of pattern recognition techniques is some background in mathematics, statistics and machine learning theory. This section gives pointers to the relevant concepts. A general and very accessible overview is, for example, given by Witten and Frank [2005], while Bishop [2006] provides a rigorous and capacious introduction.

Chapter 2. Fundamentals

The rest of this section is organized as follows: Subsection 2.5.1 explains the influence of probability theory within pattern recognition methods. Specifically, the importance of the normal distribution and the use of likelihood functions are introduced in Subsections 2.5.2 and 2.5.3, respectively. Subsection 2.5.4 focuses on the issue of numerical stability when implementing pattern recognition methods before the background of unsupervised- and supervised machine learning theory is presented in Subsections 2.5.5 and 2.5.6, respectively. Finally, Subsection 2.5.7 describes the utility of statistical tests for comparing machine learning results.

2.5.1 Statistical Pattern Recognition

Probability distributions play an important role in a part of today's pattern recognition concepts called statistical pattern recognition [Rigoll and Müller 1999]. This stems from the following reasoning: a pattern, for example, some specific vowel sound, is thought of as an abstract concept. This abstract concept cannot be measured directly because it does not exist in pure substantial form. It can, however, be observed via looking at several concrete instantiations, i.e., speech signals, that take the form of *feature vectors* within an analysis system.

In the example of the vowel sound, the speaker (more concrete: his vocal tract) is regarded as a random variable, the uttering of speech as a random experiment and a concrete feature vector from this speech as a random variate. Following the statistical reasoning, the random variable is uniquely characterized by its probability distribution. The probability distribution (figuratively, a plot of possible values vs. relative frequency) can be estimated from a large enough sample of the feature vectors. Thus, a probability distribution is regarded as a good model of a speaker's voice.

Probability distributions can be estimated using different techniques [Tüzün et al. 1994]. *Non-parametric* methods do not impose any assumptions on the data. They are typically computationally intensive and difficult to compare and store in a compact form—normally, the distribution is then represented by (a sample of) the data itself. *Parametric* methods typically result in a closed form solution, making further mathematical treatment elegant and easy. All knowledge about the random variable is encoded in the few parameters of the distribution (or model) of choice, as well as in the choice itself.

2.5.2 The Normal Distribution

The *normal* (or *Gaussian*) *distribution* plays a special role among the parametric probability distributions. This is due to several factors: for one, its elegant formulation facilitates further computations. But most importantly, it arises naturally in most of all practical situations. The reason for this is the fact that the mean of sufficiently many independent random variables tends to become normally distributed, and most practical events are caused by a great number

2.5. Pattern Recognition Basics

of previous events that can be considered to be random. This fact is known from mathematics as the central limit theorem [Stöcker 1995]. The normal distribution is predominantly used to model speech due to its convenient properties, although strictly speaking the assumption of Gaussianity is not fulfilled.

A probability distribution is accompanied by a respective *probability density function* (PDF) [NIST/SEMATECH 2003]. It is a function whose integral is overall exactly equal to one. This corresponds with the PDF's meaning that the integral over any interval of its domain equals the probability of an event occurring in this area. Hence, the probability that any event occurs equals 1. The PDF of the standard normal distribution $\mathcal{N}$ in the univariate (i.e., one-dimensional) case is defined as follows:

$$\phi(x) = \frac{1}{\sqrt{2\pi}} \cdot e^{-\frac{1}{2}x^2} \qquad (2.1)$$

This parameterless version of the PDF implies a *mean* value (center of the distribution) of $\mu = 0$ and a *variance* (spread of the distribution) of $\sigma^2 = 1$. Plotted for several values of x, this yields the well-known bell-shaped curve centered at zero and having a width such that approximately 68% of its mass are located in the area of one *standard deviation* $\sigma = \sqrt{\sigma^2} = 1$ both-way around the mean.

For later brevity, the PDF of the univariate parametrized normal distribution $\mathcal{N}(\mu, \sigma)$ is also given:

$$\phi(x, \mu, \sigma^2) = \frac{1}{\sigma} \cdot \phi\left(\frac{x-\mu}{\sigma}\right) \qquad (2.2)$$

$$= \frac{1}{\sqrt{2\pi\sigma^2}} \cdot e^{-\frac{(x-\mu)^2}{2\sigma^2}} \qquad (2.3)$$

In the multivariate case of more dimensions, the variance is expressed through the *covariance matrix* Σ that takes into account the variance in all directions of the space. The PDF of the normal distribution $\mathcal{N}(\vec{\mu}, \Sigma)$ then becomes

$$\phi(\vec{x}, \vec{\mu}, \Sigma) = \frac{1}{\sqrt[D]{(2\pi)} \cdot \sqrt{|\Sigma|}} \cdot e^{-\frac{1}{2}(\vec{x}_t - \vec{\mu})^\top \cdot \Sigma^{-1} \cdot (\vec{x}_t - \vec{\mu})} \qquad (2.4)$$

The unbiased sample mean and covariance of a set of data $X = \{\vec{x}_t | 1 \leq t \leq T \wedge \vec{x}_t \in \mathbb{R}^D\}$

Chapter 2. Fundamentals

can be estimated via the following equations:

$$\mu_d = \frac{1}{T} \cdot \sum_{t=1}^{T} x_{t,d} \tag{2.5}$$

$$\Sigma_{ij} = \frac{1}{T-1} \cdot \sum_{t=1}^{T} (x_{t,i} - \mu_i) \cdot (x_{t,j} - \mu_j) \tag{2.6}$$

Here, the equations are given such that the dth dimension of the mean vector $\vec{\mu}$ and the cell with the covariance between dimensions i and j of the covariance matrix are computed. Often in practice, only the variances of each dimension of the space with itself on the main diagonal of the matrix are needed. Then Σ becomes a *diagonal covariance matrix* and is often expressed in vectorial form as

$$\vec{\sigma^2} = diag(\Sigma) = (\Sigma_{11}, \ldots, \Sigma_{DD})^\top \tag{2.7}$$

2.5.3 Likelihoods

As soon as the imagined abstract pattern behind a set of feature vectors is characterized by the estimated PDF, newly arriving feature vectors can be tested whether they realize the same pattern. This is done by calculating the *likelihood* of these new vectors given the distribution.

Sometimes it is also necessary to compute the likelihood of the very same data that have been used before to estimate the parameters of the PDF. In this case there exists an approximate solution which is commonly used in the speech processing literature regarding a feature set's likelihood given the normal PDF. Yet, its derivation and hence its appropriateness is not intuitively clear, so that it is given here.

Let $X = \{\vec{x}_t | 1 \leq t \leq T \ \wedge \ \vec{x}_t \in \mathbb{R}^D\} \sim \mathcal{N}(\vec{\mu}, \Sigma)$ be a set of T D-dimensional vectors, obeying the given normal distribution (in fact, used to estimate its parameters). The logarithm of the set's log-likelihood given the PDF, l_G, can finally be expressed as the logarithm of the determinant of the covariance matrix Σ:

$$l_G = \log p(X|\vec{\mu}, \Sigma) = \log \left(\prod_{t=1}^{T} \phi(\vec{x}_t, \vec{\mu}, \Sigma) \right) \tag{2.8}$$

$$= \log \left(\prod_{t=1}^{T} \left((2\pi)^{-\frac{D}{2}} \cdot |\Sigma|^{-\frac{1}{2}} \cdot e^{-\frac{1}{2}(\vec{x}_t - \vec{\mu})^\top \cdot \Sigma^{-1} \cdot (\vec{x}_t - \vec{\mu})} \right) \right) \tag{2.9}$$

$$= \sum_{t=1}^{T} \left(-\frac{D}{2} \cdot \log 2\pi - \frac{1}{2} \cdot \log |\Sigma| - \frac{1}{2} \cdot (\vec{x}_t - \vec{\mu})^\top \cdot \Sigma^{-1} \cdot (\vec{x}_t - \vec{\mu}) \right) \tag{2.10}$$

$$= -\frac{T \cdot D}{2} \cdot \log 2\pi - \frac{T}{2} \cdot \log |\Sigma| - \frac{1}{2} \cdot \sum_{t=1}^{T} \left((\vec{x}_t - \vec{\mu})^\top \cdot \Sigma^{-1} \cdot (\vec{x}_t - \vec{\mu}) \right) \tag{2.11}$$

2.5. Pattern Recognition Basics

$$= -\frac{T \cdot D}{2} \cdot \log 2\pi - \frac{T}{2} \cdot \log |\Sigma| - \frac{1}{2} \cdot tr\left(\Sigma^{-1} \cdot \sum_{t=1}^{T}\left((\vec{x}_t - \vec{\mu}) \cdot (\vec{x}_t - \vec{\mu})^\top\right)\right) \quad (2.12)$$

$$= -\frac{T \cdot D}{2} \cdot \log 2\pi - \frac{T}{2} \cdot \log |\Sigma| - \frac{1}{2} \cdot tr\left(\Sigma^{-1} \cdot \Sigma\right) \quad (2.13)$$

$$= -\frac{T \cdot D}{2} \cdot \log 2\pi - \frac{T}{2} \cdot \log |\Sigma| - \frac{1}{2} \cdot D \quad (2.14)$$

$$\approx \log |\Sigma| \quad (2.15)$$

Here and later, $p(|)$ refers to a (conditional) probability and $|\ |$ stands for the determinant of a matrix if the argument is a matrix. The skillful transformation in this derivation lies in the introduction of the trace function $tr()$ between (2.11) and (2.12). This does not change the term's value, but allows for a reordering of the factors inside the trace function, as is done in (2.12): note the position of the transposed term $(\vec{x}_t - \vec{\mu})^\top$. This yields a second covariance matrix in (2.13), and if the vectors $\vec{x}_t \in X$ have also been used to estimate the covariance matrix of the PDF, the product inside the trace function yields the identity matrix I (otherwise, this is already an approximation). Omitting constant terms in (2.14) yields the final approximation of the log-likelihood $l_G \approx \log |\Sigma|$.

2.5.4 Numerical Stability in Software Implementations

It has already been reminiscent in the equations above: likelihoods (and probabilities) are normally expressed by their logarithms. This is due to the fact that the involved numbers typically get very small very fast. The *log domain* thus provides a way to treat the small numbers in a software implementation and to make numerical computations stable. Besides, working in the log domain in the almost omni-presence of the Gaussian function renders many computations of exponentials unnecessary because typically the base-e logarithm ln is used where log is written. Additionally, instable (and expensive) products are turned into sums. Logarithms are also used to express signal energies and powers: the high dynamic range of the ear has been mentioned before, and likewise does an electronic mimicry of the ear compress the wide range of numerical values by expressing them logarithmically.

Besides numerical issues, there exists another source of algorithmic instability known as the *curse of dimensionality* [Köppen 2000]. It refers to the fact that feature vectors typically comprise many dimensions, but working in high-dimensional space has several drawbacks: for instance, distance computations become very questionable because the space is only sparsely populated by the high-dimensional feature vectors and everything is far distant. This does not induce numerical problems, but makes the algorithms instable, i.e., not working as expected, when presented with higher-dimensional input.

This leads to the paradox situation that adding good additional dimensions to a good feature vector can actually decrease recognition performance. Additionally, the more dimensions a data set comprises, the more data is necessary to estimate its distribution. Thus, generally, it is good practice to work with as little dimensions as possible and to be cautious with adding new ones. *Feature selection* may be used to arrive at a concise set out of many promising candidates [Arauzo-Azofra et al. 2008; Zhao and Liu 2007].

A good resource for implementing efficient and stable algorithms for all aspects of automatic speech processing are the works of Press et al. [1988], Skiena [2008] and Sedgewick [1990].

2.5.5 Unsupervised Machine Learning

Machine learning, which is presented with a very clear structure by Mitchell [1997], splits into approaches for unsupervised- and supervised learning. Unsupervised learning refers to the case where no additional information about the data is available. Hence, an algorithm has to learn structure just from the data itself. This is also called *clustering*.

The most common clustering algorithm is the *k-means* algorithm, probably due to its simplicity rather than good performance. It receives a set of feature vectors (or any data in vectorial form) along with a parameter k provided by the user and referring to the number of groups expected in the data. The algorithm performs several steps iteratively in order to group the data into the k clusters. Prior to the iterations, the k cluster centers (called *centroids*) are initialized most often by a random selection of k points out of the training data.

In each iteration, the distances of each feature vector to each centroid are measured. Then, each vector is assigned to the cluster whose centroid has the smallest distance. Finally, the centroids are reestimated as the averages of all belonging vectors.

The algorithm terminates after a certain number of iterations (typically 10) or if no vector changes its assigned cluster. Several improvements exist in the literature, like performing more sophisticated statistical initialization or doing several random initializations and subsequent clusterings in a row to finally chose the best result. Also, it is possible to take only vectors from the training data set as centroids instead of (artificial) averages. In this case, the vectors nearest to the average cluster centers are used as centroids and the algorithm is called *k-medoids*.

2.5.6 Supervised Machine Learning

Supervised learning approaches receive the training data along with user-provided *labels* that indicate for each training vector its learning target. If the label constitutes a real number, the learning task is called *regression*, but in the context of speech processing, a label typically refers to a discrete category or *class* the feature vector belongs to [Pardo and Sberveglieri 2002]. The aim of learning is then to find a function that associates feature vectors with labels in a way that generalizes well to previously unseen data. Supervised learning algorithms are hence general

2.5. Pattern Recognition Basics

function approximators that learn from examples. Their application naturally splits into the two separate phases of training and evaluation. Because the final goal is to deduce the class of a newly arriving feature vector, the task is commonly known as *classification* [Kotsiantis et al. 2006].

There exists a large set of learning algorithms that differ in the way they search (and prune) the *hypothesis space* of possibly learnable functions. This implies that some algorithms are better suited for certain problems or are not expressive enough for others [Mitchell 1997]. Nevertheless, a more complex system is not always the best choice [Holte 1993].

A classic supervised machine learning approach is the decision tree. It is widely employed in data mining applications due to the learned *model* (another name for the trained classifier) being easily interpretable by humans [Küsters 2001]. It is, however, mostly irrelevant to speech- and speaker recognition systems, unlike the neural net approach [Munakata 2008]. Its model is not comprehensible by humans, but is proven to be able to approximate any function with arbitrary precision [Cybenko 1989].

Since its introduction, the support vector machine (SVM) learning algorithm [Schölkopf and Smola 2002] has become the most popular learner. Basically, it learns an optimal hyperplane that linearly separates data from two classes, but can be extended to a multi-class scheme [Rifkin and Klautau 2004]. The hyperplane is chosen such that the *margin* between the closest instances of both classes is maximized, and it is characterized completely by those *support vectors*.

The *kernel trick* makes the approach both computationally efficient and applicable to more challenging scenarios: linearly unseparable training vectors are implicitly mapped into a higher-dimensional space via a kernel function. In this space, the data can be separated using a linear (higher-dimensional) hyperplane, but without ever computing it explicitly. The most common kernel function is the *radial basis function* (RBF) kernel employing a Gaussian function and implicitly mapping the data into an infinitely-dimensional space.

The supervised approaches presented so far all belong to the category of *discriminative* learners: labels for two (or more) classes are provided, and the model learns to separate them. A second class of algorithms is known as *generative* approaches. They are only provided with examples of one class and subsequently learn what it is that makes up this class. Figuratively, while discriminative approaches learn the boundary between several classes, generative models learn the center of one class. As the name "generative" suggests, it is possible to sample new instances of the learned class from the model.

Generative models typically try to estimate the probability distribution of the training data. A distinguished exponent of this class of algorithms in speaker recognition is the Gaussian mixture model to be introduced later. Recently, the one-class SVM has been established as a competitor: it uses the many advantages of the SVM learning algorithm to determine the level set, i.e., the $\nu\%$ densest area, of the distribution as represented by a few support vectors. This is in accordance with the machine learning principle of never trying to solve a more general task than necessary, because the available information might only suffice for the easier task [Vapnik 1998].

Generative models can be used to subsequently build a discriminative approach by constructing a *maximum likelihood* (ML) classifier: the likelihood of evaluation data to each trained generative model is calculated, and the class of the model yielding the highest likelihood is chosen as the final classification.

2.5.7 Statistical Tests

The outcome of a classification run is called a *hypothesis* about the data: the classifier hypothesizes the class or group each data point belongs to. Using a statistical test (also called a hypothesis- or significance test) it can be evaluated how significantly the outcome of, for example, a newly created algorithm deviates from a baseline, i.e., if it is really better if the figures of merit are improved to a certain extend.

In this case, the computed figures of merit (e.g., accuracy or error-rate) for each classifier are treated as a realization of a random variable. The actual assumption, that the newly created algorithm is better than the baseline, is called the H_1 hypothesis. It is "accepted" if the contrary unwanted outcome (that both systems are actually equal and any deviations in figures of merit are due to chance), called the H_0 hypothesis, can be rejected with a probability of more than 95%. The complement of this probability is called the α-*level* and denotes the probability of rejecting a true H_0 hypothesis, thereby committing a type-I error.

Different statistical tests exist that hold different assumptions on the data. The *t-test* is used to test whether two Gaussian distributed, independent samples of continuous variables (like, e.g., figures of merit) with equal variance do have the same expected value. The χ^2 *test* does the same for enumeration data. This means that it can be used, for example, to compare cells in contingency tables as they occur when listing the number of vectors that have been classified into a certain class.

2.6 The Pattern Recognition Process

The pattern recognition process for speech processing follows a typical design and flow of events. It is depicted in Figure 2.6 and can be recognized in every respective algorithm or system in speech processing. An understanding of the purpose of each stage helps in comprehending the complete structure of one of its instances more quickly. It enables the observer to focus on the individualities of the algorithm under consideration rather than on the similarities it has

2.6. The Pattern Recognition Process

in common with all its relatives.

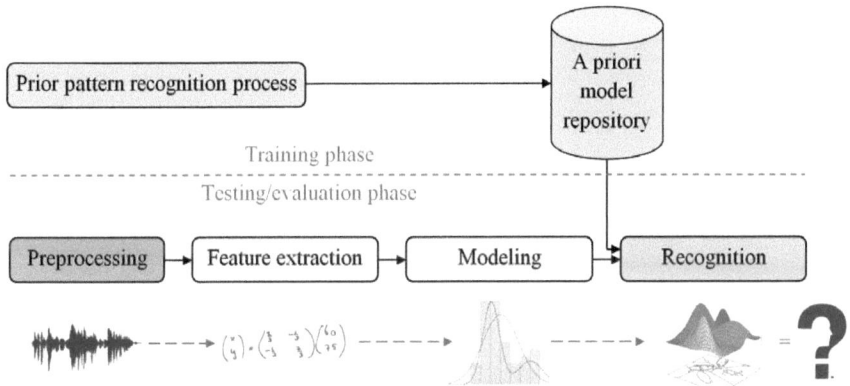

Figure 2.6: Overview of the pattern recognition process.

In this section, the fundamental techniques for automatic speaker recognition are introduced at their respective stage in the pattern recognition process. The process starts with signal *preprocessing*, described in Subsection 2.6.1. Basically, the signal is loaded and conditioned here to be suitable for the subsequent phase of *feature extraction*. This stage is responsible for making the properties of the sought pattern more explicit. Feature extraction is introduced in Subsection 2.6.2.

Based on the extracted features, models of the patterns are built as described in Subsection 2.6.3. The purpose of *modeling* the feature vectors is again to compress and focus the information regarding the pattern. Trained models can then be used to subsequently recognize newly arriving patterns based on certain comparisons of newly arriving feature vectors and prebuilt models. The *recognition* stage as highlighted in Subsection 2.6.4.

2.6.1 Preprocessing

The pattern recognition process begins with several tasks that are summarized with the term preprocessing [Picone 1993]. Generally, everything until the feature extraction stage is regarded as preprocessing, for instance, the cleaning of signals from noise via speech enhancement methods [Ephraim et al. 2005; Niederjohn and Heinen 1996].

Another example is signal acquisition: when the signal is loaded, it has to be decoded and possibly decompressed in order to extract the samples stored in some container format. Then, resampling and normalization may take place: 16 kHz sample rate on a mono (single) channel are a common basis for speaker recognition. In Matlab, for example, automatic normalization to a maximum sample value of 1 takes place when a signal is loaded with the wavread function.

When the signal samples reside in an array within the analyzing software system, a last preprocessing step is to *pre-emphasize* the signal. This means to pass the N signal samples $S = \{s_n | 1 \leq n \leq N \land s_n \in \mathbb{R}\}$ through a high-pass (or first-order difference) filter that performs the following operation:

$$s'_n = s_n - \alpha \cdot s_{n-1} \tag{2.16}$$

Here, α is chosen close to 1, with typically values being between 0.96–0.97. The aim of pre-emphasis is to boost the high frequencies in the signal in order to improve the SNR and strengthen the high formants [Vergin and O'Shaughnessy 1995].

2.6.2 Feature Extraction

The aim of feature extraction within the sought pattern recognition process is to lossily compress the information in the signal such that the relevant information regarding the pattern is emphasized while irrelevant information is removed. This way, the pattern is hoped to stand out more explicitly in a feature vector than in the original signal.

In the following, typical features for speaker recognition are briefly introduced. All features presented here are the result of a frame-based analysis at a fixed frame rate. Although not being optimal, this approach is predominantly used with few exceptions [Jayanna and Prasanna 2009] due to its simple nature and good results.

Mel Frequency Cepstral Coefficients

The by far most popular features not only in speaker recognition, but also in speech recognition and general audio analysis are the *mel frequency cepstral coefficients* (MFCC) introduced by Davis and Mermelstein [1980] ("mel" being an abbreviation for "melody"). They provide a compact representation of the spectral envelope of a frame of speech which accounts for the frame's perceived timbre. This is achieved the following way, starting with the power spectrum of the predominantly Hamming-windowed frame:

The spectrum is first broadly summarized by a bank of triangular filters. Typically, 24 filters for the range of 0–8 kHz are used. The filters are linearly spaced with 50% overlap on the mel scale, which is a percpetually motivated frequency scale that approximates the frequency weighting of the human auditory system. The mel scale is roughly linear below 1 kHz and then logarithmically spaced, meaning that the 24 mel filters, if measured on a linar Hertz scale, get broader with increasing frequency. This corresponds well with the finding from psychoacoustics that timbre corresponds with the relative level in each of the 27 critical bands, compared across filters in a process called profile analysis. Each critical band has a breadth of approximately one third of an octave.

A filter can be imagined as a triangle having the value 1 at its top, with both sides slowly and linearly decreasing to zero. The amplitude of each filter's output is then measured by multiplying each spectral component with the "height" of the filter triangle at its position, and then adding up the weighted components. The resulting 24-dimensional vector is logarithmized and then known as a *log-filterbank energy* (FBE) vector.

The FBE vector still contains information both from the vocal tract (filter during speech production) and vocal cords (excitation source), which are associated via the operation of convolution. The convolution of the source signal with the filter response is turned into addition when the spectrum of the FBE vector (which is already a resident of the spectral domain) is computed, for example, via the *discrete cosine transform* (DCT). To distinguish this second spectrum linguistically from the original one, it is called a *cepstrum* [Childers et al. 1977]— the inversion of some of the letters thereby refers to its property of dissolving convolutions [Oppenheim and Schafer 2004].

The (mel) cepstrum is preferred over the FBE vector in speech technology because it is more noise robust and higher voice specific. Additionally, due to its components being DCT coefficients, they are completely decorrelated (statistically independent), which is an advantage as well as a common prerequisite for further modeling. MFCCs are also made more compact than FBEs by only keeping the first 12–19 coefficients and throwing away higher order components of the vector. This corresponds to a low-pass filtering of the encoded spectral envelope: the higher level coefficients account for small fluctuations in the spectrum (because they are the high-frequency components of the frequency analysis of the spectral curve) and are detrimental to further analysis.

The cepstral smoothing via a circumcision of the DCT coefficients additionally has the effect of removing pitch information from the feature vector: together with the ambiguous fluctuations in the spectrum the harmonics of F_0 are removed, such that a sensation of pitch is most completely eliminated.

Overall, the preference for cepstral feature vectors over simpler spectral vectors results in higher recognition rates and better compatibility with other parts of current state-of-the-art voice processing systems. They have the disadvantage of not corresponding straightforwardly with articulation.

Linear Predictive Coding

Linear predictive coding (LPC) analysis is the second prominent way to arrive at parametric feature vectors. Basically, in this approach, each sample in a frame of speech is predicted by a linear combination (i.e., weighted sum) of the previous p samples in the frame. The coefficients

α_1–α_p of the analysis are estimated such that the *residual* (i.e., the difference signal between the predicted- and actual signal) for the whole frame is minimized. The precision of the analysis increases with increasing order of the prediction.

LPC analysis has the advantage of implicitly decoupling the speech source and filter: while the LPC coefficients are the direct estimates of a digital filter resembling the vocal tract, all influences from the source as well as phase information are concentrated in the residual. This makes this kind of feature not only relevant for speech analysis, but also for synthesis [Furui 2001].

LPC coefficients can be further processed to arrive at LPC cepstrum coefficients (LPCC) or the more compact, robust and efficient *line spectral pairs* (LSP) [McLoughlin 2008]. The literature is not unambiguous on whether the performance of the LPC family of features is marginally inferior to MFCCs in speaker recognition or not, but it is generally believed that both features capture similar parts of the speech signal quite well.

Time-Domain Features

While the speech signal reveals most of its information when surveyed in the frequency domain, there is also useful information exploitable in the time domain. One possible feature is the *short-term energy* (STE), a measure of signal loudness, gained by summing up the squared sample values in a frame.

A second feauture is the *zero crossing rate* (ZCR), being a simple measure of frequency that for a mono-component signal corresponds with its pitch. A mono-component signal thereby is any signal consisting only of one frequency component (sinusoid) at a time. ZCR is calculated by counting the number of sign changes within the samples of one frame.

Pitch and Formants

If the analyzed signal is not mono-component, its pitch (or rather F_0, the acoustic correlate of pitch) can be determined using the time-domain approach of *autocorrelation*: the signal is multiplied with a lagged version of itself and summed up in a series of autocorrelation coefficients, indexed by lag. A peak in the series of coefficients happens if the waveform has a repeating pattern at a period corresponding with the respective lag.

The F_0 range of a speaker roughly spans the width of $\mu \pm 2\sigma$ Hertz assuming a Gaussian distribution, which is not totally true. In fact, the distribution of pitch is skewed to the high-frequency side, so that taking the square root of the estimated frequency before using it as a feature is advisable. For a good estimate of a speaker's F_0 statistics, 60 s of speech are necessary.

Because the creation of pitch involves a vibration of the vocal cords, reliable detection of pitch corresponds with good classification of speech as being voiced or unvoiced. But it is difficult to measure the perceptual sensation of pitch automatically. This gives rise to a great variety of approaches. The algorithm presented by Talkin [1995] can be regarded as a competitive baseline. It works in the frequency domain and is based on LPC analysis. This has the advantage of being extensible also to formant tracking.

From a psychoacoustic point of view, pitch detection is also triggered by different cues: depending on whether the pitch is below or above 5 kHz, temporal- (i.e., phase locking) or place mechanisms (on the basilar membrane) are at work. The detected pitch is then, for example, used for speaker change detection by the auditory system: each time a pitch transition does not comply with the rules of intonation, a change point is triggered [Moore 2004, p. 291].

Regarding the use of formants for speaker identification, it has been determined that the third formant, F_3, indicates the length of the vocal tract, while F_4-F_5 correspond with individual voice quality. The problem is that the higher formants with center frequency above 4 kHz cannot be extracted reliably automatically and are difficult to interpret. This applies partly already to the fourth formant, so that generally it is believed that cepstra are better suited than formants for speaker recognition. Nevertheless, formant center frequencies and their amplitudes as well as bandwidths and the coupling of the first two formants carry speaker specific information [Rose 2002].

Phase Features

While the power- or magnitude spectrum has received great attention in frequency-domain speech processing, the phase spectrum ins typically discarded due to its perceptual irrelevancy [Kim 2001]. Yet, a growing body of research examines the usefulness of the short-term phase as surveyed by Alsteris and Paliwal [2007]: for example, Hegde et al. [2004] as well as Thiruvaran et al. [2007] use it for speaker recognition and Murthy and Gadde [2003] perform phase-based phoneme recognition.

The meaning conveyed in the phase spectrum is the information about the locality of events in the waveform of a frame, i.e., about its shape and the position of "edges". But the short term phase spectrum's susceptibility to smallest variations in the signal due to noise or window position is problematic. Therefore, a derived, robust feature is sought. The first step towards such a feature is the unwrapping of the phase: the removal of the coarse discontinuities due to the phase values being confined to the interval of $[-\pi, \pi]$.

Then, the *group delay function* (GDF) [Banno et al. 1998] can be computed. The GDF is defined as the time delay of each frequency component of the original signal, represented as a function of frequency. Such, it is a measure of the non-linearity of the phase spectrum. The GDF is speech- and speaker specific and offers the additional opportunity to detect the instants of glottal closure [Prasanna et al. 2006].

Results using the GDF in the approaches mentioned above are split: On the one hand, performing speech recognition using a combination of GDF and MFCCs sometimes worsens the overall result, but sometimes also improves it [Alsteris and Paliwal 2007]. This may be induced by the noisiness of the GDF due to zeros in the vocal tract filter's spectrum [Smith 2003]. On the other hand, using the derived feature of log-GDF cepstral coefficients (LGCC), it is possible to linearly separate several speakers in the 2D space derived from a Sammon's mapping of the LGCCs (a certain technique for distance-preserving dimensionality reduction [Sammon 1969]). This has not been possible using MFCCs [Hegde et al. 2004].

Human Used Features

It is interesting to consider the features and cues humans use for recognizing events in speech. As Moore [2004] enumerates, a variety of features is employed by the auditory system to detect certain sound classes like vowels, nasals and so forth. The list contains positions like changes in frequency, loudness, gross spectral shape or the presence of low-energy periodicity and corresponds well with already presented automatic features. Interestingly, almost exclusively not the absolute feature values, but their rate of change is evaluated or compared with the value at the onset of the next detected unit. Prosodic features in contrast tend to play a minor role at this stage of auditory processing.

Rose [2002] adds a list of features that is explicitly used within forensic phonetic analysis. Here, automatically extracted parametric features like cepstra are not considered very useful— but if used, they are strongest for nasal consonants. Instead, simple long term statistics are considered useful which are seldom available in automatic analysis. Also in contrast to the custom in automatic voice recognition is the result that source features (derived from vocal cord activity like pitch and phonation type) are very strong.

Besides spectrogram analysis, a very robust feature is deemed to be the speech rate and related features like speech tempo, breath patterns, syllable grouping or hesitation that take the temporal evolution of speech into account, although speech rate does not have a high discriminability. F_0 averages and ranges are highly discriminative if taken over longer segments, but pitch is subject to intonation. Overall, it is concluded that a significant part of the between-speaker variability is linguistic in nature rather than acoustic, so that linguistic knowledge is needed to detect the differences. The primary acoustic correlates of voice quality are then the lowest three major peaks in the smoothed spectrum.

2.6.3 Modeling

If the aim of feature extraction within the pattern recognition process is to lossily compress the signal while making the sought patterns explicit, this is the more true for the modeling stage. A voice model summarizes the information contained in a set of feature vectors such that the primarily present linguistic information contained in each frame is averaged and the speaker-specific content stands out that otherwise is only playing a minor role in the signal.

This way, the voice model is the container of the voice-biometric signature of the speaker. It shall contain what makes up the voice, even if it is difficult to specify from a non-technical perspective what exactly it is that characterizes a voice. The ideal voice model would, if it were possible to draw samples of the voice's sound from it, generate a stream of speech-like sounds that would not convey any understandable content, but would sound familiar to a human analyzer knowing the original.

The role of a voice model thus is to be the basic unit for comparison when it comes to computing the similarity of two speakers based on their voice. This has also speed reasons: comparing two (parametric, thus compact) models bears the potential of being less costly than comparing two high-dimensional sets.

The remainder of this subsection is devoted to introducing common voice modeling methods.

The Gaussian Mixture Model

The *Gaussian mixture model* (GMM) as introduced by Reynolds and Rose [1995] is the predominantly used speaker model due to its ability to model arbitrarily shaped PDFs via a superposition of multivariate Gaussians. This is even true when using a diagonal covariance matrix: the loss in expressibility induced by the Gaussians being confined to a circular area can be alleviated using more Gaussians. Using diagonal covariances additionally boosts recognition performance because the fewer parameters of the model can be estimated more reliably from limited training data.

The rationale behind the following model formulation is that each mixture models an underlying broad phonetic class present in a speaker's voice: a GMM consists of a mixture of M Gaussians, where M depends non-linearly on the size and content of the training data set and has to be provided by the user. A typical value is $M=32$ for characteristic feature dimensions in the range of 12–36. Each mixture employs a D-dimensional mean vector $\vec{\mu}$ and typically a diagonal covariance vector $\vec{\sigma^2}$, weighted by a factor w so that the overall mass is 1 and the model forms a distribution. The log-likelihood l_{GMM} of a set of D-dimensional feature vectors $X = \{\vec{x_t} | 1 \leq t \leq T \ \wedge \ \vec{x_t} \in \mathbb{R}^D\}$ is given by the probability $p(X|\lambda_{GMM})$, where λ_{GMM} represents the GMM by its parameters. It can be computed per dimension using the univariate Gaussian

Chapter 2. Fundamentals

PDF due to the diagonal covariances:

$$\lambda_{GMM} = \{w_m, \vec{\mu_m}, \vec{\sigma_m^2} | 1 \leq m \leq M \ \wedge \ w_m \in \mathbb{R} \ \wedge \ \vec{\mu_m}, \vec{\sigma_m^2} \in \mathbb{R}^D\} \quad (2.17)$$

$$l_{GMM} = \log p(X|\lambda_{GMM})$$
$$= \prod_{t=1}^{T} \sum_{m=1}^{M} w_m \cdot \prod_{d=1}^{D} \phi(x_{t,d}, \mu_{m,d}, \sigma_{m,d}^2) \quad (2.18)$$

Here, $x_{t,d}$ refers to the dth component or dimension of the tth feature vector, and $\phi(..)$ is the univariate Gaussian density as in (2.3).

GMMs are typically trained using the *expectation maximization* (EM) algorithm [Dempster et al. 1977]. It can be viewed as being a probabilistic variant of k-means: the model parameters are initialized to some basic values (typically using either k-means or randomness) and iteratively improved to arrive at their *maximum likelihood estimates*. While it is not guaranteed for EM to converge to a global optimum, it typically converges very quickly at least to a local optimum. The reestimation equations for each round are given below [Reynolds and Rose 1995]:

$$\overline{w_m} = \frac{1}{T} \cdot \sum_{t=1}^{T} p(m|\vec{x}_t, \lambda_{GMM}) \quad (2.19)$$

$$\overline{\vec{\mu_m}} = \frac{\sum_{t=1}^{T} p(m|\vec{x}_t, \lambda_{GMM}) \cdot \vec{x}_t}{\sum_{t=1}^{T} p(m|\vec{x}_t, \lambda_{GMM})} \quad (2.20)$$

$$\overline{\vec{\sigma_m^2}} = \frac{\sum_{t=1}^{T} p(m|\vec{x}_t, \lambda_{GMM}) \cdot \vec{x}_t^2}{\sum_{t=1}^{T} p(m|\vec{x}_t, \lambda_{GMM})} - \overline{\vec{\mu_m}}^2 \quad (2.21)$$

$$p(m|\vec{x}_t, \lambda_{GMM}) = \frac{w_m \cdot \prod_{d=1}^{D} \phi(x_{t,d}, \mu_{m,d}, \sigma_{m,d}^2)}{\sum_{u=1}^{M} w_u \cdot \prod_{d=1}^{D} \phi(x_{t,d}, \mu_{u,d}, \sigma_{u,d}^2)} \quad (2.22)$$

Here, (2.22) refers to the a-posteriori probability of the acoustic class (mixture) m modeling the training vector $\vec{x}_t$, and $\overline{\vec{\mu_m}}$ is the reestimated version of last round's $\vec{\mu_m}$. A very accessible description of the algorithmic details is given by Mitchell [1997, pp. 197–202].

An improvement to the classical GMM approach has been contributed by Reynolds et al. [2000]: the *Gaussian mixture model with universal background model* (GMM-UBM) constitutes the state of the art in automatic speaker verification and identification. Here, a very big GMM with 1024–2048 mixture components is trained from so much data that it can be considered to model voices universally and is later referred to as the UBM. When a new voice model for far less training data shall be built, it is not trained from scratch, but the parameters of the UBM are adapted towards the newly arriving data using *maximum a-posteriori* (MAP) training. This means that a-priori knowledge in the form of the trained UBM is utilized. During evaluation, the test data is scored not only against the individual voice model in order to estimate the

2.6. The Pattern Recognition Process

likelihood, but also against the corresponding UBM. Only a limited number of top-scoring mixtures are considered in the final score (typically the top ten mixtures are considered), which is returned as the likelihood ratio between the adapted- and the universal model.

Other Voice Models

Several other model formulations have also been used for speaker recognition, for instance, the *vector quantization* (VQ) approach. While the GMM resembles a parametric estimator of a speaker's PDF, a VQ model estimates the density non-parametrically: via the Linde-Buzo-Gray (LBG) algorithm, the dataset is iteratively clustered, and the found centroids form a *codebook* that is used to represent the voice [Linde et al. 1980]. The VQ approach has the advantage of achieving good results already with very limited training data, but suffers from a lack of robustness and expressibility when encountering noise and the high variability of unconstrained speech.

Recently, the SVM has been used to model voices [Campbell et al. 2006]. It has the desirable property of handling high-dimensional feature vectors very well, in contrast to the GMM. Another possible voice model is the neural network family of classifiers, specifically the *auto-associative neural net* (AANN) [Guruprasad et al. 2003]: it measures how well a feature vector can be projected unto itself through a compressing bottleneck network layer. Only if the feature vector complies well with the training data used to establish the bottleneck's weights it can be reconstructed with reasonable accuracy.

Finally, the *hidden Markov model* (HMM) is another ambassador of the probabilistic models. It realizes a finite state machine, where each state can be described, for example, by a GMM, and the parameters of the GMMs as well as the state transition matrix is learned from the training data. Using the state transitions, it is possible to model a temporal sequence of the feature vectors complying with the sought pattern. This is the reason why it is the predominant model in automatic speech recognition [Rabiner 1989].

In speaker recognition, the HMM is often employed to model a whole recording containing multiple speakers. In an iterative process, the complete stream of speech is segmented and speaker models are built simultaneously. Thereby, each state GMM finally models one speaker, and the transition matrix and structure of the HMM learns the dialog structure of the recording. A well-known exponent of such a system architecture is the speaker diarization system of the *International Computer Science Institute* at Berkeley (ICSI) [Anguera Miró et al. 2005].

2.6.4 Recognition

After suitable voice models have been built, the recognition phase may start. This refers to applying the previously trained classification models to new data or each other. In speaker recognition, it means to compare voices with each other based on either a direct comparison of two models or a likelihood computation of feature vectors of one voice given a model of the other voice. The aim is to get a score of dissimilarity (or similarity) of the two voices under consideration.

Distance Computation

Computing simple scores of dissimilarity (e.g., likelihoods) between two voice samples is only the first step towards judging the possibility of their common origin. This is because the absolute values of such scores are not very meaningful, whereas their comparison is. This is the reason for using distance measures that employ the likelihoods and compute likelihood ratios [Iyer et al. 2007].

The standard distance measure for speaker recognition is the *generalized likelihood ratio* (GLR) [Gish et al. 1991]. Let X and Y be two sets of speech feature vectors used to build up two speaker models λ^X and λ^Y. Then, GLR is expressed as follows:

$$d_{GLR}(\lambda^X, \lambda^Y) = \log \left(\frac{l_\lambda(X|\lambda^X) \cdot l_\lambda(Y|\lambda^Y)}{l_\lambda(X \cup Y|\lambda^{X \cup Y})} \right) \quad (2.23)$$

Here, $l_\lambda(|)$ is the likelihood function (not the log-likelihood here) for the specific class λ of models (typically a single Gaussian or GMM) and $X \cup Y$ indicates the concatenation of both segments. The GLR computes the log ratio of two individual models of the two segments to a combined model of both segments. The smaller this measure gets, the better suited is a combined model, i.e., the more probable it is that both segments are uttered by the same speaker.

If the GLR is regarded as being computationally too expensive, the *cross likelihood ratio* (CLR) is commonly used [Solomonoff et al. 1998]. Since it does not require a new model to be trained, it is faster but also less accurate than the GLR [Kotti et al. 2008b]:

$$d_{CLR}(\lambda^X, \lambda^Y) = \log \left(\frac{l_\lambda(X|\lambda^X)}{l_\lambda(X|\lambda^Y)} \right) + \log \left(\frac{l_\lambda(Y|\lambda^Y)}{l_\lambda(Y|\lambda^X)} \right) \quad (2.24)$$

The CLR evaluates how good the feature vectors of each utterance fit both individual models.

Decision Making

In speaker verification and identification, it is sufficient to compute likelihood ratios of speech features and models, then choosing the best identity in a maximum likelihood sense. Here, additional care has to be taken for making the voices comparable by accounting for varying channel- and handset conditions using *score normalization* [Auckentaler et al. 2000].

2.6. The Pattern Recognition Process

In speaker clustering (using the more common alternative approach to the mentioned ICSI HMM system), distance measures as introduced before are used to create a distance matrix of all available voice samples. Then, *agglomerative hierarchical clustering* is used to iteratively merge the closest pair of speech segments. Each iteration produces one *partition* of the data, and after all segments have been merged, the best partition can be chosen according to some *model selection criterion*.

Possible criteria are, for example, the *Bayesian information criterion* (BIC) [Chen and Gopalakrishnan 1998a] and the *information change rate* (ICR) [Han and Narayanan 2007]:

$$BIC(\lambda^X, \lambda^Y) = -d_{GLR}(\lambda^X, \lambda^Y) - \frac{\alpha}{2} \cdot \log(|X \cup Y|) \cdot (\#\lambda^{X \cup Y} - \#\lambda^X - \#\lambda^Y) \quad (2.25)$$

$$ICR(\lambda^X, \lambda^Y) = \frac{1}{|X \cup Y|} \cdot d_{GLR}(\lambda^X, \lambda^Y) \quad (2.26)$$

Here, $|X|$ denotes the cardinality of the set X, i.e., the number of feature vectors in it, and $\#\lambda$ stands for the number of free parameters in the model λ, i.e., its complexity. Both measures are computed between the last two clusters that have been merged in each partition. In case of the BIC, clustering may be terminated as soon as the BIC-value for the current partition exceeds zero. The BIC penalizes the likelihood ratio with the number of parameters of the complete model, where the tunable parameter α should ideally equal 1 for theoretical reasons but needs careful adaptation to the data and problem at hand. The BIC can also be used in a single-model formulation to estimate the optimal number of mixtures for a GMM given a certain dataset.

In case of the ICR, scores for all partitions are computed. Then, searching through the stack of created partitions in reverse order, the first partition is picked where the ICR score does not exceed an a priori set threshold. In contrast to the BIC, the ICR works well in evaluating the similarity of segments whose size is far different, which otherwise would have a very detrimental effect on clustering performance [Haubold and Kender 2008].

A third possible criterion is the *within cluster dispersion* (WCD) [Jin et al. 1997]. It is computed not by using just the information of the closest pair of clusters, but rather of the complete partition $P = \{(\lambda^{X_c}, X_c) | 1 \leq c \leq C\}$ of overall C clusters and their covariance matrix W:

$$WCD(P) = |W| + \alpha \cdot \log(C) \quad (2.27)$$

$$W = \sum_{c=1}^{C} |X_c| \cdot Cov(X_c) \quad (2.28)$$

Here, X_c refers to the feature vectors of the segment of speech used to build the model λ^{X_c}.

Note the different meaning of | | depending on the context: $|X_c|$ is again the cardinality of a set while $|W|$ is the determinant of the weighted sum of covariance matrices $Cov(X_c)$. The reasoning behind the WCD is to pick a partition that reveals small intra-speaker variability as expressed in the covariances. Hence, the partition is picked as the final clustering result that produces the minimum WCD score.

Several other issues need consideration in speaker clustering. For example, how shall a cluster be represented during distance computation? A unified model of all segments belonging to the cluster could be built, known as *average linkage* and obviously very exact. This is expensive in terms of computational costs, and experiments suggest that some other form of linkage for the points (segments or models) in the cluster might even be more suitable: *complete linkage*, for instance, means to compute the distance between two clusters based on the greatest distance of individual points in the cluster. *Single linkage*, on the other hand, refers to using the distance of the closest pair of individuals to represent the distance of a pair of clusters [Ester and Sander 2000].

Figures of Merit

After the decision about the speaker identity is made for a database of test utterances, the quality of the result can be assessed using different figures of merit. It depends on the concrete background of the experiment and the conducting researcher which figures of merit are given in a certain paper. Most practical choices are discussed and defined by Kotti et al. [2008b].

For speaker identification experiments, the *identification rate* or *accuracy* is helpful: it is the ratio of correctly identified speakers, possibly expressed in percent. Additionally, adapted version of the well-known *recall* and *precision* measures from the information retrieval domain can be used [van Rijsbergen 1979]. They may also apply to speaker clustering experiments:

Recall is a measure of the completeness of the result. In the context of clustering, this measures the ability of a clustering system to summarize all utterances of one speaker in a single cluster instead of splitting them into several clusters. Precision is an indicator of exactness or purity, measuring the ability of a clustering algorithm to only summarize segments from one speaker in a cluster instead of mixing utterances from different speaker together.

In the remainder of this book, used figures of merit are to be defined when required.

2.7 A Complete Speaker Identification System

It is one thing to know possible methods for a certain task together with their pros and cons, and a totally different thing to implement a software system that performs this task well. In speech processing, it is said, 20% of the effort towards success goes into method development

2.7. A Complete Speaker Identification System

and 80% is inherent in the engineering of the targeted system.

It is beyond the scope of this chapter to convey engineering skills, which is more than mere knowing. But it serves the aim of this chapter to survey a complete, yet simple pattern recognition process for speaker recognition at work: it develops understanding of voice modeling methods in their respective contexts.

This section summarizes the concepts presented so far by introducing a real-world speaker identification system in Subsection 2.7.1. Building upon this basis, the connection line is drawn to the current state of the art in Subsection 2.7.2.

2.7.1 A Classic System and Setup

The work of Reynolds [1995] can be regarded as the seminal paper in automatic speaker recognition: in a clear, concise and reproducible manner it describes a high-performance system using simple methods that still work as building blocks in current implementations. This is true also for speaker verification and for identification. The rest of this subsection concentrates on the latter case.

Front end analysis (a phrase lend from automatic speech recognition and referring to the preprocessing- and feature extraction stages) is carried out the following way: 20 ms long frames are extracted every 10 ms and treated with a pre-emphasis filter. Each frame is processed to arrive at 13 MFC coefficients of which the zeroth is discarded: it just represents log-energy, and modeling loudness may be detrimental.

This yields 100 12-dimensional feature vectors per second of training- and evaluation data. The vectors are filtered with an adaptive energy-based speech activity detector to sort out "silence" frames only containing (low-energy) background noise. This step is crucial for the models to adapt to the different speakers instead of the background activity.

The training data is modeled with GMMs employing 32 mixtures. Several issues arise in GMM training [Reynolds and Rose 1995], such as initialization. Because no difference can be observed in the final likelihood scores whether a sophisticated initialization scheme is used or not, it is done here by random values followed by one single iteration of k-means prior to 10 rounds of EM training. Care has to be taken for the variances to not becoming too small. This is avoided by defining a minimum variance value used as a replacement for spurious estimates. It has a value in the range of $\sigma^2_{min} = [0.01..0.1]$ here. The order of the model is found to be relatively irrelevant to the final result on a wide range of values: a number of 16 mixtures worked "well", i.e., equal or better than other numbers, for various training utterance lengths between 1 and 90 seconds. However, 1 minute of training data has been found necessary for high speaker identification rates.

The TIMIT database (the name being an abbreviation of the two founding organizations,

Chapter 2. Fundamentals

Texas Instruments and the Massachusetts Institute of Technology) [Fisher et al. 1986; Linguistic Data Consortium 1990] is used in order to asses how well text-independent speaker identification can perform in a near-ideal environment: the database has a relatively large population size of 630 speakers from 8 US dialect regions, parted 70/30 between males and females. Ten sentences are recorded from each speaker under noise-free studio conditions. They are supplemented by detailed aligned acoustic-phonetic transcriptions down to the sample-based boundaries of single phonemes.

Identification is performed using maximum likelihood classification among all $S = 630$ speakers. After application of Bayes' theorem on the optimal Bayes' decision rule, the problem can be formulated as follows [Bayes 1763]:

$$\overline{s} = \arg\max_{1 \leq s \leq S} l_{GMM}(X|\lambda^s) \qquad (2.29)$$

Here, $\overline{s}$ refers to the sth speaker from the training set and implicitly represents his identity, while X is the set of evaluation feature vectors as defined earlier. Using the described setup, the system is able to achieve 0.5% closed set identification error, or conversely, 99.5% speaker identification rate. The term "closed set" here refers to the fact that no *impostors* have been considered in the experimental setup, i.e., each test utterance is considered to belong to one of the enrolled training speakers. This is a very competitive result: according to Rose [2002, p. 95], the forensic phonetic software VoiceID achieves 0.48% *equal error rate* (EER) on the same data set. EER thereby refers to the fact that both the error rates of type I and II, i.e., of falsely rejecting an enrolled speaker and falsely admitting an impostor in a verification scenario, are equal.

2.7.2 The State of the Art

The current state of the art in automatic speaker recognition has recently been surveyed by Kotti et al. [2008b] and Kinnunen and Li [2010]. The development in the last decade has also been closely escorted by the NIST speaker recognition evaluation campaigns, which are summarized by van Leeuwen et al. [2006]. All authors demonstrate that contemporary systems are still based on the methods used by Reynolds and Rose [1995], but surpass them in several aspects. The trend has been to incorporate more knowledge from more sources and joining them in a sort of higher-level processing made possible by the increase in computational power. For instance, in speaker verification and identification, a priori knowledge is used to build GMM-UBM models [Chao et al. 2009], and anchor models are used to represent alternative hypotheses [Sturim et al. 2001].

Another front line of development has been the improvement of feature extraction. While

MFCCs are still indispensable, work towards enriching them with higher-level features has shown good results when plenty of data is available [Zhang et al. 2007]. Additionally, the exploitation of ASR results to perform feature alignment and -normalization has been examined with positive outcome [Campbell et al. 2004]. Descriptions of complete up-to-date speaker recognition systems of four of the most active research groups in the field are given by Kajarekar et al. [2009], Sturim et al. [2009], Han and Narayanan [2009] and Gales et al. [2006].

Kotti et al. point out in their survey that for state-of-the-art speaker clustering performance the quality of the basic speech segments is crucial. For agglomerative hierarchical systems this means that a high-quality *speaker change detection* algorithm (SCD) must be employed. The next section enlarges on this topic. Additional information on the state of the art in special areas of speaker recognition is given in the following chapters together with respective improvements.

2.8 Speaker Change Detection

Speaker change detection is the task of segmenting an audio stream according to speaker turns: each time the speaker of the current frame differs from the one of the last speech frame, a change point is to be reported. SCD acts upon the results of speech activity detection algorithms that segregate speech- from non-speech segments. Together, both segmentation algorithms provide the basis for speaker clustering: respective algorithms work with the initial segments as provided by SCD to find clusters of segments uttered by the same speaker.

This section provides an overview and outlook of current and future SCD algorithms. Subsection 2.8.1 introduces the popular BIC-based segmentation algorithm together with its strengths and weaknesses. Subsection 2.8.2 then presents promising directions for future research.

2.8.1 BIC-Based Segmentation

The Bayesian information criterion (2.25) has been introduced for the task of speaker segmentation by Chen and Gopalakrishnan [1998b]. Delacourt and Wellekens [2000] added a second pass to the process to refine the result, thereby establishing the approach. Since then, much work on related concepts has been published, allowing the conclusion that BIC-based algorithms are the predominant approach to speaker change detection. Algorithmic as well as implementation details are given by Cettolo et al. [2005], and an overview of competing variants is provided by Moschou et al. [2007]. Kotti et al. [2008a] finally present a contemporary state-of-the-art system with some improvements. The basic processing steps have, however, stayed the same over the years.

Basically, the (voiced- and unvoiced speech-only) stream of feature vectors is analyzed with a

Chapter 2. Fundamentals

sliding window having an initial size of 3–6 seconds. The feature vectors are thereby comparable to those used by Reynolds as presented in the last section. The sliding window is subsequently divided into two parts at reasonable intervals. The boundary starts with, for example, only 50 frames on the left side of the window and is shifted with a step size depending on the feasibility of high computational costs (typically between 1 and 25 frames) until the same small amount of frames is left in the right half.

For each division of the sliding window, a BIC score is computed between the two halves, each modeled by a single multivariate Gaussian using the derivation of the Gaussian log-likelihood in (2.8)–(2.15). This yields a series of BIC values for the initial sliding window. If this series shows a clear peak that exceeds a certain preset threshold, the peak's position is regarded as a change point. Then, the sliding window is reset and shifted to the position directly following the change point, and the process starts again.

If no change point is found, the sliding window is first iteratively enlarged in steps of, for example, 75 frames until a final size of maximal 20 seconds. For each size, the previously explained search for a change point is conducted. If finally no change point is found in the outgrown sliding window, its position is shifted by approximately 100 frames and the search starts again.

The prerequisite for this process is that each initial sliding window contains a maximum of 1 change point, and that no overlapping of speech of different speakers occurs. Additionally, the assumption of the mono-Gaussian model on each half of the sliding window should be rudimentary fulfilled.

Figure 2.7 shows plots of the detectability of speaker change points under two different conditions. The detectability of a change point is thereby defined as the length of the shortest of its two neighboring segments, because this one limits the possible quality of one of the involved voice models and hence of the whole comparison. The density in the plot is estimated using the non-parametric *Pareto density estimation* method (PDE) [Ultsch 2003a] and plotted via an sclib method (see Chapter 8). As can be seen in the plot, the detectability in a "real-world" movie lies mostly below one second, whereas the detectability of concatenated sentences from the TIMIT corpus has its peak somewhere around 25 seconds.

BIC-based SCD algorithms are well suited for (and often evaluated on) data sets as the latter one. For more unconstrained data like encountered in general multimedia footage analysis, they are rather unsuited. This is due to the fact that usually more than one change point will fall into an initial sliding window, but sliding windows cannot be made arbitrarily small in order to arrive at reliable estimates of the Gaussians and hence of the voice: the statistical approach and the used features demand a certain minimum size as indicated above.

The performance of the BIC approach can be visualized using the self-similarity matrix [Foote 1999] depicted in Figure 2.8. Here, each 1.5 seconds long segment has been compared

2.8. Speaker Change Detection

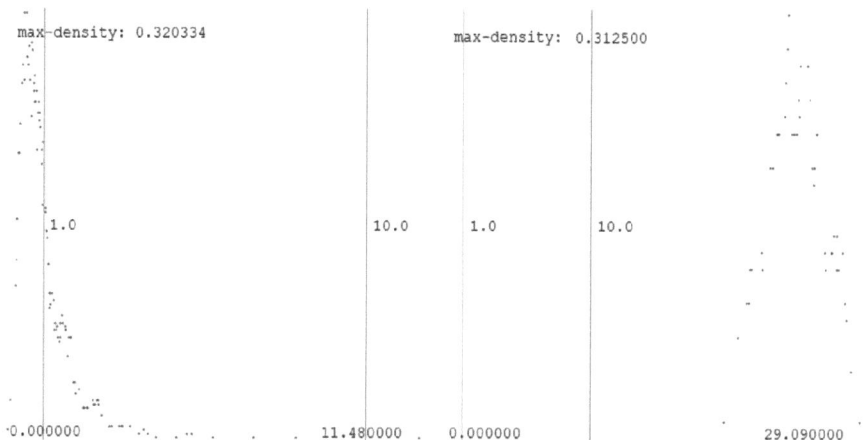

(a) First half of the cinematic motion picture "The Legend of the Fall" [Li et al. 2004].

(b) Subset of 800 utterances from the TIMIT corpus, concatenated ordered by speaker.

Figure 2.7: PDE plots of the detectability of speaker change points in different data sets. The abscissa is scaled in seconds from the lowest to the highest measured value, wheres the ordinate gives the estimated density. Orders of magnitude on the abscissa are plotted as red lines.

with all others, yielding a "sliding window" of overall 3 seconds of length. A BIC score is evaluated once in the middle of each comparison unit. A subset of the TIMIT corpus is used as the data basis and is presented in detail in Section 6.2.2. The BIC scores have been turned into a gray-scale image, where a dark pixel implies high similarity between the two segment-positions as indicated by the position of each pixel: the upper-left pixel represents the first consecutive 3-seconds window, the lower left pixel a comparison of the first- with the last 1.5 seconds in the corpus, and the main diagonal shows the score for all the consecutive sliding windows. Red crosses mark the real speaker change points as indicated by *ground truth*, i.e., by human annotators.

As can be seen from Figure 2.8, the BIC score for consecutive segments does not show much structure for the relatively short overall window size of 3 seconds. But when regarding the temporal neighborhood of each segment as shown off the main diagonal, dark boxes indicate similar segments of greater size. They correspond well with the manual change point marks and hence make change point detection possible. It can even be seen that the first 5 speaker seem to have something in common, and that the last 3 also form a group of some sort. This corresponds well with the fact that the first 4 speakers are females and the last 3 speakers are male, whereas the fifth speaker has an unusually high-pitched voice for a male talker. Thoughts like this are summarized in the next section in order to improve speaker change detection in

Chapter 2. Fundamentals

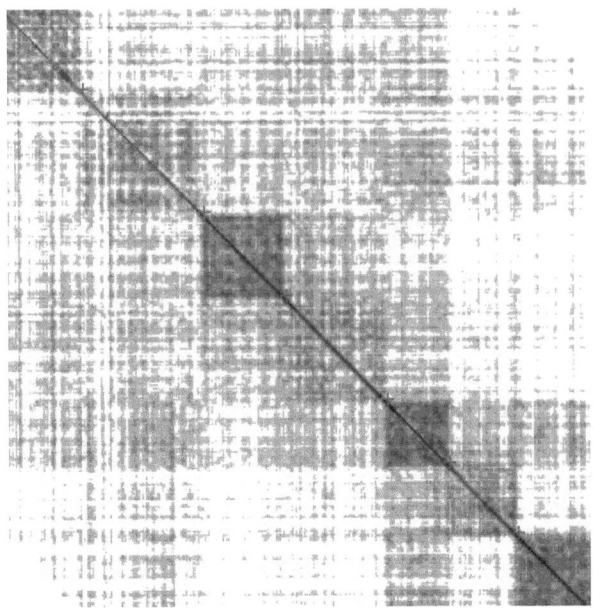

Figure 2.8: A self-similarity matrix of the first 7 speakers of the TIMIT test set based on BIC scores within a 3 seconds long comparison "window".

the presence of short segments and decreased detectability.

2.8.2 Promising New Ways

The problem in speaker change detection is that speaker change points are only one sort of boundaries in a pyramid of different segmentations at different levels of granularity: there are phoneme change points, word change points, sentence boundaries and acoustic change points, to name a few. Therefore, longer-term averaging seems necessary to arrive at speaker-level information. But sometimes speaker change points occur already after each word or syllable—this is the problem of the fractal nature of speech.

Another problem in SCD is that an optimal feature set and metric is unknown. Besides the dominant role of MFCCs and the BIC, several other methods are evaluated here and there with varying degrees of success, for example, by Fergani et al. [2006] or Kartik et al. [2005]. This is similar to the problem of face detection, where faces are sought on different scales, and the meta learning algorithm *AdaBoost* [Freund and Schapire 1997] is applied with great success to find good features given a broad class of possibilities [Viola and Jones 2004]. A transfer of the

2.8. Speaker Change Detection

principles learned in the face detection domain to the problem of speaker segmentation in the spirit of Fink et al. [2006] seems promising.

Such an approach would need to solve several research questions: for instance, a way must be found to work with the fractal nature of speech. Classifiers trained on different levels of granularity would be one possible solution. Then, the question arises how the detectability of a piece of evaluation data could be estimated in order to weigh the results of these different classifiers: if the detectability is high, much weight should be given to a classifier working on long segments of speech and vice versa. Last, if supervised learning is used to train a classifier, what are good negative examples for speaker change points?

A literature survey considering works on speaker change detection as well as general change point detection literature from the fields of video segmentation and data stream analysis has revealed the following additional factors of success in individual systems. Future speaker segmentation algorithms, accomplishing a crucial preprocessing step for speaker recognition, could regard some of the following factors:

- **Temporal neighborhood**. Use the area surrounding a change point, for instance, by using a self-similarity matrix [Foote 2000] or a continuity signal [Yuan et al. 2007], at least as a post-processing step to refine the results.

- **Multi-step analysis**. Iteratively refine an initial segmentation result using different classifiers working on complementary features. Reduce the type-I error on each step while simultaneously creating multiple chances for each change point to be detected. Even use different sources of information (i.e., different features, metrics and models) at each step [Kotti et al. 2008b].

- **Simplicity first**. Employ simple first-order statistics (e.g., T^2) at the first stage of the cascade to handle limited data [Kotti et al. 2008b].

- **Source features**. Use AANN models for glottal source features to account for speech segments with less than 1 second of length [Dhananjaya and Yegnanarayana 2008].

- **A priori knowledge**. Model the expected duration of segments and use this knowledge to weight classifier decisions [Kotti et al. 2008a]. Use domain knowledge to perform unsupervised classification [Aggarwal 2007; Ewerth and Freisleben 2004].

- **Holistic view**. Employ methods like Viterbi resegmentation [Gupta et al. 2007] or genetic algorithms [Salcedo-Sanz et al. 2006] that hold a holistic view of the speech stream instead the limited view of only one sliding window when faced with a decision.

Chapter 2. Fundamentals

2.9 Current Trends in Audio Processing

To conclude this section on fundamental concepts in automatic speaker recognition, an outlook is given to current trends in the general field of audio processing. It is challenging to define what makes a trait of research appear in this list—in the end, it is a combination of several factors: frequency of occurrence in the literature, together with a growing circle of adopters; a fresh and promising look on the subject; and discussions at conference banquets.

One trend is the use of *supervectors*: it primarily refers to the method of training GMM speaker models, then concatenating their parameters to a large (super) vector and feeding a SVM with those speaker-model-vectors in order to discriminate them [Kinnunen and Li 2010]. The concept may be extended to all approaches that take the result of some classifier (called mid-level features) as the input to some higher-level knowledge forger (see Chapter 9).

Overall there seems to be much progress in the way features are extracted and used: different *prosodic features* are evaluated as supplements to traditional MFCCs [Friedland et al. 2009] in order to capture suprasegmental speaker-specific information. Additionally, research intended to get *beyond "bags of frames"* is formulated in the music information retrieval community [Aucouturier et al. 2007]. This is rooted in several problems (e.g., "hub" songs that appear similar to almost every piece of music) arising when comparing sounds based on global averages of independent- and identically distributed (*iid*) features.

In multimodal analysis, the trend is towards building highly coupled, but specialized multimodal approaches instead of early fusing low-level features (which is again beyond a bag-of-frames approach, see Section 9.4). Additionally, several techniques originally developed for text- or video retrieval are adapted to the audio domain, like, for example, the application of *probabilistic latent semantic analysis* (pLSA) on dictionaries of audio features [Hofmann 1999; Peng et al. 2009].

The sparse matrices created by dictionary-approaches also play a role in the rapidly growing field of *compressive sampling* [Candès 2006]. The new theory already had an impact on face recognition methods [Kroeker 2009; Yang et al. 2007], and may also be relevant for audio applications. Especially the way features and classifiers are viewed in this light opens new possibilities: imagine there is no curse-, but a blessing of dimensionality...

2.10 Summary

In this chapter, the fundamental concepts and basic methods necessary for the understanding of the remainder of this book have been presented. The focus has been on fostering understanding for the interconnection of the individual stages in the pattern recognition process. To this end, the threads from many contributing ares to this multidisciplinary field have been brought

2.10. Summary

together. This unique composition of ideas might as well inspire new approaches as it stands out over other introductions to the field, for example, in the way it admits involvement from the fields of psychoacoustics and forensic phonetics.

The important message of this chapter has been the way the pattern recognition process for speech processing works: first, the signal is preprocessed in order to be suitable for feature extraction. Here, MFCC extraction is the predominant method. Then, models are built, which typically dissolves to creating GMMs. They can be used directly for speaker identification using a maximum likelihood approach, or within agglomerative hierarchical clustering to answer the question "who spoke when" for an audio stream without any prior knowledge. For the latter case, some distance measure is needed in order to compare the models, for example, the GLR, and a clustering termination criterion as the BIC.

On several occasions this chapter has widened its view beyond currently applied, well understood fundamental technologies to the borders of research in niches of the field. For instance, nonlinear and non-stationary speech processing has been discussed, and the use of phase features or new approaches to speaker change detection as well as current trends in audio processing have been explained. These niches will not be picked up later in this book. The discussions have rather been given to show a harmonious overall picture also of research frontiers beyond the scope of the methods presented in this book. They are pointers to future work as well as the context in which the developed methods from the next chapters fit in.

A performance-oriented summary of the presented state of the art in speaker recognition reads as follows: automatic speaker verification and identification have matured into robust applications, for example, for the task of access control. Also, the analysis of broadcast news material works reasonably well. More unconstrained data, however, still induces problems for all contemporary algorithms and systems: mainly due to short utterances and background noise, the performance under such "real-world" conditions as met within conversational speech drops below what humans consider an acceptable result. This might be caused by, for example, inexpressive base features or the ineptness of the statistical approach as some literature suggests. Another reason is the fractal nature of speech. These concepts will be examined in the remainder of this book.

"Therefore, since brevity is the soul of wit..."
William Shakespeare (1564–1616)

3
Short Utterance-Tolerant Voice Models

3.1 Introduction

Furui [2009] states that one of the two major challenges in automatic speaker recognition today is to cope with the lack of available data for training and evaluating speaker models. For instance, in automatic speaker indexing and diarization of multimedia documents, unsupervised speaker clustering has to deal with the output of speaker segmentation algorithms that chop the signal into chunks of typically less than 2-3 seconds. In speaker verification and identification, enrollment and evaluation data is expensive in the sense that the system should bother a user as little as possible. This is in conflict with the general finding that one needs 30-100 seconds of training data to build a state-of-the art model of high quality that can be evaluated using approximately 10 seconds of test data. This state-of-the-art model refers to the GMM approach with diagonal covariance matrices used in almost all current systems, together with MFCC feature vectors [Kinnunen and Li 2010; Reynolds 1995].

Several approaches exist in the literature to cope with short utterances. For instance, Merlin et al. [1999] propose to work in an explicit speaker feature space in order to overcome the intra-speaker variability omnipresent in acoustic features due to the phonetic structure of speech; less ambiguity and variability in the transformed space is believed to lead to more stable model estimates with less training data. A prototypical implementation of the acoustic space transformation via projection to anchor model scores shows promising results. Larcher and his

Chapter 3. Short Utterance-Tolerant Voice Models

colleagues criticize the GMM-UBM approach for its insufficiency for mobile appliances in terms of data demands for training and evaluation [Larcher et al. 2008]. Their solution includes using temporal structure information (i.e., word dependency) and multimodal information (video) to compensate for short training and evaluation samples. Vogt et al. [2008a] use a factor analysis technique to arrive at subspace models that work well with short training utterances and can be seamlessly combined with the optimal GMM-UBM model when plenty of training data is available. In subsequent work, they suggest to estimate confidence intervals for speaker verification scores, leading to accurate verification decisions after only 2–10 seconds of evaluation data where usually 100 seconds are needed [Vogt and Sridharan 2009; Vogt et al. 2008b].

In this chapter, a different approach is presented to address the problem of small sets of training and evaluation data: a novel way is proposed to reduce the number of necessary free parameters in the GMM with the aim of obtaining more stable statistical estimates of model parameters and likelihoods using less data. Furthermore, better—i.e., closer to truth—estimates improve recognition accuracy, and less complex models have a strong positive effect on runtime, too. Additionally, the approach can be combined with other short utterance approaches proposed in the literature.

The chapter is organized as follows. In Section 3.2, the motivation for the proposed approach is explained by looking at feature distributions. Section 3.3 introduces the dimension-decoupled GMM. In Section 3.4, experimental results are presented. Section 3.5 concludes the chapter and outlines areas for future work.

Parts of the work presented in this chapter have been published in a paper by Stadelmann and Freisleben [2010a].

3.2 Feature Distributions

Figure 3.1 depicts the plot[1] of a diagonal covariance GMM with 32 mixtures, trained on the set of 19-dimensional MFCCs extracted from 52.52 seconds of anchor speech from a German news broadcast. While the first several coefficients show a multimodal or skewed distribution, many of the later dimensions look more Gaussian-like. Different feature types like linear prediction-based cepstrum coefficients (LPCC) show a similar characteristic. Others, like line spectral pairs (LSP) or filterbank energies are more Gaussian-like in any of their dimensions, while Pitch's single dimension is quite non-Gaussian. In combination, the marginal densities of most practical feature sets exhibit a similar structure as shown in Figure 3.1.

This leads to the following reasoning: different coefficients obviously have different distributions, so different (often small) numbers of 1D Gaussian mixtures are necessary to approximate

---
[1]Produced with *PlotGMM*, see Section 7.3.3 and http://www.informatik.uni-marburg.de/~stadelmann/eidetic.html.

3.2. Feature Distributions

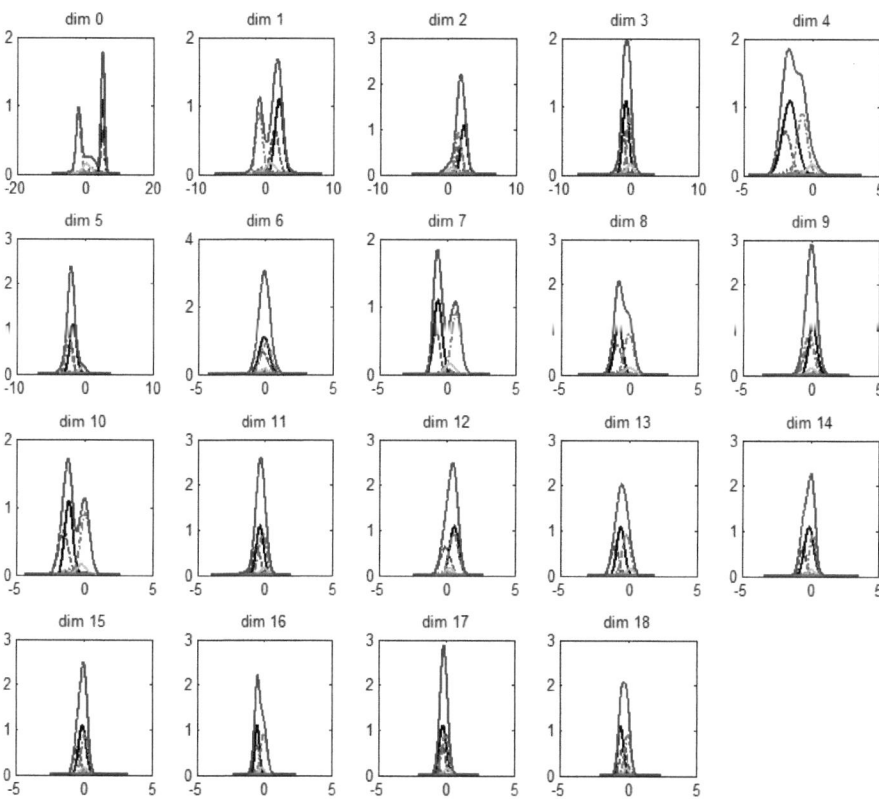

Figure 3.1: A 32-mixture GMM of 19-dimensional MFCCs. The topmost solid blue line shows the joint marginal density.

their true marginal density. In contrast, a standard GMM uses a certain (high) number of multivariate mixtures, giving equal modeling power to each dimension, also to those with very simple marginal densities. Visual inspection suggests: several parameters could be saved by modeling the dimensions independently, i.e., decoupling the number of mixtures for one dimension from the number of mixtures for any other dimension.

Accomplished in a straightforward fashion, to decouple the dimensions means to fit a one-dimensional GMM to each dimension of the feature vectors instead of training a single multimodal mixture model; the complete model would then be the ordered set of univariate GMMs, renouncing to model any interrelation of the marginals. In fact, practical GMMs use diagonal covariance matrices, assuming that the features are uncorrelated (as is the case with MFCCs)

Chapter 3. Short Utterance-Tolerant Voice Models

or that this information is unimportant or can be modeled via more mixture components. The only correlation information still possibly present in such a multivariate model is introduced by the training procedure: a complete (multivariate) mixture is always trained based on complete (multivariate) feature vectors. Thus, the togetherness of values for different dimensions in one mixture component allows inferring the co-occurrence of these values in the training data. However, this information is currently not used for speaker recognition and might only play a role in speech synthesis.

3.3 The Dimension-Decoupled GMM

The dimension-decoupled GMM (DD-GMM) λ_{DD} can be formalized as follows:

$$\lambda_{DD} = \{(M_d, \lambda_d) \,|\, 1 \leq d \leq D\} \cup \{\Omega\} \tag{3.1}$$

$$\lambda_d = \{(w_m, \mu_m, \sigma_m^2) \,|\, 1 \leq m \leq M_d\} \tag{3.2}$$

The DD-GMM is essentially a set of tuples, one for each dimension d within the dimensionality D of the feature vectors. Each tuple contains an univariate GMM λ_d and the number of mixtures M_d in this dimension. Ω is the matrix of *eigenvectors* of the covariance matrix of the training data, used to perform an *orthogonal transformation* on the (training and evaluation) data prior to modeling/recognition in order to further decorrelate the features and thus to justify the decoupled modeling, as suggested by Liu and He [1999]. After transforming the training set this way, each λ_d is trained on only the dth dimension of the training vectors using the standard EM-based maximum likelihood training procedure as introduced in Section 2.6.3. The optimal number of mixtures M_d for each model is estimated via the BIC by training all pooesible different candidate models with $1 \leq m \leq 32$ mixtures, penalizing the likelihood of the training data with their number of parameters and choosing the candidate that maximizes the BIC score [Chen and Gopalakrishnan 1998a]. The model is evaluated, then, on the Ω-transformed evaluation set of feature vectors by calculating the log-likelihood l_{DD} according to (3.3):

$$\begin{aligned} l_{DD} &= \log p(X|\lambda_{DD}) \\ &= \log \left(\prod_{d=1}^{D} \prod_{t=1}^{T} \sum_{m=1}^{M_d} w_{m,d} \cdot \phi(x_{t,d}, \mu_{m,d}, \sigma_{m,d}^2) \right) \end{aligned} \tag{3.3}$$

Here, $x_{t,d}$ is the dth dimension of the tth feature vector from $X = \{\vec{x}_t | 1 \leq t \leq T \wedge \vec{x}_t \in \mathbb{R}^D\}$, $\phi(..)$ is the univariate parametrized normal distribution as in (2.3), and $w_{m,d}$, $\mu_{m,d}$ and $\sigma_{m,d}^2$ are the weight-, mean- and variance-parameters of the mth mixture in GMM λ_d, respectively.

The DD-GMM has been implemented within the C++ class library `sclib` presented in

Chapter 8 as a mere wrapper around the existing GMM class; using the code of Liu and He [1999] for the orthogonal transform, the essential parts constitute less than 80 lines of code. On the one hand, this leaves room for speed optimizations (e.g., by integrating the DD-GMM with the GMM); on the other hand, this shows that the approach can easily be integrated with any existing GMM implementation.

3.4 Experimental Results

Several experiments have been conducted to validate that the DD-GMM improves speaker recognition performance while saving free parameters and reducing computational cost. Reynolds' experimental speaker identification scenario is used as the basic setting [Reynolds 1995]: The 630 speakers of the TIMIT database are split into a training- and a separate test set, leading to an average of 21.67/5.09 seconds of training/evaluation utterance length. The minimum and maximum length are 14.57/2.93 and 33.54/8.18 seconds, respectively, leading to a standard deviation of 2.82/0.90 seconds for the two phases. The utterances are transformed to MFCC feature vectors (20 ms frames with 50% overlap, coefficients 1–19 discarding the 0th). For the 630 training utterances, models are built a priori, then an identification experiment is run for the 630 test utterances. As models, the standard 32-mixture GMM from Reynolds (called 32-GMM in the figures) and a BIC-tuned multivariate GMM with $1 \leq m \leq 32$ mixtures (BIC-GMM) is used as baselines to compare with the proposed DD-GMM. To simulate various short utterance conditions, the training- and/or evaluation data lengths are reduced in steps of 5% from 95% of their original length to 5%, and the corresponding models' behavior is observed.

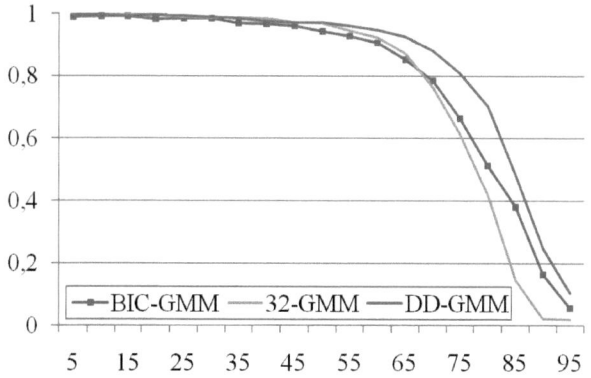

Figure 3.2: Speaker identification rate (vertical) versus removed percentage of training- and evaluation data (horizontal).

Chapter 3. Short Utterance-Tolerant Voice Models

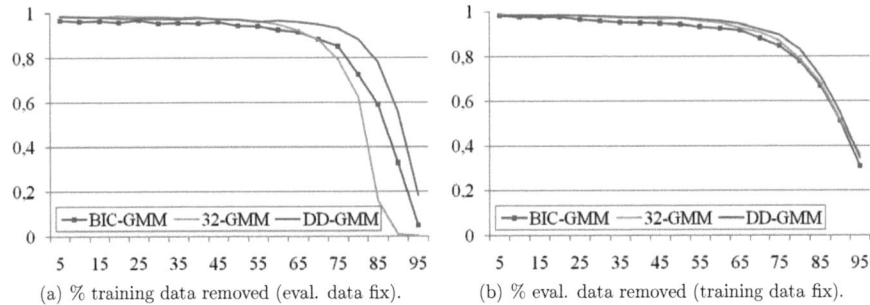

(a) % training data removed (eval. data fix).

(b) % eval. data removed (training data fix).

Figure 3.3: Speaker identification rate (vertical) versus changing data availability conditions (horizontal).

First, Figure 3.2 shows speaker identification rate (or accuracy) for all three models as training and evaluation utterance length drops simultaneously. While until 45% reduction the models' identification performance is about the same (with the 32-GMM having a small advantage), the DD-GMM then outperforms the other two competitors clearly. With $\geq 50\%$ reduction, the DD-GMM performs on the average 7.56% better then the best competitor using the same amount of data (vertical distance), while it achieves similar recognition scores as the best competitor with an average of 4.17% less data (horizontal distance) in this general short utterance case. This effect increases in the case of merely reducing training data (with evaluation data fixed at reasonable 50%), as depicted in Figure 3.3(a), while it is smaller, yet still visible, when only the evaluation data rate drops, as in Figure 3.3(b). In this case, training data is fixed at 50%, too. This result validates the dimension-decoupled modeling scheme at least for MFCC features.

Second, Figure 3.4 shows the evolution of the parameter count in the three model types as the utterances get shorter. The drop in the 32-GMM's number of parameters towards the end is due to the fact that here the amount of data is too small to find even enough distinct cluster centers for 32 mixture candidates. Thus, the mixture count is reduced in this case until a valid model can be trained. Besides this anomaly, the figure shows the efficiency of the DD-GMM in reducing the number of free parameters in the model, even more so in comparison with the standard parameter optimization via the BIC: the saving here still constitutes 90.98% on the average. For comparison, Liu and He [1999] achieved a parameter saving of about 75% using their orthogonal GMM without additionally enabling short utterance support or boosting accuracy.

Finally, runtime plots given in Figure 3.5 show the computational efficiency of the proposed approach: due to the BIC parameter search (training essentially 32 times as many models as

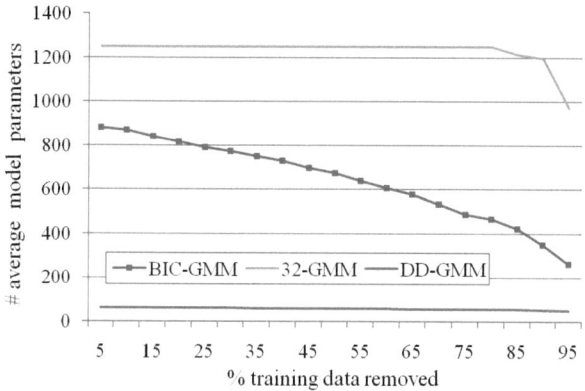

Figure 3.4: Effect of utterance length on the number of model parameters.

for the 32-GMM), the DD-GMM's training time is on the average 2.3 times longer than for the 32-GMM, but 5.1 times faster than with the BIC-GMM and still 13.5 times faster than real-time. In the evaluation phase, which occurs more often in practice and thus has the higher relevance, the DD-GMM is the fastest, outperforming the BIC-GMM and 32-GMM by a factor of 2.1 and 3.6, respectively, taking only 54.5% of real-time. All measurements have been taken on a usual contemporary PC having a 3 GHz Intel Core2Duo CPU and 2GB of memory, running a C++ implementation under Fedora 12 Linux exclusively on one core.

3.5 Conclusions

The dimension-decoupled GMM has been presented as a novel approach to cope with short (training and evaluation) utterances in speaker recognition tasks. The fundamental idea is to find a more compact model that describes the data using less parameters in order to be estimated more reliably. The achieved good results support the thesis of Schmidhuber [2008] that striving for compression progress is a successful driver behind many natural phenomena.

In the case of lacking data, the DD-GMM gives more reliable results (i.e., higher recognition rate) than the baselines, while it is computationally more efficient even in the case of having plenty of data, where it also gives competitive accuracy. The DD-GMM allows to recognize speakers in regions where baseline GMM approaches are not usable anymore (i.e. more than 80% identification rate with less than 5.5 seconds of training- and 1.3 seconds of evaluation data). At the same time, the proposed approach can easily be integrated into other short utterance schemes, allowing for synergetic effects, and can straightforwardly be implemented in any GMM environment.

Chapter 3. Short Utterance-Tolerant Voice Models

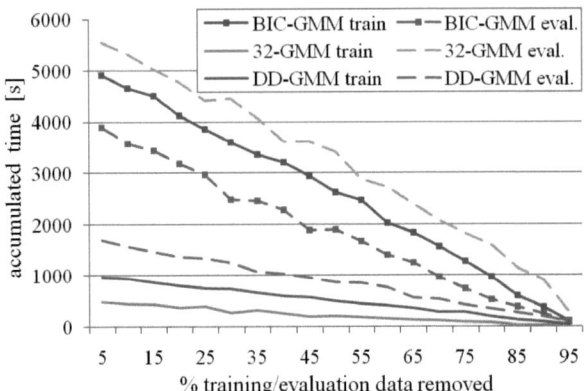

Figure 3.5: Effect of utterance length on computing time.

Areas for future work are: testing the DD-GMM with other feature types, evaluating its performance using further data sets, and applying it as a classifier in other domains than speaker recognition.

"A man's errors are his portals of discovery."
James Joyce (1882–1941)

4

Noise Robust Modeling

4.1 Introduction

In supervised speech- or voice recognition tasks, several existing approaches suffer from the mismatch between training and evaluation conditions caused by interfering background signals called noise. A prominent technique to deal with such conditions in the modeling- or recognition stage is the MixMax model. Nádas et al. [1989] have introduced it as a technique for speech recognition in the presence of noise. It provides a way to build a statistical mixture model, normally a GMM, of a signal, while simultaneously keeping a model of the accompanying noise. Through the interaction of both models, noise compensation is achieved via a statistical variant of noise masking [Klatt 1976]: the noisy speech mixtures get "masked" by the background mixtures rather than cleaned. In the likelihood computation, the feature vectors are scored against the combined speaker-background model. The more a speaker mixture is masked by noise, the less it contributes to the final likelihood score. As a consequence, testing previously unseen signals against models built from training data under different noise conditions is possible as long as a model for the current noise exists.

Varga and Moore [1990] have developed the same idea independently of Nádas et al. for the decomposition of speech and noise to facilitate speech recognition. Rose et al. [1994] have used the MixMax model for robust speaker recognition and called it the *Gaussian mixture model with integrated background* (GMM-IB). They placed it in a framework of general signal–

noise interaction and modeling. Burshtein and Gannot [2002] have used the approach for speech enhancement on embedded devices, focusing on accelerating the necessary computations. Tsai et al. [2004] have employed the MixMax model for singer's voice modeling within music information retrieval in several works [Tsai and Wang 2004, 2005, 2006]. Afify et al. [2001] have derived upper and lower bounds on the mean of noise-corrupted speech signals using the MixMax' modeling assumptions. Furthermore, the MixMax equations have been extended and evaluated by Deoras and Hasegawa-Johnson [2004] for simultaneous speech recognition (i.e., source separation) and Logan and Robinson [1997], Erell and Weintraub [1993] as well as Erell and Burshtein [1997] for noisy speech recognition, enhancement and adaptation, among others.

This chapter provides a survey of the MixMax model. It reviews the existing literature and thus prepares the ground for the next chapter, but mainly makes the following contribution: an in-depth discussion is given of the suitability of the MixMax model for the cepstral domain, inspired by contradicting views expressed in several recent publications. The contradictions are dissolved by experiments, arguments and proofs in the following sections. Additionally, small errors in the corpus of the model's training equations are corrected that have been repeated in the literature since their initial publication in 1994.

The chapter is organized as follows: Section 4.2 introduces the idea behind the MixMax model, followed by the model's formal definition and an explication of its corpus of training- and evaluation equations in Section 4.3. Section 4.4 then introduces the problem of contradicting views about the MixMax model's suitability for cepstral features. They are investigated by providing an alternative explanation for publications claiming to use the MixMax model on MFCC features in Section 4.5, and a proof that the other publications refraining from doing so are actually right in Section 4.6. Section 4.7 concludes the chapter and outlines areas for future research.

Parts of the work presented in this chapter have been published in a paper by Stadelmann and Freisleben [2010b].

4.2 The MixMax Idea

The principal idea behind the MixMax model is as follows: given is an (unobserved) acoustic feature vector $\vec{z}'$ that is formed as the addition of independent pure signal and noise vectors $\vec{x}'$ and $\vec{y}'$, i.e., $\vec{z}' = \vec{x}' + \vec{y}'$, but the actual observations are logarithms of (possibly linear transformations of) these vectors ($\vec{z} = \log t(\vec{z}')$, $\vec{x} = \log t(\vec{x}')$, $\vec{y} = \log t(\vec{y}')$, where $t()$ is some linear transformation or the identity). Then, the following approximation can be used to model the signal–noise interaction in the new (transformed, logarithmized) domain to simplify and speed up subsequent modeling computations:

$$\vec{z} = \log(t(\vec{x'}) + t(\vec{y'})) = \log(e^{\vec{x}} + e^{\vec{y}}) \approx \max(\vec{x}, \vec{y}) \quad (4.1)$$

Note that both the log-function and the max-function are meant to operate component-wise if used with vector arguments, i.e., (4.1) is a shorthand notation for all components $\{z_d | 1 \le d \le D\}$, of $\vec{z} \in \mathbb{R}^D$.

Consider the following concrete situation: two frames of speech signal $\vec{x'}$ and noise $\vec{y'}$ are purely additive in the time-domain. This happens, for example, when two different sound recordings are mixed together after they have been recorded, as it is done within music (singing and diverse instruments) or movies (soundtrack or effects and possibly dubbed voices), or when different sound sources are recorded with a single microphone. Therefore, signal and noise are also additive in the FFT domain (i.e., $t() = FFT()$), because the FFT is linear with respect to addition. Thus, the signal is really additive in the frequency domain. But when the power-spectrum $|\ |^2$ is then computed of some Fourier-transformed signal $a = b+c$, it yields $|a|^2 = |b|^2 + |c|^2 + 2 \cdot |b| \cdot |c|$, which can be approximated by $|a|^2 \approx |b|^2 + |c|^2$. This (approximate) additivity in the power-spectral domain remains after passing the power-spectrum through a bank of (probably mel-scaled) filters. But after taking the logarithm ($\vec{z} = \log FFT(\vec{z'})$, etc.) of these filterbank energies, the signal–noise interaction function becomes $\log(e^{\vec{x}} + e^{\vec{y}})$, which is approximated by $\max(\vec{x}, \vec{y})$ for the sake of computational simplicity.

Thus, the MixMax model is appropriate, for example, if signal and noise are additive in the time domain, but the observations are log-filterbank energy (FBE) features. The max()-approximation leads to manageable mathematical expressions and good results, explaining its application to numerous problems in the audio processing domain. It also explains the name: via GMMs, mixtures of maxima of signal and noise are modeled.

4.3 Definition of the MixMax Model

A MixMax model λ_{MM} consists of two separate GMMs λ^s and λ^b and specialized algorithms for training and testing. It is defined as follows [Rose et al. 1994]:

$$\lambda_{MM} = \{\lambda^s, \lambda^b\} \quad (4.2)$$

$$\lambda^s = \{(w_i^s, \vec{\mu}_i^s, \vec{\sigma_i^2}^s) | 1 \le i \le I\} \quad (4.3)$$

$$\lambda^b = \{(w_j^b, \vec{\mu}_j^b, \vec{\sigma_j^2}^b) | 1 \le j \le J\} \quad (4.4)$$

Here, λ^s is the signal model with I mixtures and λ^b is the background model with J mixtures, each having a weight w, a mean vector $\vec{\mu}$ and a diagonal covariance matrix $\vec{\sigma}^2$ per mixture.

4.3.1 Model Training

The background model has to be trained in advance using samples of the expected noise and a standard GMM training procedure as described in Section 2.6.3. Then, training the signal model via the EM algorithm and the specialized equations derived in the literature [Burshtein and Gannot 2002; Rose et al. 1994] can be accomplished independently for each dimension, taking into account the diagonal covariance matrix of the Gaussians:

$$\overline{w_i^s} = \frac{1}{T} \sum_{t=1}^{T} \sum_{j=1}^{J} \prod_{d=1}^{D} p(i,j|z_{t,d}, \lambda_{MM}) \tag{4.5}$$

$$\overline{\mu_{i,d}^s} = \frac{\sum_{t=1}^{T} \sum_{j=1}^{J} p(i,j|z_{t,d}, \lambda_{MM}) \cdot E\{x_{t,d}|z_{t,d}, i, j, \lambda_{MM}\}}{\sum_{t=1}^{T} \sum_{j=1}^{J} p(i,j|z_{t,d}, \lambda_{MM})} \tag{4.6}$$

$$\overline{\sigma_{i,d}^{2\,s}} = \frac{\sum_{t=1}^{T} \sum_{j=1}^{J} p(i,j|z_{t,d}, \lambda_{MM}) \cdot E\{x_{t,d}^2|z_{t,d}, i, j, \lambda_{MM}\}}{\sum_{t=1}^{T} \sum_{j=1}^{J} p(i,j|z_{t,d}, \lambda_{MM})} - \overline{\mu_{i,d}^s}^2 \tag{4.7}$$

where $\overline{w_i^s}$, $\overline{\mu_{i,d}^s}$ and $\overline{\sigma_{i,d}^{2\,s}}$ are the new (reestimated) parameters of the signal GMM λ^s for the next round of the EM algorithm. D is again the dimensionality of the feature vectors $\vec{z} \in \mathbb{R}^D$ and d the index for the dimension. To apply the formulas, several other terms must be defined:

$$p(i,j|z_d, \lambda_{MM}) = \frac{p(z_d|i,j,\lambda_{MM}) \cdot w_i^s \cdot w_j^b}{\sum_{i=1}^{I} \sum_{j=1}^{J} p(z_d|i,j,\lambda_{MM}) \cdot w_i^s \cdot w_j^b} \tag{4.8}$$

$$E\{x_d|z_d, i, j, \lambda_{MM}\} = \frac{z_d}{p(x_d = z_d|i,j,\lambda_{MM})^{-1}} + \frac{E\{x_d|x_d < z_d, i, j, \lambda_{MM}\}}{(1 - p(x_d = z_d|i,j,\lambda_{MM}))^{-1}} \tag{4.9}$$

$$E\{x_d^2|z_d, i, j, \lambda_{MM}\} = \frac{z_d^2}{p(x_d = z_d|i,j,\lambda_{MM})^{-1}} + \frac{E\{x_d^2|x_d < z_d, i, j, \lambda_{MM}\}}{(1 - p(x_d = z_d|i,j,\lambda_{MM}))^{-1}} \tag{4.10}$$

Here, $z_{t,d}$ is the dth dimension of the tth observation vector in the transformed, logarithmized domain, while x_d is its implicit clean signal estimate in the same domain. The meaning of (4.9) is as follows: the expected value $E\{x|z, i, j\}$ of a clean speech component, given the noisy observation and a specific foreground–background state combination, is the weighted mean of the noisy observation z and the signal's expected value given that its amplitude is below the noisy observation's amplitude ($E\{x|x < z\}$). The weights are defined by the probability that the current observation is already a clean signal ($p(x = z)$) and its complementary event. These equations already make use of the max assumption (in the formulation of the expected value for x, which needs its amplitude being smaller than the amplitude of z), which becomes evident in the following equations:

$$p(z_d|i,j,\lambda_{MM}) = b_j(z_d) \cdot S_i(z_d) + s_i(z_d) \cdot B_j(z_d) \tag{4.11}$$

4.3. Definition of the MixMax Model

$$p(x_d = z_d | i, j, \lambda_{MM}) = \frac{s_i(z_d) \cdot B_j(z_d)}{b_j(z_d) \cdot S_i(z_d) + s_i(z_d) \cdot B_j(z_d)} \quad (4.12)$$

$$E\{x_d | x_d < z_d, i, j, \lambda_{MM}\} = \mu_{i,d}^s - \sigma_{i,d}^{2\ s} \cdot \frac{s_i(z_d)}{S_i(z_d)} \quad (4.13)$$

$$E\{x_d^2 | x_d < z_d, i, j, \lambda_{MM}\} = \left(\mu_{i,d}^{2\ s} + \sigma_{i,d}^{2\ s}\right) - \sigma_{i,d}^{2\ s} \cdot \frac{s_i(z_d) \cdot (z_d + \mu_{i,d}^s)}{S_i(z_d)} \quad (4.14)$$

Here, $b_j()$ and $s_i()$ are the univariate Gaussian PDFs for mixtures j and i of the background- and signal GMM, respectively (see (2.3) for the definition of the PDF $\phi(..)$ of the normal distribution). $B_j()$ and $S_i()$ are the corresponding *cumulative density functions* (CDFs) as defined below. Note the squared form $\sigma_{i,d}^{2\ s}$ in (4.13): this has been incorrectly given un-squared in the original paper by Rose et al. [1994] and in the subsequent literature.

$$b_j(z_d) = \phi(z_d, \mu_{j,d}^b, \sigma_{j,d}^{2\ b}) \quad (4.15)$$

$$B_j(z_d) = \Phi\left(\frac{z_d - \mu_{j,d}^b}{\sigma_{j,d}^b}\right) \quad (4.16)$$

$$s_i(z_d) = \phi(z_d, \mu_{i,d}^s, \sigma_{i,d}^{2\ s}) \quad (4.17)$$

$$S_i(z_d) = \Phi\left(\frac{z_d - \mu_{i,d}^s}{\sigma_{j,d}^s}\right) \quad (4.18)$$

The Gaussian CDF $\Phi()$ is defined in terms of the error function erf as follows:

$$\Phi(x) = \frac{1}{2} \cdot \left[1 + erf\left(\frac{x}{\sqrt{2}}\right)\right] \quad (4.19)$$

$$= \frac{1}{\sqrt{2\pi}} \cdot \int_{-\infty}^{x} \phi(x) dt \quad (4.20)$$

4.3.2 Model Evaluation

During training, the mixtures of the signal model λ^s in the individual frequency bands (dimensions) get masked by the background mixtures at the points where both distributions overlap. During testing of the combined model against evaluation data, the probability of noise corruption for each feature vector, frequency band and state (mixture) in the combined signal–background mixture lattice is computed. The higher this probability is, the less does this component contribute to the final log-likelihood score l_{MM} in (4.21):

$$l_{MM} = \log p(Z|\lambda_{MM})$$
$$= \sum_{t=1}^{T} \log \left(\sum_{i=1}^{I} \sum_{j=1}^{J} w_i^s \cdot w_j^b \cdot \prod_{d=1}^{D} p(z_{t,d}|i,j,\lambda_{MM}) \right) \quad (4.21)$$

where $Z = \{\vec{z}_t | 1 \leq t \leq T \wedge \vec{z}_t \in \mathbb{R}^D\}$ is the set of evaluation feature vectors.

4.4 MixMax and MFCC Feature Vectors

The MixMax model has shown its effectiveness in reducing the influence of noise in the tasks mentioned above. Nevertheless, it suffers from not using the best possible input: by design, the MixMax assumption is not appropriate for cepstral features like MFCCs that have many advantages over conventional filterbank features (see Section 2.6.2). These advantages can typically cause a drop in the final error rate as high as 5–10% absolute reduction and must be left unexploited in the case of the MixMax model.

Several researchers acknowledge this constraint, e.g., Nádas et al. [1989], Varga and Moore [1990] and Rose et al. [1994]. Nevertheless, in a series of publications on singer identification in popular music databases, authors report on good results using MixMax models in conjunction with MFCC feature vectors [Tsai and Wang 2004, 2005, 2006; Tsai et al. 2004].

As a motivating example, consider the power envelopes depicted in Figure 4.1: the good concordance of FBEs with the max-assumption can be seen as well as its violation within the MFCCs. Loosely speaking, the inappropriateness of the MixMax model for MFCC features is due to the MFCC vector being the cosine transform of a FBE vector. Thus, every single component of a MFCC vector is a weighted linear combination of all components of the FBE observation ($\vec{z} = DCT(\max(\vec{x}, \vec{y}))$), such that a highly non-linear coherence between $\vec{x}$ and $\vec{y}$ through the nested call to the max(.) function is created. No good results can be expected when this relationship is ignored.

4.5 Explaining Good Results Using "MixMax" and MFCCs

In this section, one part of the mentioned contradiction is dissolved by explaining Tsai et al.'s good results. The approach taken here is to show that in fact a different model ("the actual model used", AMU) has unawarely been applied by the authors, and to discover what this AMU looks like. Subsection 4.5.1 begins with the extraction of the AMU's training and evaluation equations from the authors' source code. The equations deviate strongly from the MixMax model's formulation, and the implementation suggests that they might have evolved

4.5. Explaining Good Results Using "MixMax" and MFCCs

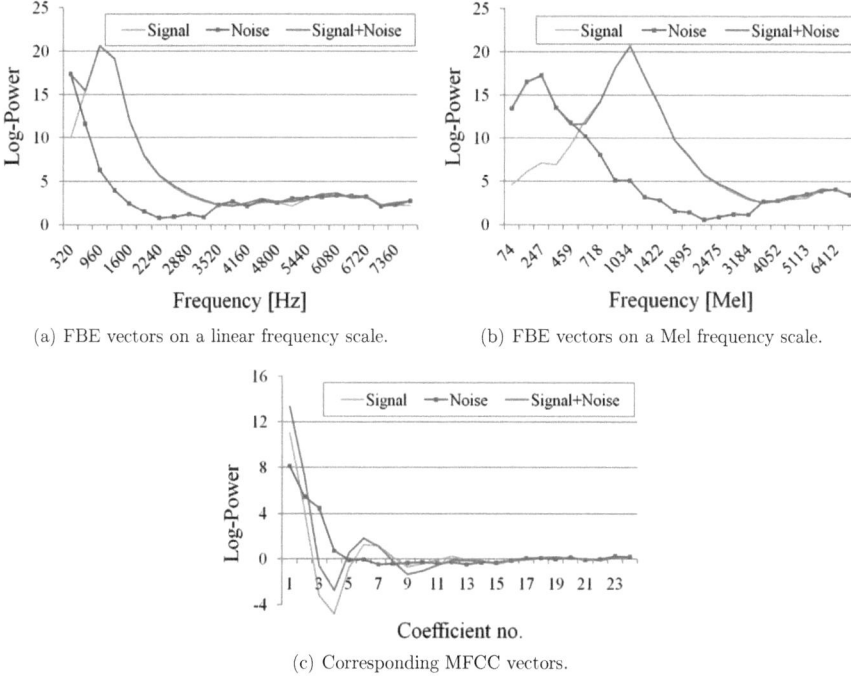

(a) FBE vectors on a linear frequency scale.

(b) FBE vectors on a Mel frequency scale.

(c) Corresponding MFCC vectors.

Figure 4.1: Example of the power envelopes of FBE and MFCC vectors of some pure signal, pure noise and the corresponding combined observation.

unintentionally. Then, Subsection 4.5.2 reports on extensive experiments comparing the results using these equations with the MixMax- and other models. The experiments allow to draw the following conclusions:

a The actual model used by Tsai et al. in conjunction with MFCCs indeed performs significantly better than MixMax & FBE, GMM & MFCC and (of course) MixMax & MFCC on quite diverse data sets; this shows its *suitability* (to some extent) for noise compensation in the cepstral domain.

b The actual model used does not perform significantly different than a particular extension of the GMM baseline; this indicates its *identity* as being more related to this baseline extension rather than to the MixMax model.

Based on this analysis, it is suggested to dissolve the contradiction in the literature by arguing that Tsai et al. seem to have used the model extracted here, but have described the

Chapter 4. Noise Robust Modeling

MixMax model in their publications. Publishing the actual model used in the next subsection is meant to clarify which method actually produces good results in compensating noise and modeling voices in the cepstral domain. In straightens the body of literature regarding the MixMax model and its area of application: the MixMax model is not applicable in the cepstral domain.

4.5.1 The Actual Model Used

Tsai et al. thankfully provided the source code of their published singer recognition system in order to pursue the question why it shows good results in a context where it is not supposed to do so. Careful analysis revealed a set of equations for the actual model used that deviates from the MixMax equations given in (4.5)–(4.21).

Let λ_{AMU} denote the actual model used, defined as in (4.2)–(4.4). The following expressions are used to train its integrated signal model λ^s as revealed by reverse engineering:

$$\overline{\mu_{i,d}^s} = \mu_{i,d}^s \tag{4.22}$$

$$\overline{\sigma_{i,d}^s} = \sigma_{i,d}^s \tag{4.23}$$

$$\overline{w_i^s} = \frac{1}{T} \cdot \sum_{t=1}^{T} \frac{w_i^s \cdot \sum_{j=1}^{J} w_j^b \cdot p_{train}(\vec{z}_t | i, j, \lambda_{AMU})}{\sum_{u=1}^{I} w_u^s \cdot \sum_{v=1}^{J} w_v^b \cdot p_{train}(\vec{z}_t | u, v, \lambda_{AMU})} \tag{4.24}$$

$$p_{train}(\vec{z}_t | i, j, \lambda_{AMU}) = \prod_{d=1}^{D} p(z_{t,d} | i, j, \lambda_{AMU})$$

$$= \prod_{d=1}^{D} (b_j(z_{t,d}) \cdot S_i(z_{t,d}) + s_i(z_{t,d}) \cdot B_j(z_{t,d})) \tag{4.25}$$

Here, $p(z_{t,d}|i,j,\lambda_{AMU})$ is defined as in (4.11). The difference (apart from the domain of the observation vector, which is MFCC here) to the equations given by Rose et al. [1994] and in Section 4.3 for the MixMax model is that the means and variances are not re-estimated, i.e., they remain as initialized prior to EM training. The expression for the log-likelihood function l_{AMU} has been determined to be

$$l_{AMU} = \log p(Z|\lambda_{AMU})$$

$$= \sum_{t=1}^{T} \log \left(\sum_{i=1}^{I} \sum_{j=1}^{J} w_i^s \cdot w_j^b \cdot p_{eval}(\vec{z}_t | i, j, \lambda_{AMU}) \right) \tag{4.26}$$

with

$$p_{eval}(\vec{z}_t|i,j,\lambda_{AMU}) = \left(\prod_{d=1}^{D} b_{j,d}(z_{t,d})\right) \cdot \left(\frac{\sum_{d=1}^{D} S_{i,d}(z_{t,d})}{D}\right) + \left(\prod_{d=1}^{D} s_{i,d}(z_{t,d})\right) \cdot \left(\frac{\sum_{d=1}^{D} B_{j,d}(z_{t,d})}{D}\right) \quad (4.27)$$

Note that different equations are used during training and evaluation to compute the "likelihood" $p_{train/eval}(\vec{z}|i,j,\lambda_{AMU})$ of the current vector to a given state of the model. The equation for $p_{eval}()$ differs from (4.25) in that it gives up the component-wise max() assumption. Instead, its meaning is "the probability that the components of the signal are *on the average* greater than the components of the noise or vice versa". Though this "average maximum" signal–noise interaction is also not generally true for the coherence of signal and noise in the MFCC domain, it might approximate the strongly non-linear behavior.

4.5.2 Experimentation

It is the purpose of this subsection to

a show that the equations nevertheless point to an effective method for noise compensation in the cepstral domain as indicated by the positive results;

b give evidence about what this effective method might be.

First, it is reported on the datasets used in the experiments that partly resemble those presented in Tsai et al.'s publications, but largely exceed them. Then, experiments are presented supporting the view that the AMU is in fact an effective model, before another set of experiments is performed that aims at revealing its "true" identity. Conclusions from these experiments are drawn within the discussion in the next subsection. All experiments follow the setup that Tsai et al. used, i.e., closed set singer/speaker identification experiments are conducted in the spirit of Reynolds [1995].

Databases

Three different datasets are used to provide a broad basis for extensive computational simulations. Therefore, each dataset has a distinct focus: singing voice with music, spontaneous conversations or noisy telephone quality speech. In particular, the following datasets are utilized:

The DB-S-1 database introduced by Tsai and Wang [2006] has been primarily designed for singer recognition experiments. It splits into the training set DB-S-1-T and the evaluation set

Chapter 4. Noise Robust Modeling

DB-S-1-E, each consisting of a total of 100 Mandarin pop songs, 5 by each of 10 male and 10 female distinct solo singers. The data has been downsampled from CD quality to 22 kHz. Each song is between 2:15 and 6:30 minutes in length. However, in case of FBE features, only 7 male and 8 female distinct artists with 4 to 5 songs each are present in the database as provided by the authors, resulting in 72 songs per subset.

The Portuguese TV soap opera "Riscos SL" is part of the "MPEG-7 Content Set" [MPEG 7 Requirement Group 1998]. All speech from speakers occurring more than once has been extracted, resulting in a population of 5 male and 6 female speakers in the set called MPEG7 in the rest of this section. It is further divided such that each speaker has an equal number of utterances in his/her training- and evaluation set, resulting in 3–47 seconds of training speech per speaker from 1–10 utterances (18.4 seconds in 4.3 utterances on the average) and 2–28 seconds of test data from 1–10 utterances (15.3 seconds in 4.2 utterances on the average). The speech within this database can be characterized as short, spontaneous and emotional in nature, accompanied by background noise such as speech babble and ambient sounds as well as music. This forms a challenging scenario for speaker identification experiments. The data is converted from an 44 kHz 192Kbps MPEG-1 layer II compressed audio stream to a 16 kHz waveform before further processing.

The NOIZEUS corpus has been introduced by Hu and Loizou [2006] for the comparison of speech enhancement algorithms. It consists of read speech from 3 male and 3 female speakers. Each of them uttered 5 phonetically rich sentences that were later mixed with 5 different noise types from the AURORA database at 4 different SNRs from 15 dB to 0 dB. These studio-quality recordings were further processed to have telephone speech quality at 8 kHz sample rate. To use this data for voice recognition, it is split into a training and evaluation set as follows: the first two sentences of all speakers with accompanying restaurant ambient noise at 15 dB and 0 dB are used for model training, while the last 3 sentences with airport-/station-/train- and exhibition-noise at SNRs of 10 dB and 5 dB are used for testing. This way, there is no co-occurrence of sentences, SNRs or noise-types in both training and testing, making the task of speaker identification more difficult due to unforeseen circumstances.

The datasets are not proprietary and are also used by other works or are actually available to the public (in case of MPEG7 and NOIZEUS), so that the experiments are repeatable. For the purpose of noise model training, each set also contains samples of pure interfering noise, collected from the parts before, in between and after the speech in case of DB-S-1 and MPEG7, and from the pure noise samples in case of NOIZEUS.

4.5. Explaining Good Results Using "MixMax" and MFCCs

Experiments Confirming the AMU's General Suitability

These experiments are designed to assess the performance of the MixMax model and the AMU on both log-filterbank energy- and cepstral features and to give evidence of their respective strengths and weaknesses. Following the setup of Tsai et al., the input data is first processed by HTK [Young et al. 2005] to produce 20 MFCCs or 28 FBEs per frame. Each frame is preemphasized with a factor of $\alpha = 0.97$ and Hamming-windowed, with a frame length of 32 ms and a frame step of 10 ms. All voice (singer, speaker) models comprise 32 mixture components, while in case of noise models 8 mixtures are used. All models are initialized via 10 iterations of the k-means algorithm and trained using 20 iterations of the EM algorithm. As a baseline for comparison, scores for a standard GMM recognition system (EM-trained, without UBM score normalization) are also reported.

Features	Model	Recognition rate		
		DB-S-1 [%]	MPEG7 [%]	NOIZEUS [%]
FBE	GMM	88.89	54.35	45.83
	MixMax	91.67	56.52	64.58
	AMU	91.67	60.87	47.22
MFCC	GMM	93.00	63.04	70.13
	MixMax	75.00	39.13	68.05
	AMU	98.00	73.91	71.53

Table 4.1: Singer/speaker identification rate on all three databases.

The first recognition rate column of Table 4.1 shows the results of voice recognition (in fact: closed set singer identification) on the DB-S-1 database. Several facts can be noted: looking at the performance of the GMM system with the different features, the superiority of MFCCs over FBEs can be seen. For the MixMax model, the predicted drop in recognition rate when using MFCCs is quite obvious. The AMU scores equal to the MixMax model when used with FBEs, but scores best in conjunction with MFCC features. This last result is comparable (except for small variations due to model initialization, score normalization etc.) to the one reported by Tsai and Wang [2006] for the solo modeling case with automatic segmentation, validating the used implementation within the sclib as well as the experimental setup.

In the second recognition rate column of Table 4.1 the results for the MPEG7 test set are reported. They are qualitatively equal to those on the DB-S-1 database, though the recognition rates are consistently shifted down by 20–30 percentage points. This may be due to very short training and evaluation utterance lengths as well as highly non-stationary noise, as reported earlier.

Finally, the results for the NOIZEUS corpus are shown in the last column of Table 4.1. There are two differences to the previous results: The MixMax model, in combination with MFCC features, works better than with FBE features, though it is still the worst classifier on MFCCs.

Chapter 4. Noise Robust Modeling

Also, the AMU is clearly outperformed on FBEs by the MixMax model. Again, note that the utterances here consist of only one short sentence.

In general, the new AMU & MFCC combination always performs best. Compared to the results of the formerly best combination, MixMax & FBE, an average relative improvement in identification rate of 16.14% is achieved (6.19% on DB-S-1, 30.77% on MPEG7 and 10.76% on NOIZEUS, respectively). This corresponds to an average increase of the scores as high as 10.22 percentage points. Table 4.2 gives the raw identification results for these two systems and all three databases.

System	Correct ID [#]	Wrong ID [#]	Σ [#]
MixMax & FBE	185	77	262
AMU & MFCC	235	55	290
Σ	420	132	552

Table 4.2: Raw identification results for all 3 databases in a contingency table.

These experiments support already expressed arguments: the MixMax model's inappropriateness in case of MFCCs is demonstrated by means of low recognition rates, and the general preference of cepstral features over log-filterbank energies can be seen. The results are novel with regard to the AMU. Here, empirical evidence is given for a certain suitability of the specific model formulation in Section 4.5.1 in conjunction with MFCC features by means of high recognition rates in difficult voice recognition scenarios. A χ^2-test based on the values of Table 4.2 suggests that the H_0 hypothesis of these results being not significantly better than those of the MixMax & FBE approach has to be rejected with 99.5% confidence. This and the qualitative homogeneity of the results over all three highly different databases also gives evidence that the outcome is not data-dependent or random, but somewhat models the non-linear interaction of signal and noise in the transformed domain.

On the other hand, (4.22)–(4.27) or in fact the AMU's model formulation, look too contrary to reason (i.e., too random) at some points. There seems to be another—yet hidden—model that still needs to be discovered, as described below.

Experiments Indicating the AMU's "True" Identity

A closer look at the AMU equations reveals that in the training part (4.22)–(4.25), only the weights are changed during subsequent EM iterations. Equation (4.24) uses (4.25), the probability that an observation vector at time t is reflected by the state (i, j) under the component-wise maximum assumption of signal–noise interaction, which is an unchanged adoption from the corresponding MixMax equation in (4.11). Two conclusions can be drawn:

a since this assumption is wrong for MFCC features, the meaning of (4.24) is questionable;

b since (4.25) is also used in the MixMax training equations for reestimating the mean- and variance-vectors, it is obvious that the omitted training of the means and variances in the AMU should be beneficial to the model's performance (in the sense of rather doing nothing than doing something wrong).

These findings directly suggest two changes in the AMU formulation with respect to training: First, adjusting the means and variances of the model in a non noise-specific, standard GMM sense should further amplify the effect gained by leaving them as initialized by k-means (because initializing the parameters via k-means roughly clusters the training data by using a distance measure; EM training refines this clustering in a maximum likelihood sense, so reestimating $\vec{\mu}_i^s$ and $\vec{\sigma}_i^s$ via non noise-compensating equations should just improve the initialization). This direction has not yielded promising results in preliminary experiments, so it is excluded from further analysis.

Model	Recognition rate		
	DB-S-1 [%]	MPEG7 [%]	NOIZEUS [%]
GMM (32)	93.00	63.04	70.14
GMM (40)	92.00	58.70	73.61
GMM (32/8, per dim.)	78.00	58.70	63.19
GMM (32/8, per frame)	95.00	65.22	73.61
MixMax (32/8)	75.00	39.13	68.05
AMU (32/8)	98.00	73.91	71.53
w/o eval. CDFs	94.00	69.57	71.53
w/o both CDFs	97.00	65.22	74.31
w/o both CDFs, ∨	97.00	65.22	74.31
w/o both CDFs, ∨, both per dim.	92.00	65.22	71.53
w/o both CDFs, ∨, both per frame	97.00	65.22	71.53

Table 4.3: Singer/speaker identification rates for AMU variants and baselines using MFCC features on all three databases.

Second, the use of p_{train} (4.25) in the reestimation of the weights (4.24) should be exchanged by a more suitable formulation. An option is to use (variants of) the adapted form p_{eval} (4.27) applied during the evaluation of an AMU. Results are reported in Table 4.3 for MFCC feature vectors and several reasonable baselines (the MixMax model, too, for comparison) and a couple of such variants, as described below:

"GMM (32)" indicates voice modeling with a 32-mixture GMM without regarding the background noise. "GMM (40)" describes the same system using 40 mixtures, thereby reaching the same number of used parameters as a model with 32 foreground- and 8 background mixtures. Thus, the statistical expressibility (in terms of number of parameters) is equal to all background-modeling techniques, and any difference in performance must be attributed to the expressive power (i.e., goodness of fit) of the specific model under consideration rather than to the model's size. "GMM (32/8, per dim.)" stands for a system comprising two separate standard GMMs,

Chapter 4. Noise Robust Modeling

a 32-mixture GMM trained on the noisy speech samples, and an 8-mixture one trained on the pure noise. During recognition, for each dimension in each vector it is decided if it is better fitted by the noise- or the voice model, and only scores from a better fitting voice model contribute to the final likelihood; thus, it can be viewed as a non-probabilistic, on/off-like noise masking scheme per dimension. "GMM (32/8, per frame)" makes the same decision based on a complete vector (all its dimensions). The MixMax model and AMU are already known from above.

The six variants of the AMU are all chosen with respect to finding "the original formulation" to (4.27), i.e., to find an improvement. Because of the mathematically questionable "average maximum" assumption expressed in the equation via the CDFs, the variants depict several approaches to reformulate the CDF part of the equation. First, "w/o eval. CDFs" describes the variant that eliminates all calls to CDFs in p_{eval}, i.e. they are replaced with a factor of 1. Second, "w/o both CDFs" stands for the variant without any CDFs in both p_{train} and p_{eval}. Third, "w/o both CDFs, ∨" describes the alternative that both in training and evaluation, the CDFs are omitted and the remaining two PDFs are joined not just via addition (meaning a probabilistic "or", denoted ∨, in the case of mutually exclusive events). Instead, the formulation models the probability that the vector $\vec{z}$ is speech or noise given that the two events are *not* mutually exclusive: $b(z)+s(z) - b(z) \cdot (z)$ (dropping all indices). The remaining difference between training and evaluation equations is now only the fact that during training, the equation correctly regards the multivariate nature of $\vec{z}$ by calculating the product over all dimensions of the diagonal-covariance Gaussians; during evaluation, however, the multivariate nature is oddly treated by building the product of the individual terms independently. This difference is resolved in the cases "w/o both CDFs, ∨, both per dim." and "w/o both CDFs, ∨, both per frame", where in the former case both training and evaluation equations work truly multivariate; in the latter case, both equations adopt the formulation of (4.27).

4.5.3 Discussion

From Table 4.3, several conclusions can be drawn:

First, all variants explored to improve the AMU and to discover a hidden meaning fail, yielding worse results than the originally found equations. This suggests that both parts, the equations for model training and evaluation, interact in their specific form to create the good results: the training stage contributes mixture means and variances resulting from pure k-means clustering, and weights that are adjusted in a manner that tends to increase the impact of few mixtures while simultaneously dropping most others to have very low impact on the result. The likelihood computation stage is built on the assumption of signal and background interaction that has previously been called the "average maximum". It departs from the paradigm of

4.5. Explaining Good Results Using "MixMax" and MFCCs

component-wise likelihood computation by operating on the whole vectors at once (which can be implemented component-wise again, as suggested by the equations, through independence of the individual MFC coefficients). It appears that the approach of "optimizing" the AMU equations failed.

Second, Table 4.3 interestingly shows that the top-scoring original AMU formulation is not far away (in terms of identification rates) from the simple but effective "GMM (32/8, per frame)" approach (denoted as the "baseline" below). In fact, a detailed analysis of the two models' individual scores of all test utterances versus the enrolled speaker models reveals that the produced scores are very similar to each other: a simple value of concordance, c, reaches 94.70% agreement according to (4.28):

$$c = \frac{\sum_{t=1}^{T} \sum_{s_1=1}^{S} \sum_{s_2=s_1+1}^{S} r(X_t, \lambda_{AMU}^{s_1}, \lambda_{AMU}^{s_2}, \lambda_{baseline}^{s_1}, \lambda_{baseline}^{s_2})}{T \cdot S \cdot \frac{S-1}{2}} \quad (4.28)$$

where X_t is the tth feature vector set out of T test utterances and $\lambda_{AMU/baseline}^{s}$ the sth enrolled speaker model out of a total of S trained models. The function $r(....)$ returns 1 if and only if the two models agree on the relative rank of two trained models (as produced by ordering them according to the achieved likelihood) for a specific test utterance:

$$r(X, \lambda_1^u, \lambda_1^v, \lambda_2^u, \lambda_2^v) = \begin{cases} 1 & \text{if } \begin{array}{l}(l_1(X|\lambda_1^u) < l_1(X|\lambda_1^v) \land l_2(X|\lambda_2^u) < l_2(X|\lambda_2^v)) \lor \\ (l_1(X|\lambda_1^u) > l_1(X|\lambda_1^v) \land l_2(X|\lambda_2^u) > l_2(X|\lambda_2^v))\end{array} \\ 0 & \text{otherwise} \end{cases} \quad (4.29)$$

Here, $l_{1/2}$ are the respective likelihood functions of the two speaker models $\lambda_{1/2}$.

The high agreement expressed by c as given above is further demonstrated in Tables 4.4–4.5 and Figure 4.2. The tables give scatter matrices for the baseline model and AMU; a coarse visual analysis of the graphical pattern created by the correct and incorrect identifications shows how similar both models work in terms of identification results and errors. This trend is further expressed in Figure 4.2, where all six cases are depicted where the two models do not agree in their final identification decision on MPEG7 data. The envelopes of the likelihood scores of both models are very similar, letting the AMU's scores appear merely as scaled versions of the baseline's results. Furthermore, as indicated by the circles, in all six (out of 46 overall) cases of non-agreement, the second best score of one of the models always resembles the winner of the other model. Additionally, quite often the difference from the best to second best score is marginally small: nearly invisible departures decide over correct identification (in a ML or nearest neighbor sense) in case of AMU and a false positive in case of the baseline several times.

Is the difference between the identification rates of the two models just random? Using a

Chapter 4. Noise Robust Modeling

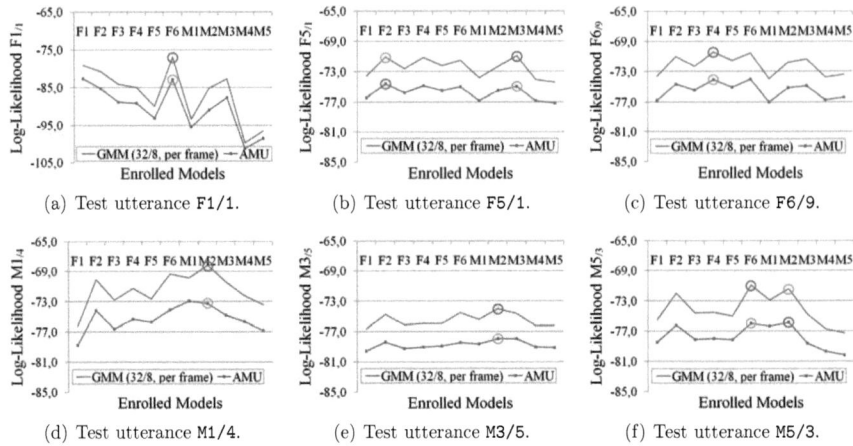

Figure 4.2: Log-likelihood scores for all misidentified test utterances from MPEG7 versus the enrolled speaker models, calculated using the AMU and baseline model. Data points encircled in red mark the highest overall score, in each case achieved by the wrong enrolled model; yellow circles mark the second-best score.

statistical χ^2 test (with and without Yates' correction for 1 degree of freedom [Yates 1934]), no significant evidence speaks against the hypothesis H_0 that "the AMU does not perform differently than the baseline model". This test result is true for the combined identification results of all three databases (α-level of $\alpha = 0.610$), and also for each single database alone ($\alpha = 0.250$, $\alpha = 0.279$ and $\alpha = 0.639$ for DB-S-1, MPEG7 and NOIZEUS, respectively). Not rejecting H_0 is not in general an evidence in support of H_0, and the resulting α-levels of this particular test result are too low to be used as counter-arguments of the test's intention. But evaluating all the available facts carefully, it is concluded that the AMU is best explained as being a distorted variant of the baseline approach "GMM (32/8, per frame)".

Thus, the explanation for the good results in Tsai et al.'s works is that not the MixMax, but a different model has been used by them; this different model appears deformed as extracted from their source code, but is best explained as resembling a non-probabilistic, multivariate noise masking scheme called "GMM (32/8, per frame)": for each feature vector of a test utterance, its likelihood to the voice model and to the noise model is computed; only those frames contribute to the final likelihood score of the integrated voice–noise model that are more likely to be modeled by the voice model.

4.6. Proving the MixMax' Ineptness for Cepstral Features

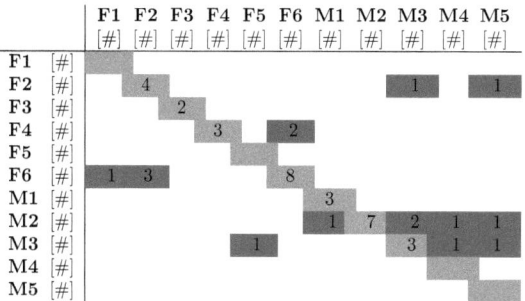

Table 4.4: Identification scatter matrix for the "GMM (32/8, per frame)" model on MPEG7 data. The numbers indicate how often utterances from specific speakers (indicated by the IDs in the column headers) are identified as coming from certain speaker models as indicated by the speaker ID in front of the rows. Correct identifications are found along the main diagonal, marked in green, while errors are individually marked in red.

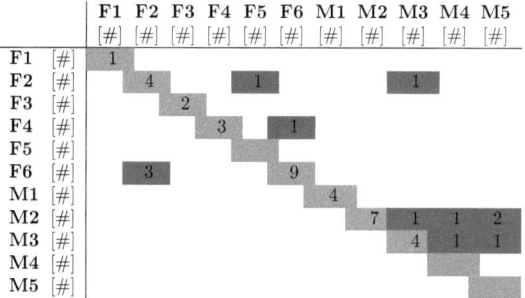

Table 4.5: Identification scatter matrix for the AMU model on MPEG7 data.

4.6 Proving the MixMax' Ineptness for Cepstral Features

In this section, the following theorem is proven:

Theorem 4.6.1. *The MixMax model is inappropriate for modeling signal–noise interaction in the cepstral domain.*

Proof. Let $\vec{x}$ and $\vec{y}$ be the FBE features of pure signal and pure noise as in Section 4.2 and let D be the dimensionality of these vectors, respectively. By reductio ad absurdum, it is shown that the following equation does *not* hold $\forall \vec{x}, \vec{y} \in \mathbb{R}^D$ and $\forall D \in \mathbb{N} \setminus \{0, 1\}$ (for $D = 1$, it is easy to see):

$$DCT\left(\max\left(\vec{x}, \vec{y}\right)\right) = \max\left(DCT(\vec{x}), DCT(\vec{y})\right) \qquad (4.30)$$

i.e., that the component-wise max-coherence between the FBEs does not remain after DCT

Chapter 4. Noise Robust Modeling

computation, such that the MixMax-model is not applicable to MFCCs in general. Knowing that the kth component $\bar{s}_k$, $1 \leq k \leq D$, of the DCT's resulting vector is computed as

$$\bar{s}_k = \alpha_k \cdot \sum_{d=1}^{D} s_d \cdot \cos\left[\frac{\pi}{D} \cdot k \cdot \left((d-1) + \frac{1}{2}\right)\right] \tag{4.31}$$

with $\vec{s}$ being the vector to be transformed and α_k a factor, the specific form (4.30) takes for the kth coefficient (MFC coefficient, if $\vec{s}$ is a FBE vector) can now be considered:

$$\sum_{d=1}^{D} \max(x_d, y_d) \cdot c_{d,k} = \max\left(\sum_{d=1}^{D} x_d \cdot c_{d,k}, \sum_{d=1}^{D} y_d \cdot c_{d,k}\right) \tag{4.32}$$

where $c_{d,k} = \cos\left[\frac{\pi}{D} \cdot k \cdot \left((d-1) + \frac{1}{2}\right)\right]$ and the α_k is dropped for simplicity.

Let $D > 1$ be arbitrary and fixed, and let $x_l < y_l$ be for l arbitrary but fixed in $\{1, \ldots, D\}$ but $x_d \geq y_d$ $\forall d \in \{1, \ldots, D\} \setminus \{l\}$. With this setting, (4.32) becomes

$$\sum_{\substack{d=1 \\ d \neq l}}^{D} x_d \cdot c_{d,k} + y_l \cdot c_{l,k} = \max\left(\sum_{d=1}^{D} x_d \cdot c_{d,k}, \sum_{d=1}^{D} y_d \cdot c_{d,k}\right) \tag{4.33}$$

Consider the case that $\sum_{d=1}^{D} x_d \cdot c_{d,k} > \sum_{d=1}^{D} y_d \cdot c_{d,k}$ to resolve the max()-function on the right hand side of (4.33). Then, (4.33) becomes

$$\sum_{\substack{d=1 \\ d \neq l}}^{D} x_d \cdot c_{d,k} + y_l \cdot c_{l,k} = \sum_{d=1}^{D} x_d \cdot c_{d,k}$$

$$\Leftrightarrow \sum_{\substack{d=1 \\ d \neq l}}^{D} x_d \cdot c_{d,k} + y_l \cdot c_{l,k} = \sum_{\substack{d=1 \\ d \neq l}}^{D} x_d \cdot c_{d,k} + x_l \cdot c_{l,k}$$

$$\Leftrightarrow y_l \cdot c_{l,k} = x_l \cdot c_{l,k}$$

$$\Leftrightarrow y_l = x_l \tag{4.34}$$

This contradicts the previous postulation that $x_l < y_l$ and therefore proves that (4.30) does not hold in general. □

In fact, the claim in (4.30) only holds in the following two unlikely cases: first, if *all* components of $\vec{x}$ are greater (smaller, equal) than *all* components of $\vec{y}$. Second, although each component x_d is related (possibly) differently to the corresponding y_d, equation (4.32) holds anyway. This means that summing up only components of $\vec{x}$ or $\vec{y}$ has always to equal the sum of a mixture of components of $\vec{x}$ and $\vec{y}$. Both cases are not existing in practice.

Thus, it is evident that the MixMax model is inapplicable to modeling the signal–noise interaction present in the MFCC domain.

Two attempts have been made in the past to overcome the MixMax' weakness of being confined to filterbank features: Gales and Young [1992] have developed an approach where the parameters of the signal model in the MFCC domain are inversely transformed to the linear spectral domain. Here, noise masking is carried out using the noise model, and the parameters are transformed back to the MFCC domain. Mellor and Varga [1993] have introduced a similar attempt, inversely transforming signal model parameters and observation vectors to the log-spectral domain for masking and back again. Both systems have the disadvantage of not directly operating on the MFCC vectors. Instead, computationally expensive bi-directional transformations or the maintenance of both MFCC- and FBE versions of the models and observations are necessary, resulting in higher memory and maintenance requirements. In the absence of a solution to these shortcomings, the method of Gales [1996] is still applied today, for example, in the recent work of Tufekci et al. [2006] on robust speech recognition. In the remainder of this book, FBE features are used in conjunction with the MixMax model.

4.7 Conclusions

In this chapter, the debate in the literature whether to use MFCC feature vectors in conjunction with the MixMax model or not has been enriched by new arguments: on the one hand, by providing a mathematical proof that shows its inappropriateness in the presented context from a theoretical point of view; on the other hand, by providing extensive experiments and a discussion suggesting how published good results on MixMax & MFCC can be explained. The result of this explanation is also to explicitly report for the first time which methods really do work as part of one of the best current systems in automatic singer recognition. Additionally, a correction of the MixMax model's training equation (4.13) has been given.

Areas for further research lie within exploring more sophisticated methods for singing voice modeling within popular music, now that the effective baseline is explicitly known, obviously offering room for improvement.

"All noise is waste.
So cultivate quietness in your speech."

Elbert Hubbard (1856–1915)

5

Fast and Robust Model Comparison

5.1 Introduction

One of the objectives of this book is to use a speaker clustering algorithm as the basis for building an audio-based person indexing system for videos. Two main challenges of this task are speed and robustness. Since speaker clustering is only one step in a chain of operations to analyze a video, its runtime has to be as small as possible. Furthermore, to obtain an approach that works under varying conditions, a speaker clustering algorithm needs to be robust against different types of noise.

Several approaches to speaker clustering exist in the literature: Jin et al. [1997] present a hierarchical speaker clustering system for ASR improvement consisting of GMMs for speaker representation and the GLR test as the distance measure. The authors report improvements in the word error rate as high as with hand labeled data using their unsupervised system. The same techniques are used by Solomonoff et al. [1998]. Ajmera and Wooters [2003] report on their unsupervised speaker-segmentation and -clustering system. They use HMMs to represent the data, where each state represents a single speech segment and is modeled by a GMM. To merge states, the BIC is used to determine the pair of nearest clusters (states). This introduces an automatic stopping criterion, so that the algorithm can be regarded as being robust against wrong parameter settings.

Liu and Kubala [2004] introduce an online speaker clustering algorithm. It clusters a new

Chapter 5. Fast and Robust Model Comparison

segment immediately after it has been processed rather than first collecting all segments. In contrast to the computational complexity of a hierarchical approach, which increases exponentially with the number of speech segments, their method's complexity increases only linearly. It also shows better results in terms of cluster purity and misclassification rate while still using GMMs and GLR. A recent overview of the state of the art in speaker clustering is given by Kotti et al. [2008b], showing that basically the same methods are still used and extended.

In this chapter, a novel approach to speaker clustering is presented that improves its speed and robustness. The basic idea to achieve speed of processing is to compare speaker models directly based on their parameters rather than relying on the underlying feature vectors by using the *earth mover's distance* (EMD) [Rubner et al. 2000], which is known from the image retrieval domain. To achieve robustness in the presence of noise, a method is proposed to use the EMD in conjunction with the MixMax model-based noise cancellation scheme. Experimental results for a 47 minute long test video show that the runtime of the proposed EMD approach outperforms a likelihood ratio based distance measure by more than a factor of 120 while the clustering performance remains nearly the same.

The chapter is organized as follows. Section 5.2 presents the new clustering method using MixMax and the EMD, while Section 5.3 reports on experimental results. Section 5.4 concludes the chapter and outlines areas for future research.

Parts of the work presented in this chapter have been published in a paper by Stadelmann and Freisleben [2006].

5.2 A New Approach to Speaker Clustering

The online speaker clustering algorithm presented by Liu and Kubala [2004] has the drawback of not having all relevant data available when making its decision about which clusters to merge. A hierarchical method that first collects all speaker models can make the globally best choice rather than working only locally. It therefore is more powerful at the expense of having exponential runtime. However, each step in the hierarchical method consists of only two single activities, distance computation and merging. Merging clusters is rather simple because it mainly consists of copying data, thus the distance computation yields most room for improvement. If one succeeds in significantly reducing the runtime of the distance computation, even hierarchical clustering can be feasible for applications where speed is required.

Let X, Y denote the sets of feature vectors (with elements in $\mathbb{R}^D$) from the two segments under consideration for comparison, and λ^X, λ^Y their respective mixture models (the specific types of features and models are not relevant at this point). It is obvious that likelihood computations for a GMM or MixMax model can take quite some time keeping in mind the specific form of l_{GMM} (2.18) and l_{MM} (4.21), since they involve nested loops over all feature

5.2. A New Approach to Speaker Clustering

vectors and states (mixtures). The problem becomes even more severe if a distance metric like the GLR is used (2.23) that first demands the training of a new model $\lambda^{X \cup Y}$ of the combined speech segments.

5.2.1 Parameter-Based Comparison

Considering these runtime problems when using likelihood-based distance measures and the effort that has been made to build a speaker model, it is appealing to compare two models directly on the basis of their parameters. Since a GMM forms a PDF, the *Kullback-Leibler* (KL) *distance* d_{KL} between distributions comes to mind, but it cannot be computed directly on GMMs because they lack a closed form solution [Goldberger and Aronowitz 2005]. Alternative metrics like the *Euclidean distance* d_E, the *Mahalanobis distance* d_M or the *Bhattacharyya distance* d_B also lack an extension to mixture models, but calculate the distance between pairs of mono-Gaussian mixtures:

$$d_{KL}(\lambda_G^X, \lambda_G^Y) = \frac{1}{2} \cdot \left[\log \left(\frac{\prod_{d=1}^{D} \sigma_d^{2Y}}{\prod_{d=1}^{D} \sigma_d^{2X}} \right) + \sum_{d=1}^{D} \frac{\sigma_d^{2X}}{\sigma_d^{2Y}} + \sum_{d=1}^{D} \frac{(\mu_d^Y - \mu_d^X)^2}{\sigma_d^{2Y}} - D \right] \quad (5.1)$$

$$d_E(\lambda_G^X, \lambda_G^Y) = \sqrt{\sum_{d=1}^{D} (\mu_d^X - \mu_d^Y)^2} \quad (5.2)$$

$$d_M(\lambda_G^X, \lambda_G^Y) = \frac{1}{D} \cdot \sum_{d=1}^{D} \frac{(\mu_d^Y - \mu_d^X)^2}{\sqrt{\sigma_d^{2X}} \cdot \sqrt{\sigma_d^{2Y}}} \quad (5.3)$$

$$d_B(\lambda_G^X, \lambda_G^Y) = \frac{1}{8} \cdot \sum_{d=1}^{D} \frac{(\mu_d^X - \mu_d^Y)^2}{\sigma_d^{2X}} + \frac{1}{2} \cdot \log \left(\frac{\frac{1}{2} \cdot \sum_{d=1}^{D} \sigma_d^{2X} + \sigma_d^{2Y}}{\sqrt{\prod_{d=1}^{D} \sigma_d^{2X} \cdot \sigma_d^{2Y}}} \right) \quad (5.4)$$

$$(5.5)$$

Here, λ_G^X is the multivariate mono-Gaussian model trained from the D-dimensional feature vector set X, and (μ_d^X, σ_d^{2X}) are its dth dimension's mean and diagonal covariance parameters, respectively.

Beigi et al. [1998] address the problem of a missing metric between collections of distributions by introducing a method that extends any distance between single mixture components of

Chapter 5. Fast and Robust Model Comparison

GMMs—a ground distance—to a distance between the entire models.

$$W_m^X = w_m^X \cdot \min_{n=1..N} \left(d_{KL}(\lambda_m^X, \lambda_n^Y) \right) \tag{5.6}$$

$$W_n^Y = w_n^Y \cdot \min_{m=1..M} \left(d_{KL}(\lambda_n^Y, \lambda_m^X) \right) \tag{5.7}$$

$$d_{BMS}(\lambda^X, \lambda^Y) = \frac{\sum_{m=1}^{M} W_m^X + \sum_{n=1}^{N} W_n^Y}{\sum_{m=1}^{M} w_m^X + \sum_{n=1}^{N} w_n^Y} \tag{5.8}$$

Here, w_m^X is the weight of the mth mixture λ_m^X in a GMM λ^X for dataset X. The Beigi/Maes/-Sorensen (BMS) distance d_{BMS} is fast and accurate and allows the comparison of GMMs with different sizes. Its major drawback is that it is not freely available for commercial applications due to patent protection rights.

5.2.2 The Earth Mover's Distance

The EMD has been introduced by Rubner et al. [1997] and in subsequent work [Rubner et al. 1998, 2000] as a metric for image retrieval. Its roots reach back to pure statistics and transportation problems [Levina and Bickel 2001]. The EMD is defined between collections of distributions S called *signatures*:

$$S = \{w_m, c_m | 1 \leq m \leq M\} \tag{5.9}$$

Here, w_m is the weight of a centroid c_m out of a total of M centroids, which can be any vector or set representing a cluster centroid.

Loosely spoken, the EMD measures the amount of work needed to transport one element of mass from one distribution (regarded as a "hill") to the other (regarded as a "hole"). This explanation and the perceptually meaningful results in its original domain inspired many authors to adopt the EMD for their problem. Among others, the EMD has been applied successfully to the tasks of music similarity computation [Baumann 2005; Logan and Salomon 2001; Typke et al. 2003], contour matching [Grauman and Darrell 2004] and phoneme matching [Srinivasamurthy and Narayanan 2003]. Kuroiwa et al. [2006] meanwhile applied it to speaker recognition using non-parametric models.

To compute the EMD, the optimal flow matrix $F = (f_{mn})$ of mass from signatures S^X to S^Y has to be found according to the following rules:

$$f_{mn} \geq 0, \quad m = 1..M, n = 1..N \tag{5.10}$$

$$\sum_{n=1}^{N} f_{mn} \leq w_m^X, \quad m = 1..M \tag{5.11}$$

5.2. A New Approach to Speaker Clustering

$$\sum_{m=1}^{M} f_{mn} \leq w_n^Y, \quad n = 1..N \qquad (5.12)$$

$$\sum_{m=1}^{M}\sum_{n=1}^{N} f_{mn} = \min\left(\sum_{m=1}^{M} w_m^X, \sum_{n=1}^{N} w_n^Y\right) \qquad (5.13)$$

$$F = \arg\min_{F}\left(\sum_{m=1}^{M}\sum_{n=1}^{N} d_{mn} \cdot f_{mn}\right) \qquad (5.14)$$

This means that the flow from each centroid m to centroid n needs to be positive (5.10), the flow away from one centroid is not allowed to excess this centroid's weight (5.11)–(5.12), and only the smaller amount of "mass" (as represented by the sum of weights in the two signatures) can be moved if they differ (5.13). The optimal flow is the one minimizing the amount of work (represented by the argument in (5.14)) to be done according to the ground distance matrix $D = (d_{mn})$, which has to be computed before: a simple distance measure between single centroids is evaluated for each cross-segment pair. Once the flow is found using the transportation-simplex method, the EMD between two signatures S^X and S^Y is given by

$$d_{EMD}(S^X, S^Y) = \frac{\sum_{m=1}^{M}\sum_{n=1}^{N} d_{mn} \cdot f_{mn}}{\sum_{m=1}^{M}\sum_{n=1}^{N} f_{mn}} \qquad (5.15)$$

Like the BMS distance, the EMD is able to compare signatures of differing size. If the overall mass of both signatures is identical, the EMD is a true metric. Furthermore, every metric between two Gaussians can be used as the ground distance. The KL distance is used in the remainder of this chapter because it showed superior results compared to other candidates in preliminary experiments.

5.2.3 Using the EMD for Speaker Clustering

By regarding each mixture component of a GMM as a cluster centroid and the mixture's weight as this cluster's mass, it is straightforward to put it in signature form and compute an EMD between two GMMs. However, problems arise when applying this simple rule to the MixMax model: its advantage of masking noisy mixtures is not fully represented in the model's parameters alone, but mainly arises from the method of likelihood computation via $p(z_{t,d}|i,j,\lambda_{MM})$ (4.11) and l_{MM} (4.21). The following method is proposed to mimic this noise masking process during the EMD computation:

The probability that the dth component of the current observation $z_{t,d}$ is modeled by speaker model mixture i and background model mixture j is given by (4.11). Furthermore, $p(x_{t,d} = z_{t,d}|i,j,\lambda_{MM})$ (4.12) gives the probability that this current observation in the state $\{i,j\}$ is equal to the unobservable, uncorrupted clean speech sample component $x_{t,d}$, i.e., that it is

Chapter 5. Fast and Robust Model Comparison

noise-free. The parameters of the speaker GMM λ^s within the MixMax model λ_{MM} are now extended by a vector $\vec{m} = (m_1..m_I)$ that is called the *mask level*:

$$m_i = \frac{\sum_{t=1}^{T}\sum_{j=1}^{J}\sum_{d=1}^{D} 1 - p(x_{t,d} = z_{t,d}|i,j,\lambda_{MM})}{T \cdot J \cdot D} \quad (5.16)$$

The mask level is computed during model estimation while the feature vectors are still available. A level of 0 for a mixture i means that this mixture is noise-free while a level of 1 means that it is fully corrupted by noise. Before EMD (or BMS distance) computation, each speaker model mixture's weight is multiplied with the factor $1 - m_i$. This way, the more a mixture is masked by noise, the less it contributes to the final distance.

5.3 Experimental Results

The test corpus for performance evaluation is composed of a subset of the MPEG-7 video content set [MPEG 7 Requirement Group 1998], namely the Portuguese night journal video jornaldanoite1. The jornaldanoite1 video includes some difficulties for a standard speaker clustering system, particularly many interviews (ca. 50% of the overall time) under non-ideal outdoor conditions, leading to a relatively low SNR.

To study the effect of additive noise on the proposed algorithms, experiments are also conducted with a short German news video called news2 and its derivatives, which have been mixed with differing types of colored noise in some scenes. Detailed information about all videos can be found in Table 5.1.

Video	Length [s]	øSNR [dB]	min SNR [dB]	max SNR [dB]
news2 (0)	244	13.6	6.3	19.7
news2 (1)	244	12.9	6.3	19.7
news2 (2)	244	11.15	6.3	16.4
news2 (3)	244	12.4	6.3	19.7
news2 (4)	244	10.27	6.3	15.08
news2 (5)	244	12.4	6.3	19.7
news2 (6)	244	9.97	6.3	14.2
news2 (7)	244	12.68	6.3	19.7
news2 (8)	244	12.09	6.3	19.7
news2 (9)	244	10.81	3.7	18.06
jornaldanoite1	2855	7.99	0.67	26.61

Table 5.1: Overview of the used corpus. The video news2 has been used in different versions: (0) is the original version, (1–9) have been partly augmented with different amounts of of colored noise: Low, medium and high energy brown noise, pink noise and white/brown noise, respectively. The SNR values are per segment.

The used speaker clustering framework operates on the 16 kHz/16 bit audio track of each video. The audio track is high- and low-pass filtered to fit into the frequency range of 50-7000 Hz, then preemphasized with a factor of $\alpha = 0.97$. It is segmented into 32 ms long frames with 16 ms overlap and each frame is converted into one of the following feature vector types using a 512 point FFT: 20 MFCCs for GMM modeling or 24 FBEs for MixMax modeling. The frequency scale for the filterbank is ExpoLog [Bou-Ghazale and Hansen 2000] in both cases. It is observed that the typical termination criteria for hierarchical clustering proposed in the literature, BIC and WCD [Liu and Kubala 2004], constantly overestimate the number of speakers in this case by far. Ground truth data is therefore used to terminate clustering at the optimal point as well as to make the speech/non-speech decision for each frame and to detect speaker changes. Silence and unvoiced speech are removed using an enhanced version of the adaptive silence detector proposed by Li et al. [2004].

The following three performance criteria are evaluated:

- Time: the elapsed time for the entire process from preprocessing until the end of speaker clustering.

- Recall: $100 \cdot \frac{\#correct\ segments}{\#available\ segments}$

- Precision: $100 \cdot \frac{\#fitting\ segments}{\#clustered\ segments}$

Here, a segment of speech is an area of continuous speech interrupted by less than 75 ms of non-speech. The number of available segments is the count of segments long enough to be analyzed (min. 1 second of length). Segments are regarded as *fitting* if they belong to any cluster in which segments of their speaker are in the majority. Segments are regarded as *correct*, if they are fitting and belong to the cluster containing the most segments of this speaker. Clustered segments are those which are included in any cluster.

The experiments on the `news2` derivatives are conducted to investigate to which extent the degradation of the SNR influences the clustering performance. With a SNR level of min. 12 dB per scene, the proposed system is able to reach 100% recall and precision using the MixMax model and any distance measure. With a SNR lower than 10.5 dB, the performance dropps heavily because segments are clustered according to background noise rather than according to voice.

The experiments with the longer `jornaldanoite1` video focus on speed. The results can be found in Table 5.2, where the time column indicates the measured wall clock time on an Intel 1.8 GHz Pentium 4 PC with 512MB memory running Windows/XP and an implementation within the `sclib` written in C++. In the case of the GMM, the EMD shows the best overall recall/precision pair while being only negligibly slower than the used reimplementation of the BMS distance according to Beigi et al. [1998]. This can be due to the fact that the reference implementation of the EMD has been used [Tomasi 1998], so it is necessary to copy all data

Chapter 5. Fast and Robust Model Comparison

Method	Time [s]	Recall [%]	Precision [%]
GMM/GLR	5 686	68.0	91.07
GMM/CLR	2 989	67.65	90.54
GMM/BMS	90	72.52	84.82
GMM/EMD	93	74.09	85.89
MixMax/GLR	74 218	74.78	92.68
MixMax/CLR	16 169	69.91	90.54
MixMax/BMS	560	63.65	76.76
MixMax/EMD	598	73.91	86.43

Table 5.2: Experimental results on the jornaldanoite1 video with SNR values as stated in Table 5.1.

into the author's format prior to distance computation. The runtime using the EMD is about a factor of 61 faster than the runtime using the GLR. When MixMax speaker modeling is used, CLR and EMD are at nearly the same performance level considering both recall and precision, only outperformed by the GLR with a 0.87 and 6.25 percentage points better recall and precision, respectively, compared to the EMD. The BMS distance performs worst, being 10.26 pp and 9.97 pp below the EMD in terms of recall and precision, respectively.

This indicates that the clustering performance of the EMD is only slightly worse than that of the GLR, but the speed differences are significant: the EMD is 61 times faster than the GLR in case of the GMM, and even 124 times faster in case of the MixMax model. This difference arises from the fact that computing a GLR using a MixMax model is much more expensive than for a simple GMM, but computing an EMD is very much the same for both (the runtime difference between the GMM/EMD and MixMax/EMD approach arises only from a longer time for model training in the MixMax case). Of course, a hierarchical clustering approach is still used with a runtime rising exponentially with the number of processed segments (for the news2 derivatives, the speed improvement factor thus is only 3.7). But in practice, waiting 10 minutes for the results of the proposed MixMax/EMD approach compared to more than 20 hours in case of MixMax/GLR is a quite significant improvement.

5.4 Conclusions

In this chapter, an approach has been proposed to accelerate hierarchical speaker clustering by using different distance measures. Commonly known likelihood-based measures (GLR, CLR) have been compared with methods which directly operate on the speaker model's parameters. For this reason, the earth mover's distance has been applied to speaker distance computation for the first time. A method to profit from the MixMax noise modeling scheme even when using the EMD has also been developed. The experimental results then showed an increase in clustering speed by a factor of more than 120 on a 47 minute test video while remaining robust to low SNR values.

There are several aspects for future work. For example, the observed failure of the commonly used clustering termination criteria on the used data deserves treatment. Furthermore, there is still room for greater noise robustness. Finally, the speed problem can be further addressed by combining the online- and hierarchical clustering schemes to take advantage of both their strengths.

"Time is free, but it's priceless.
You can't own it, but you can use it."

Harvey MacKay (1932–)

6

Modeling Temporal Aspects of a Voice

6.1 Introduction

Speaker recognition is a broad area that splits into different sub-fields, as discussed in Section 2.2.1. Its branches can be ranked according to the complexity of the task. Viewed from the speaker clustering perspective, speaker verification is the most simple task among the speaker recognition problems: the question is whether a given utterance can be assigned to a given model (identity)—a binary choice. Speaker identification is a $(1:n+1)$ choice: the question is which (if any) of the given models can the given utterance be paired with? Finally, speaker clustering is a $(m:n)$ problem in which all utterances are equally important and each utterance may be grouped together with any other utterance—or stay alone. Both the number of clusters (speakers) and the actual cluster memberships must be determined automatically.

The speaker verification and identification tasks have been studied extensively in the literature. Using MFCCs as parametric speech features and GMMs (with more recent modifications like the UBM) as speaker models has become the quasi-standard, although other methods have been proposed [Faúndez-Zanuy and Monte-Moreno 2005]. This is due to quite satisfactory results with just moderate demands for the data: the utterances should be relatively noise-free (telephone speech works) and long enough (minimum 10 seconds, better more than 30 seconds per utterance) [van Leeuwen et al. 2006]. The canonical example is the experiment in Reynolds' classic paper on GMMs [Reynolds 1995] (see Section 2.7.1): The 630 speakers

Chapter 6. Modeling Temporal Aspects of a Voice

of the TIMIT database are split into a training set (8 sentences per speaker concatenated to one utterance) and a separate test set (2 sentences per speaker form one utterance). Each sentence is approximately 3 seconds long. The utterances are transformed to MFCC feature vectors. For the 630 training utterances, GMMs with 32 mixtures are built a priori, then an identification experiment is run for the 630 test utterances. It yields a satisfactory 0.5% closed set identification error.

Speaker clustering has also been studied extensively for more than a decade [Jin et al. 1997; Reynolds et al. 1998]. The basic techniques used for speaker clustering are largely along the lines of the previously discussed verification/ identification techniques: MFCC features are modeled by GMMs [Kotti et al. 2008b; Tranter and Reynolds 2006]. Upon this, a step-by-step scheme using agglomerative hierarchical clustering is usually built using some metric (often the GLR) and a termination criterion (frequently based on the BIC) [Meignier et al. 2006]. Evaluations typically concentrate on data sets built from broadcast news/shows and meeting recordings, where diarization error rates ranging from 8% to 24% are reported [Kotti et al. 2008b; Meignier et al. 2006; Reynolds and Torres-Carrasquillo 2004]. These results are confirmed by more recent approaches that otherwise deviate from the standard methodical scheme (e.g. by using genetic algorithms instead of agglomerative clustering [Tsai et al. 2007] or SVMs instead of GMMs [Fergani et al. 2008]).

From the definition of the task of speaker clustering it is evident that speaker clustering has a much higher complexity than the other two tasks. This fact certainly affects the anticipated outcome in terms of higher expected error rates and/or applicability only to less complex data. Both implications can be observed in the literature:

- Error rates for clustering and identification are significantly apart from each other, as indicated above.

- Data sets for clustering have a considerably smaller speaker population size: for example, in the approaches surveyed by Kotti et al. [2008b], the number of speakers (with several segments each) per run ranges from 2 to 89, with an average of 28 speakers (and a standard deviation of 31) as compared to 630 in the speaker identification example above. As pointed out by Reynolds and Rose [1995], a smaller number of speakers eases the task considerably.

- Several authors notice that the current clustering or diarization systems are not very robust to data variations and thus are poorly portable [Han et al. 2008; Reynolds and Torres-Carrasquillo 2005; Zhang et al. 2008]. This is in contrast to the wide applicability of speaker verification and identification techniques [Benesty et al. 2008; Przybocki and Martin 2004].

6.1. Introduction

In the following paragraphs, an experiment is presented to determine what exact impact the change in the experimental setting (i.e., from identification to clustering) has on the results. The basic settings of Reynolds' identification experiment on TIMIT [Reynolds 1995] are used and re-ran with a reimplementation of the complete speaker identification chain. This yields 0.0% closed set identification error rate (attributing the difference to Reynolds' original results to subtle varieties in the implementations of the signal processing and model initialization parts). Then, the experimental setting is changed from an identification scenario to clustering (i.e., each of the 1260 utterances can now be grouped with any other utterance; before, there was prior knowledge that 630 utterances are distinct speakers and each of the remaining 630 utterances has to be grouped with an utterance of the first group). The sclib provides the speaker clustering software and uses the same framework as the identification module, implementing a state-of-the-art system comparable to the one described by Han et al. [2008] (of course without the "selective clustering" part that would nearly reduce the clustering experiment to the identification task for optimal parameter settings).

The system scores a misclassification rate of 99.84% with respect to utterances, which effectively shows that the task is too complex for the used techniques. In contrast to the identification task before, efforts were made to find optimal parameter settings for the values that did not correspond to settings in Reynolds' experiment and thus should not be altered for the sake of comparability. Finally, for 16 kHz data (Reynolds used 8 kHz), the following settings were used: MFCCs 1–19 (coefficient 0 discarded) extracted from 20 ms long frames every 10 ms using a 512 point FFT on the Hamming-windowed, pre-emphasized ($\alpha = 0.97$) signal and a mel filterbank of 24 triangular filters ranging from 0 to 7600 Hz. GMMs with 32 mixtures and diagonal covariances were initialized via a maximum of 10 iterations of k-means seeded by the deterministic Var-Part method [Su and Dy 2007] and trained with a maximum of 15 EM steps (or until the increase in log-likelihood dropped below 100, whatever happened first) having a variance limit of 0.01. Individual models were compared using the distance measure described by Beigi et al. [1998] (in conjunction with the Euclidean distance between single mixtures). Clustering was performed based on these distances using complete linkage and stopped by the ICR criterion (2.26) tuned to the optimal threshold using ground truth data. The choice of the metric, linkage method and termination criterion was motivated by comprehensive experiments comparing most of all reasonable options and choosing the best for this task on a subset of the data.

The encountered complexity is distinct (in fact: additive) in nature to what is described by Morris et al. [2004] to make identifying voices on TIMIT data a challenge: the pure quantity of speakers seems to exhaust the expressive power of the clustering system in the presence of an increased number of degrees of freedom. This view is supported by the fact that the same clustering experiment performs relatively well (12.50% misclassification rate) for a reduced subset of only the first 40 speakers out of the original 630 and even perfect for 20 speakers and less.

The hypothesis of this chapter is: the techniques originally developed for speaker verification and identification are not suitable for speaker clustering, taking into account the escalated difficulty of the latter task. However, the processing chain for speaker clustering is quite large—there are many potential areas for improvement. The question is: *where* should improvements be made to improve the *final* result?

In this chapter, first it is shown which part of the processing chain bears how much potential for further improvement. This part of the answer implies that improving other parts of the chain will probably not show the full potential of that improvement: an improvement at the beginning of the pattern recognition process is probably not able to propagate until its end if it is succeeded by an even greater source of failure. Second, it is stated explicitly what this improvement has to look like qualitatively. Third, an implementation of a speaker clustering system is presented that experimentally supports this proposition by improving existing results on a `TIMIT` benchmark test. The proposed approach is based on an analysis of the operating mode and capability of the best speaker clustering automaton available: the human being, according to the principle of biomimetics [Bar-Cohen 2006].

The chapter is organized as follows. The design of a speaker grouping study with human participants is described in Section 6.2. The evaluation and interpretation of the results of the study follow in Section 6.3. Section 6.4 presents a technical implementation of the findings in the mentioned speaker clustering systems along with corresponding results. Section 6.5 concludes the chapter and outlines areas for future research.

Parts of the work presented in this chapter have been published in a paper by Stadelmann and Freisleben [2009].

6.2 Analyzing the Process

This section reports on the motivation, design, and results of a study that puts humans in the role of a speaker clustering software: participants are asked to group together utterances based on their inferred speaker identity within variants of the same data set. These variants are the internal representations of the original speech signal at different levels of the pattern recognition process in an actual speaker clustering software made audible again.

6.2.1 Motivation

The poor results of the speaker clustering experiment on the full `TIMIT` database raise the question what kind of information is actually missing in the applied methods. The feature extraction method at the beginning of the pattern recognition chain lossily compresses the information included in the original signal [Bishop 2006], and the later speaker modeling (i.e., classifier training) stage basically does the same. The basic idea of the proposed approach is to use the qualitative judgment of humans based on their experience as listeners to determine the lacking information in the different pattern recognition stages. This requires to represent the acoustic signal at these stages such that the participants can listen to it, i.e., *resynthesis*. From the evoked sensation, the level of discernability present in the data is determined: signals sounding very similar might also be difficult to distinguish by a computer. This is measured by asking probands to perform a speaker clustering experiment that is evaluated in the same way a software system would be evaluated.

The rationale is: it has already been demonstrated above that the clustering software succeeds for a reduced `TIMIT` data set of less than 40 speakers. If humans find a reasonable clustering for the original speech signal but cannot distinguish the data as used by the computer—showing that the computer essentially does not have some information that was still present in the original signal—there is some unused potential. This potential lies in the information that was removed in the course of processing.

Several arguments support this approach: humans may not be trained to analyze synthetic speech features, but in contrast to machine learning techniques that need well-posed learning problems [Mitchell 1997] as well as an appropriate training data basis—human learning is generalizing well and adaptive [Goertzel and Pennachin 2007]. Information is best (i.e., very quickly and reasonably accurately) grasped with our auditory system as a guide in an otherwise unstructured search in a large hypothesis space [Demuynck et al. 2004]. A similar view is advertised by Aucouturier [2009] in the field of music information retrieval, and understanding multimedia data by surveying human behavior and decision has also been successfully applied by Cherubini et al. [2009].

6.2.2 Design

The primary goal of this study is to show which stage of the processing chain of speaker clustering bears how much potential for improvement (then, what can and has to be improved). The two stages of feature extraction and modeling are the most promising candidates, since there the main information reduction takes place. Further candidate stages are signal (pre-)processing (which is added here to feature extraction), segmentation (into e.g. silence/speech/noise, which are complete pattern recognition processes in themselves and therefore are likely to benefit from this study rather than contribute to it) and clustering (which is not considered here for reasons explained later in Section 6.3). To accomplish the goal, the biomimetic approach of observing human behavior is applied. To obtain relevant results, a feasible data set has been created

Chapter 6. Modeling Temporal Aspects of a Voice

along with a test philosophy and a reasonable group of participants has been acquired.

The data set is based on a subset of the TIMIT data introduced in Section 2.7.1 with a meaningful but manageable size. It contains 7 speakers, hence 14 utterances, with 3 male and 4 female voices from the same dialect region. The first 7 speakers are taken in lexicographical ordering of the file names: FAKS0, FDAC1, FELC0, FJEM0, MDAB0, MJSW0 and MREB0 from TEST/DR1. The data set (and additional material for reproducing the study) is publicly available on the web[1]. Reynolds' procedure is used to concatenate the 10 sentences to 2 utterances per speaker (see Section 6.1). This material is the input to the already introduced speaker clustering system, scoring perfectly with 0.0% error. As side products, the system outputs altered versions of the input data (equal to it in length), namely resynthesized features and resynthesized models (the technical details of this process are presented in Section 7.3.1). This yields "dataset 1" (resynthesized speaker models, sounding similar to "bubbling/boiling liquid"), "dataset 2" (resynthesized feature vectors, sounding like a "robot voice") and "dataset 3" (original speech, sounding "normal") for the human speaker grouping study.

According to the test plan, the three data sets are presented to the participants in the order described above. The task is the same for each data set: within 30 minutes or less (to set an upper bound on the time for participation), a participant is supposed to group the 14 utterances by the inferred speaker identity. This is done by drawing lines between the utterances in question on the assessment sheet (as depicted in Appendix A.3), where their file names (i.e., numbers) are arranged on a circle.

The participants are told to "engage" with the sound and "not to focus on maybe unfamiliar patterns that all recordings of a run have in common, but on the more subtle differences, like the ones used when, for example, distinguishing two low-pitched male voices. The decision to group recordings together must be taken solely based on the acoustical similarity of the voices". By hearing the more unfamiliar sounds first, it is ensured that no participant is tempted to transfer findings from an earlier data set to a later one. To further minimize such effects, the arrangement of the utterances on the assessment sheet's circle is permuted randomly between runs. Together with the actual grouping, the participants are asked to describe "in 1–3 short sentences how [they] tried to solve the task and how [they judged their] own result". The freedom offered by this formulation is intentional so that driving the participants in any direction by asking specific questions on used features, methods or experienced difficulties is prohibited. These instructions are given to the participants together with the data and reprinted in Appendix A.2 for reference.

The acquired group of participants consists mainly of students and university staff ranging in age from 21–64 years (mean: 30.7, standard deviation: 8.98). Overall, 20 people participated,

---

[1] http://www.informatik.uni-marburg.de/~stadelmann/download/sg_experiment.zip

6 of them being female and 14 male, giving a representative sample in size and composition. Each participant is told to read the instructions and act accordingly. This effectively eliminates prior knowledge on the design and goal of the study. The comprehensibility and sufficiency of the instructions and the feasibility of the task has been approved in a pretest.

Although it is reported on a study with human participants, a technical challenge to deal with is the reconversion of features and models to speech. To this end, the tool *WebVoice*[2] has been used, which is described in detail in Section 7.3.2.

6.2.3 Results

This subsection presents the results of the human speaker grouping study. Both quantitative and qualitative results will be discussed, starting with the quantitative outcomes showing how "well" the participants did the job.

Quantitative Results

Table 6.1 contains some statistical measures: mean and standard deviation of the time (in minutes) used to solve the task, the number of clusters created, the number of correctly drawn connections between utterances (considered transitively) and the number of connections drawn overall (without considering transitivity).

Means	Dataset	Time [m]	Clusters [#]	Correct [#]	Connections [#]
human $\mu(\sigma)$	1	22.95 (7.44)	6.05 (2.39)	3.0 (1.72)	8.05 (2.52)
random $\mu(\sigma)$	1	-	6.49 (1.48)	1.04 (1.05)	7.51 (1.48)
human wins?	1	-	no	0.0005	0.1
human $\mu(\sigma)$	2	17.33 (7.71)	6.35 (1.31)	3.3 (1.92)	7.75 (1.41)
random $\mu(\sigma)$	2	-	6.77 (1.23)	0.85 (0.91)	7.23 (1.23)
human wins?	2	-	no	0.0005	0.1
human $\mu(\sigma)$	3	8.95 (5.19)	7.20 (0.77)	6.55 (1.05)	6.75 (0.72)
random $\mu(\sigma)$	3	-	7.37 (0.57)	0.51 (0.72)	6.63 (0.57)
human wins?	3	-	no	0.0005	no

Table 6.1: Comparison of human- and random clustering using statistical measures.

Furthermore, the probability for the two segments of each of the 7 speakers to be joined (also considering transitivity) is presented in Table 6.2. These are stated for human annotations and "random" clustering (see next paragraph for an explanation of the meaning of randomness in this context) for all three data sets. A third line per data set shows the result of a one-sided t-test (H_0: human figure at most equals random figure; H_1: human figure is better than

---

[2]Available at http://www.informatik.uni-marburg.de/~stadelmann/eidetic.html.

Chapter 6. Modeling Temporal Aspects of a Voice

random) in terms of the minimal α-level possible to reject the null hypothesis (or "no" if it cannot be rejected). The t-value is computed using a pooled variance due to the small sample size of 20 on the side of the human annotations.

Means	Dataset	p(FAKS0) [0..1]	p(FDAC1) [0..1]	p(FELC0) [0..1]	p̂(FJEM0) [0..1]	p(MDAB0) [0..1]	p(MJSW0) [0..1]	p(MREB0) [0..1]
human μ	1	0.25	0.4	0.55	0.45	0.4	0.25	0.7
random μ	1	0.14	0.15	0.15	0.15	0.14	0.14	0.14
human wins?	1	0.1	0.001	0.0005	0.0005	0.0005	0.1	0.0005
human μ	2	0.25	0.6	0.7	0.35	0.4	0.4	0.6
random μ	2	0.12	0.12	0.13	0.13	0.13	0.12	0.11
human wins?	2	0.05	0.0005	0.0005	0.005	0.0005	0.0005	0.0005
human μ	3	0.85	1.0	0.95	0.85	0.95	0.95	1.0
random μ	3	0.07	0.08	0.08	0.08	0.07	0.07	0.07
human wins?	3	0.0005	0.0005	0.0005	0.0005	0.0005	0.0005	0.0005

Table 6.2: Comparison of human- and random clustering using individual speaker's probabilities of being grouped together.

It is important to know whether the human results deviate from pure human guessing. But what is a guessed result on a clustering task, where both the number of clusters as well as the affiliations to clusters must be guessed and both choices interdepend? It is observed that a human will never choose cluster sizes and numbers totally at random, but will follow some intuition like "there will be more than one and less than the maximally possible number of clusters" and "there must be clusters having a 'reasonable' number of members". Therefore, the distributions of numbers and sizes are taken as created by the participants for each data set, and then the guessed numbers and sizes of clusters are drawn at random from them. The members of the created empty clusters are then picked at random (i.e., uniformly distributed) from the set of still unassigned utterances. In this Monte Carlo way, 10 000 independent random clustering runs per data set are simulated and their outcome is presented, getting results that are less purely random but more like human guessing [Doucet and Wang 2005].

The results can be summarized as follows:

a **Improvement.** Human performance improves from run to run as indicated by more correct connections using less time as well as cluster and connection numbers approaching the real values (7/7) with less variability.

b **Individuality.** Nevertheless, individual speakers differ in how well their voices could be recognized: FELC0 and MREB0 have a consistently higher probability of being grouped

6.2. Analyzing the Process

correctly by humans among all data sets, whereas there is a consistently lower probability for FAKS0.

c **Purpose.** Human results deviate positively (i.e., are better) from the random outcomes with a confidence of at least 99.5% in terms of the number of correct connections drawn and also in the probability of grouping together the correct utterances for almost all speakers on all three data sets.

Due to the fact that the random cluster sizes and numbers of clusters were drawn from the discrete distribution per data set created by the human participants, those figures do not deviate significantly; the small deviation is because the distributions are not Gaussian, but somehow skewed and multimodal, so that with increased sample size in the random case (10 000 as compared to 20) it becomes obvious that mean and standard deviation are inappropriate measures to describe these distributions.

Quantity as Expressed in Common Figures of Merit

Tables 6.3 and 6.4 evaluate the achievements of human and random annotators in terms of several figures of merit as defined in the survey by Kotti et al. [2008b] (except for overall recall and precision): overall recall rec_o and overall precision $prec_o$ are extensions of the usual recall and precision measures of the information retrieval community used for the task of clustering as defined in Section 5.3. The misclassification rate MR gives the likelihood of an utterance not getting assigned to the correct cluster. Average cluster purity acp is the likelihood of the utterances in one cluster really belonging together, whereas average speaker purity asp is the likelihood of utterances being assigned to speaker x really being spoken by x; the *purity* is the geometric mean of both. The Rand index γ is an unnormalized number decreasing with the number of correctly clustered utterances, whereas the BBN metric I_{BBN} increases (unnormalized, too) with the number of big, pure clusters. The diarization error rate DER finally depicts the ratio of *samples* assigned to the wrong speaker, including speaker error time, missed speaker time, and false alarm speaker time (but due to the fact that only clustering is evaluated here, the latter two sources of error are eliminated).

There are several possibilities of selecting entities for computing figures of merit: audio samples would be the most accurate way, then segments (as created by silence detection, which would reduce to sentences here) or utterances (i.e., entire files consisting of concatenated sentences in the used database). It is decided to choose utterances because they reflect most naturally what a human considers to be a good achievement; sample- or segment-level computation would introduce biases towards (or against) the longer segments, whereas this way each utterance is weighted equally.

Several observations are noteworthy:

Chapter 6. Modeling Temporal Aspects of a Voice

Means	Ds.	rec$_o$ [%]	prec$_o$ [%]	MR [%]	acp [%]	asp [%]
human $\mu(\sigma)$	1	52.14 (10.65)	56.79 (15.80)	47.86 (10.65)	56.85 (15.95)	71.43 (12.26)
random $\mu(\sigma)$	1	41.45 (10.09)	43.93 (12.50)	58.55 (10.09)	50.64 (10.50)	57.18 (7.36)
human wins?	1	0.0005	0.0005	0.0005	0.005	0.0005
human $\mu(\sigma)$	2	61.79 (19.43)	63.22 (19.29)	38.21 (19.43)	64.22 (18.18)	73.57 (13.73)
random $\mu(\sigma)$	2	41.86 (10.01)	44.29 (11.97)	58.14 (10.01)	52.17 (9.20)	56.19 (6.52)
human wins?	2	0.0005	0.0005	0.0005	0.0005	0.0005
human $\mu(\sigma)$	3	96.07 (7.85)	97.86 (4.69)	3.93 (7.85)	97.74 (4.85)	96.79 (7.50)
random $\mu(\sigma)$	3	42.16 (9.90)	45.14 (11.25)	57.84 (9.90)	56.40 (6.23)	53.69 (5.11)
human wins?	3	0.0005	0.0005	0.0005	0.0005	0.0005

Table 6.3: Performance of human- and random clustering in terms of different figures of merit.

Means	Dataset	purity [%]	γ (unbound, <)	I_{BBN} (unbound, >)	DER [%]
human $\mu(\sigma)$	1	62.72 (0.68)	16.4 (8.37)	4.13 (1.78)	33.13 (9.50)
random $\mu(\sigma)$	1	53.37 (6.35)	18.3 (6.52)	3.42 (1.25)	34.84 (9.71)
human wins?	1	0.0005	0.1	0.01	no
human $\mu(\sigma)$	2	68.41 (15.04)	12.7 (7.18)	5.39 (2.5)	27.57 (14.26)
random $\mu(\sigma)$	2	53.87 (6.01)	16.4 (4.48)	3.63 (1.1)	33.77 (9.74)
human wins?	2	0.0005	0.0005	0.0005	0.005
human $\mu(\sigma)$	3	97.21 (5.70)	0.9 (1.8)	10.1 (0.88)	2.38 (5.00)
random $\mu(\sigma)$	3	54.99 (5.31)	12.74 (1.67)	4.19 (0.76)	32.00 (9.93)
human wins?	3	0.0005	0.0005	0.0005	0.0005

Table 6.4: Performance of human- and random clustering in terms of more figures of merit.

d **Monotonicity.** Confirming the statistical results above, the human figures of merit get consistently and strictly monotonically better across runs.

e **No big picture.** There are three important exceptions to the fact that all other human results are with at least 99.5% confidence better than random: for γ, I_{BBN} and DER on dataset 1, there is considerably less or no basis to deduce that they deviate from pure guessing; all three measures have in common (in contrary to the other ones) that they evaluate clustering in total.

f **Humaneness.** Average human performance on dataset 3 (the natural, "easy" one) is not perfect, but almost perfect.

g **Grouping.** The biggest increase in performance seems to be between run (dataset) 2 and 3 (the latter is nearly perfect), which is on average 4.72 (with a standard deviation of 1.46) times greater than the gain between run 1 and 2 (the performance on the former is near guessing). But careful analysis reveals: the standard deviation for all measures in run 2 is considerably higher than for run 1 (and, less important, run 3). Looking inside the individual participant's results as given in Appendix A.4 shows that there are two groups of participants that are distinct: the major group (17 out of 20 persons) gives results as indicated by Tables 6.3 and 6.4; but two subjects score perfectly (IDs mhm and abf), another one (ID rsm) has made only one wrong connection. These three participants have in common that they nearly exhausted the given time limit (median of 30 minutes), in contrast to everyone in the first group (median of 14 minutes).

h **Diligence.** In run 1, the top 3 participants (there is no clear division of the subjects into groups here) in terms of Rand index also use considerably more time (median of 30 minutes) than the rest (median of 20 minutes).

i **Equality.** There is no correlation of a participant's individual properties (sex, age or time taken to complete a task) with scoring considerably better or worse in any other run.

Qualitative Results

The qualitative results exhibit "how" the participants accomplished each task. They are assembled from the free text fields for each run on the assessment sheet. Due to the nature of free text, phrasing among the participants differs (and many have not commented on all of the indirect inquiries). Nevertheless, the results are very homogeneous, as confirmed by several oral inquiries consulting randomly selected participants.

Feature	Dataset 1 [#]	Dataset 2 [#]	Dataset 3 [#]
rhythm/velocity	7	11	8
pitch	7	11	7
timbre/sound	3	6	14
perceived gender	0	2	13
perceived age	0	0	5
visual imagination	0	1	3
volume	2	1	0
nasalization	0	1	0
holistic judgment	0	0	1

Table 6.5: Popularity of human-used features.

Table 6.5 reports on the features used by the participants on the different data sets. The popularity values display how often respective features are mentioned by the participants after summarizing similar references. Some broader categories include more detailed features besides and beyond the pure meaning of their names after summarization: rhythm/velocity includes concentrating on frequency *changes* as well as the accentuation and use of pauses; pitch includes separating "high" from "low" voices, which extends the psychoacoustical notion of pitch [Moore

Chapter 6. Modeling Temporal Aspects of a Voice

2004] to a broader view of main spectral components; timbre/sound includes articulation, accent, speaking style and intonation.

The following findings are noticeable:

j **Growth.** With the data set's number, the usage of features that allow for a vivid perception of the voice increases. It basically starts on dataset 2 with the mentioning of "imagining the speaker behind the voice" and the use of gender detection (although other participants state that this is impossible on this data set) and is used on dataset 3, where participants even clustered based on inferred attractive appearance of female speakers.

k **Speech mode.** An appeal to the normal human speech perception mode (i.e., holistic hearing), which is distinct in nature from perceiving other sounds being judged based on simple patterns and features as described by Moore [2004], is only made for dataset 3.

l **Confusion.** The features used for dataset 1 mostly confused the participants: rhythm/velocity as well as timbre/sound do not convey speaker-related information on dataset 1 because any inter-frame relationships are purely random by design.

m **Methodology.** Regarding the methodology, the participants broadly adopt a systematic way of pairwise comparison of voices by adding them up to clusters until a certain threshold of dissimilarity is reached. The process then restarts with the next free utterance.

n **Multi-pass.** In some cases, a multi-pass scheme that first skims a whole data set and then clusters utterances based on a process of elimination can be observed.

o **Hierarchy.** For dataset 3, a hierarchical scheme that first presorts utterances by gender (a cue described as most helpful by several participants) before building groups can be observed.

p **Intuition.** Some participants do not use any systematic strategy on dataset 3 but just "do it naturally".

The findings from the self-assessment of participants are summarized as follows:

q **Affirmation.** The quantitative results from above are largely confirmed: judgments are between "impossible" and "very unsure" on dataset 1 and do not vary much for dataset 2, where the range is from "very unsure" to "mediocre" with an emphasis on the first one. For dataset 3, the self-assessment is "quite correct" and predominantly "sure".

r **Humility.** The self-assessment for the second data set partly contradicts the measured clustering performance in that even the participants of the group of well-doing subjects do not regard themselves as being able of clustering the data.

6.3 Harnessing the Results

The aim of this chapter is to identify speaker clustering stages that need to be improved and the order in which these improvements have to take place such that a maximum performance gain is obtained. The findings of Section 6.2 are now evaluated with respect to this aim.

6.3.1 Interpretation

First, the results of Section 6.2.3 confirm the choices made earlier in this chapter as well as the popularity of common techniques:

- The result 6.2.3.i (equality) and the homogeneity of the qualitative results indicate that the choice of the set of participants is appropriate.

- The results 6.2.3.m–6.2.3.o (methodology, multi-pass, hierarchy) indicate that humans apply, in the absence of the subconscious speech mode used when everything is familiar, a way of accomplishing the task of grouping that resembles the algorithm in an automatic hierarchical clustering system: evaluating pairwise distances, grouping the closest clusters until a termination criterion is met, guided by any available additional information like sex. This justifies the omission of the clustering stage in the list of potential stages for improvement.

- Several results give evidence that the used MFCC features capture speaker-specific information quite well: 6.2.3.c (purpose) and 6.2.3.e (no big picture) show that humans clearly perform better than guessing on dataset 2, and 6.2.3.g (grouping) and 6.2.3.h (diligence) suggest that achieving even better results on unfamiliar data might be a concentration issue rather than a matter of missing cues in the features. Moreover, Rose [2002, p. 103] reports on experiments showing that human performance normally nearly doubles when exposed to familiar voices as opposed to unfamiliar ones. It is argued that this performance loss in the presence of unfamiliarity is even more present when the sound itself is unusual.

- As indicated by 6.2.3.c (purpose), modeling is effective in the sense that GMMs even contain human-exploitable speaker-related information (although the main statement of 6.2.3.e (no big picture) needs further treatment below).

- The last two remarks allows to conclude that humans are capable of analyzing this kind of sounds in principle, which supports the biomimetic approach. Further justification comes from Furui [2005], who points out that breakthroughs in speech technology will rather come from a better understanding of speech and the way it is produced and *perceived* rather than from mere improvements in statistical pattern recognition; and from Wu et al. [2009], who also use the opportunity of learning from human speech processing abilities.

Second, there is evidence for a specific answer to the opening question. From 6.2.3.a (improvement), 6.2.3.d (monotonicity) and 6.2.3.q (affirmation) it is clear that it is appropriate to view the pattern recognition chain as a process of information compression: exploitable as well as useless information with respect to speaker identity is abolished in each step. Via 6.2.3.g (grouping), the main argument of this chapter is introduced by showing where the most useful information disappears: it is in the modeling stage. At first glance, 6.2.3.g (grouping) seems to contradict this finding, but even though the figures of merit deviate more among dataset 2 and 3 than between dataset 1 and 2, there is a fundamental difference between both transitions. From dataset 3 to 2, average human performance drops from nearly perfect to below what is considered acceptable for a clustering system; but there is still this group of three candidates scoring nearly perfectly also on the audible features. On dataset 1, however, the complete clustering performance for all participants tends towards guessing (6.2.3.e, no big picture) and no one considers himself able of accomplishing the task in contrast to dataset 2 (6.2.3.q, affirmation). The fundamental difference is this: what is difficult on the audible features becomes impossible on the audible models. This does not contradict the conclusion that exploitable information is found in the models; individual voices can still be recognized quite well even on dataset 1 (6.2.3.b, individuality)—but the task of clustering dataset 1 *as a whole* becomes impossible.

What is it that produces this frontier between the feature extraction and modeling stage? 6.2.3.j (growth) suggests that participants find no features within audible models that help making the "voices" vivid. Table 6.5 shows what these features are: the timbre or sound of a voice, as well as the rhythm and velocity of the stream of speech (the latter ones have also been used by participants on dataset 1, but in a wrong way, see 6.2.3.l (confusion)). These features have in common that they are essentially supra-frame based—they are not grasped in a single instant of time, but the sensation needs an evolution of frames to emerge. What is crucially missing in the modeling stage is an account for time.

Another point for optimization lies in the feature extraction stage: participants found the preclassification of utterances by perceived gender most helpful (6.2.3.o, hierarchy), and gender is strongly correlated with the pitch of a voice. A sensation of pitch, though, is largely eliminated by design in MFCCs.

To summarize, it is found that the used features include what it takes to identify a voice (at least for a human analyst; no proposition is made that to be useful for machines, it might not be necessary to make certain parts of the vectors' content more explicit). But they would benefit from providing further cues for gender detection, i.e., pitch (or its acoustic correlate, F_0). But this improvement must be succeeded by an enhancement of the applied models to incorporate an account for the temporal succession of frames without modeling speech instead of a voice. This is the area with the highest potential for improvement.

6.3.2 Discussion

There are several promising approaches for finding better features, e.g., by Pachet and Roy [2007], Thiruvaran et al. [2007] or Prasanna et al. [2006]. But until modeling is capable of capturing the fundamental relationships among individual vectors, these approaches will not yield what might be expected. This is also true for examples of accompanying MFCCs with pitch (or better: F_0) as done by Lu and Zhang [2005], whose results are not better than those of comparable approaches [Kotti et al. 2008b] without an account for pitch. Nevertheless, F_0 is an important feature also for forensic phoneticians, from whom striving for a better understanding of speech instead of improving technical solutions can most likely be expected: it is the most often mentioned single feature in Rose' book [Rose 2002, pp. 41, 161/162, 246, 249/250]. However, apart from spectral (cepstral) features, all other features mentioned there have one thing in common: they exploit the temporal coherence of speech. Those features are: temporal factors (p. 113), breath patterns (p. 113), speaking tempo (p. 115), syllable grouping (p. 133), speech rate (p. 169) and hesitation (p.172).

Lindblom et al. [2008] use the temporal context of spectral frames to improve the extraction of formant center frequencies and conclude that the "temporal fine structure of the signal plays a very significant role [...] in speech perception". In a current attempt to identify future traits of research in biometrics, Schouten et al. [2008] put the demand for context inclusion on top of their list of 19 urgent topics. The need for and the realization of the integration of temporal context has also recently been discovered by Aucouturier [2009] and Joder et al. [2009], respectively, for the field of music information retrieval. It follows that there is a widespread awareness of the importance of time-based information for audio processing.

The easiest way of modeling time dependencies is by accompanying feature vectors with their temporal derivatives of first and second order (δ and $\delta\delta$ features). Malegaonkar et al. [2008] show that this has some potential, but the positive effect is not consistently observable [Kotti et al. 2008b]. Another approach lies in the area of prosody modeling for speaker recognition: approaches there try to capture intonation, stress, rhythm and velocity of speech by modeling the trajectories of F_0 and/or short time energy over the duration of syllable-like units (50–100 ms according to Rose [2002, p. 167]). Adami [2007] gives a good overview and presents his approach of modeling the joint distribution of pitch and energy gestures along with their durations via bigrams. A gesture lasts until either the pitch or energy contour changes direction and is

Chapter 6. Modeling Temporal Aspects of a Voice

quantized into one of 5 states encoding the joint pattern of rise and descent of the two features. Mary and Yegnanarayana [2008] presegment the speech by detecting vowel onset points (VOP) before extracting mean-, peak- and change in F_0, peak distance to VOP, amplitude and duration tilt and finally change in log-energy per segment as features for prosodic behavior. They model them via auto-associative neural nets. Further systems come, for instance, from Reynolds et al. [2003, 2005], Ferrer et al. [2003] and Soenmez et al. [1997]. They all have in common that the prosodic features and models complement conventional (cepstrum-based) systems and improve the final result; that they are robust to noise and other variations; and that they need much data for training and testing in the region of several minutes.

Modeling prosodic speaker-dependent information heads into the right direction, but does not cover completely what is claimed by this study. First, not all of the features mentioned by the participants fall into the category of prosody: timbre and sound, for example, account for more than what is covered by energy- and pitch contours; they emerge with time, but likely with the time evolution of gross spectral shapes instead of just amplitude and fundamental frequency. Second, the features used by the participants could readily be evaluated with small amounts of training and test data (some participants reported to have used only the first 5–10 seconds to judge an utterance), whereas current prosodic systems suffer from the need for vast data consumption, as pointed out by Chen et al. [2005]. Rose seems to bridge this gap with the following suggestion: the quality of a voice is best viewed in contrast to (or deviation from) an idealized neutral vocal apparatus configuration [Rose 2002, p. 279] and the analysis might better focus on individual outstanding events rather than on global averages [Rose 2002, p. 73]. A human listener with general knowledge of how speech sounds can find those outstanding speaker-specific sounds in a short utterance and reliably recognizes the voice based on them. Current prosodic systems do not possess this general knowledge and hence cannot find the few interesting parts of the signal, eventually needing more data for compensation.

6.4 Implementation and Results

Several ways are imaginable to implement the exploitation of time and pitch information in the spirit of the presented results. In this section, an implementation of a speaker clustering system is presented that incorporates this kind of information.

The proposed *time model* replaces the GMM in the diarization framework presented in Section 6.1; everything else is left unchanged. The following new processing steps are incorporated in the time model:

- Speaking rate normalization

- Transformation of basic features to *trajectories*

6.4. Implementation and Results

- Estimation of the support of the trajectory's distribution in time and frequency
- Comparison of different trajectory models

The central idea is trajectory modeling: feature vectors of one utterance are not independent of each other, but belong to their temporal context. This context can be grasped by concatenating several subsequent single frames to a *context vector*. It depends on the viewpoint whether this can be considered as improving the features instead of the modeling—in this implementation, the modeling stage receives a set of feature vectors in their original order that is then exploited further, hence it is spoken of improving the modeling stage. Previous approaches to trajectory modeling include the work of Chengalvarayan and Deng [1998], Saul and Rahim [1998], Vlachos et al. [2002] or Sekhar and Panaliswami [2004]. Here, it is deviated from their approaches in the way models are created and/or trajectories are compared.

The ordered sequence of 19-dimensional MFCC feature vectors, enriched with the F_0 contour extracted via the RAPT algorithm [Talkin 1995], is taken as the basic features and input to the time model. The sequence represents a single utterance as described in Section 6.1. Each dimension is normalized to the range [0..1] using the min/max values found on all the TIMIT data.

Then, the speaking rate is normalized so that the same sound uttered in different tempi results in the same sequence of feature vectors. This is performed by first clustering the frames into $\frac{2T}{3}$ clusters via k-means, where T is the number of feature vectors in the utterance under consideration (this way, speaking rate normalization works adaptive). The factor of 66% has been found optimal in informal listening experiments. Each vector is then replaced with its centroid, and a sequence of identical centroids in the feature set is cut to length one, thus reliably shortening stretched sounds.

Then, 13 subsequent vectors are concatenated to form one context vector. This corresponds to a syllable length of 130 ms and is found to best capture speaker specific sounds in informal listening experiments over a range of 32–496 ms (in intervals of 16 ms). The context vector step is one original frame, i.e., 10 ms. This way, two subsequent trajectories share $\frac{23}{24}$ identical speech samples (one frame difference, and frames have 50% overlap), such that the time/frequency information is spread into different corners of the 260-dimensional context vector space. This makes it more probable for a differently aligned context vector in the evaluation phase to be recognized. Experiments showed that the remaining 5 ms possible displacement lead to very similar context vectors on otherwise identical data.

The set of context vectors of one utterance is then fed into a one-class SVM [Tax 2001] training step. Using only positive examples to identify the $100 \cdot (1-\nu)\%$ densest data points, it can (in contrast to a GMM) handle very high dimensional data. The implementation available in libsvm [Chang and Lin 2001] is used in conjunction with the RBF kernel. For all the

Chapter 6. Modeling Temporal Aspects of a Voice

speaker models, a common outlier factor of $\nu = 0.4825$ has been found effective; for the γ parameter of the SVM, a grid search optimization framework is adopted for each training set/model separately, using 5-fold cross validation in 25 logarithmically spaced steps between the minimum and maximum pairwise distances of all trajectories in the set. This individual parameter search is mainly responsible for the increased runtime, but appears to be crucial for the result.

After having built a time model for each utterance, the clustering procedure is applied using the CLR as the metric between two models. CLR works considerably better in pretests than the *contrast measure* d_c presented by Desobry et al. [2005a,b], a direct measure between model parameters, and better than GLR as well. The likelihood of a set of MFCC+F_0 to a time model is computed as follows: feature vectors are transformed to context vectors using the methodology described above, and classified using the previously trained one-class SVM model. The ratio of positively classified trajectories is the desired "likelihood".

This is a novel approach to voice modeling for the purpose of recognition. The processing steps inside the model as well as the various parameter settings originate from sound considerations but only preliminary experiments, leaving room for improvement. The time model has been applied to the clustering task on the reduced `TIMIT` data set with 40 speakers and 80 utterances that was used as an example to show when the baseline GMM approach starts to fail. Comparisons are made with the baseline MFCC & GMM approach presented in Section 6.1 and with several common approaches for time and pitch exploitation, namely enhancing the MFCC vectors by δ, $\delta\delta$ and F_0 columns. All experiments have been carried out on a computer with 2 GB memory and an Intel Core2Duo processor at 2.4 GHz running a C++ based implementation within `sclib` under Fedora 10 Linux. Results are presented in Table 6.6.

Approach	Runtime [m]	rec$_o$ [%]	prec$_o$ [%]	MR [%]	DER [%]
baseline	2.70	87.50	98.75	12.50	4.527
baseline+δ	4.95	35.00	35.00	65.00	58.33
baseline+δ+$\delta\delta$	7.98	50.00	98.75	50.00	17.31
baseline+F_0	2.15	73.75	90.00	26.25	15.51
baseline+δ+F_0	4.98	51.25	51.25	48.75	40.84
baseline+δ+$\delta\delta$+F_0	7.97	28.75	28.75	71.25	61.76
time model	523.13	93.75	97.50	6.250	1.962

Table 6.6: Experimental results.

First, the standard baseline system itself scores better than the enhanced baseline systems, which is in line with the previous reasoning, the results presented by Kotti et al. [2008b], and partly due to the curse of dimensionality letting GMMs perform poorly on higher-dimensional inputs [Fergani et al. 2008]. Overall, the proposed time model approach yields 56.66% and 50.00% relative DER and misclassification rate improvement over the standard baseline, respectively. These results indicate that time coherence exploitation (combined with pitch) as suggested by the presented study improves the performance of current speaker clustering systems.

6.5 Conclusions

The work presented in this chapter is based on the observation that speaker clustering (diarization) approaches work considerably less satisfactory than approaches for the related tasks of speaker verification and identification. Therefore, a study has been presented to answer the following two questions by means of observing human behavior in a speaker clustering task: (a) where in the processing chain of speaker clustering has an improvement to take place to maximally improve the final outcome? (b) How does this improvement look like qualitatively?

The interpretation of the results has shown that it is the stage of modeling that bears the highest potential: the inclusion of temporal context information among feature vectors is what is crucially missing there. Furthermore, the inclusion of pitch information into feature vectors (in order to enable systems to better exploit gender information) is found to be a subordinate improvement—it will only have an effect after the major problem within modeling has been solved.

These results have led to an implementation of a speaker clustering system that demonstrates the validity of the presented approach by outperforming common MFCC & GMM-based approaches on the reduced **TIMIT** benchmark with a relative improvement of 56.66% DER and 50.00% misclassification rate, respectively.

Two things should be noted about the approach: on the one hand, its design allows improvements in speaker clustering systems—time coherence, e.g., clearly is a currently unexploited source of important information, and MFCCs modeled by GMMs will certainly not score above some glass ceiling in the spirit of Aucouturier and Pachet [2004]. On the other hand, the biomimetic approach is not the only possible way to determine areas of improvement; other approaches may certainly be discovered.

There are several questions for future work: is the time succession of frames best grasped by concatenating several frames together? What are good conditions and parameter settings for the one-class SVM model and how can they be found? How can, according to Rose [2002, p. 73], the outstanding trajectories of a speaker be found and technically exploited? How can the increased runtime of the time model approach be improved? Finally, how can the entire temporal context be considered, just as in the popular forensic phonetic method of analyzing spectrograms in a Gestalt-based manner [Rose 2002, p. 116]?

"Intuition (is) perception via the unconscious."

Carl Gustav Jung (1875–1961)

7

Perceptually Motivated Algorithm Design

7.1 Introduction

Contemporary speech processing systems are complex, typically consisting of several algorithms. These often contain sub-algorithms, with numerous processing steps whose effects and parameter settings are not intuitively understandable by humans. This leads to several problems when designing new and adapting or replicating existing algorithms. Taking the MFCC feature extraction algorithm as a concrete example, parameters such as the number of coefficients to keep are relatively easy to understand, but other parameters, such as the window type or the size of the filter bank, are more abstract, making it difficult to intuitively judge their importance and their effects on the complete processing chain. When the parameterization is fixed, the choice of the concrete implementation may offer variability, too [Ganchev et al. 2005; Zheng et al. 2001].

When adapting an existing algorithm to a new environment, there is usually no instant success due to such misconceptions. The same is true for designing a new algorithm based on theoretical results or reimplementing a published algorithmic description for comparison. For example, Keogh et al. [2004] report on the problems arising when new data is used in conjunction with published parametrized algorithms. When the results do not meet the expectations, several questions arise:

Chapter 7. Perceptually Motivated Algorithm Design

- What effect does a change of a parameter in a component of an algorithm have?
- What does the selection of a particular algorithmic technique in the presence of several possibilities do with the overall functionality?
- What is the contribution of a specific algorithmic step?
- Is it actually the right algorithm for this data?
- If not, how should a valid one be designed?

These questions are aimed at finding a hypothesis—the beginning of the scientific process. But how to arrive at a promising hypothesis? Some disciplines have developed their own methodologies to assist human creativity in this process. They conceptualize a principle that in its core is as appealing as common sense, then add to it formal procedures and ready-to-use tools. One such methodology, from the discipline of data mining, can be summarized by the phrase "know your data": the approach of striving for (visual, mathematical, expertise-like) insight into the data set belongs to every data miner's toolbox, making the mining process more amenable to planning and success more likely [Thearling et al. 2001].

In this chapter, a related methodology for speech processing is conceptualized that systemizes the search for hypotheses about the reasons of unexpected algorithmic behavior. This captures a spirit that may also have existed partially and unmatured before, and elaborates, formulates and formalizes it in order to be applicable. Based on this methodology, a set of tools is introduced that facilitates the proposed workflow. These tools comprise a novel algorithmic framework for audio resynthesis as well as new service-oriented ways to deploy the software.

The chapter is organized as follows: the core principle, its relevancy, formalized methodology and practical applications are shown in Section 7.2. The corresponding tools, `WebVoice` and `PlotGMM`, are introduced with theoretical background and implementation details in Section 7.3. Section 7.4 draws conclusions and outlines areas for future work.

Parts of the work presented in this chapter have been published in papers by Stadelmann et al. [2009] and Stadelmann et al. [2010].

7.2 A Methodology for Speech Research & Development

This section provides the background for- and embedment of an approach to speech processing algorithm design that is strongly motivated by perception. Algorithm design thereby comprises all aspects between research—acquiring an appropriate idea about some phenomenon—and development—the process of putting an idea to work. This approach is the condensate of the paths taken in order to arrive at the results presented in the previous chapters.

7.2. A Methodology for Speech Research & Development

In Chapter 3, the improvement of the GMM was triggered by looking at a visualization created with a tool to be introduced below in this chapter. The same is true for the heart of the approach in Chapter 6, made possible by a tool for audio resynthesis and inspired by the striving for intuition into a complex problem. The occupation with the EMD in Chapter 5 was initially motivated by its intuitive working; and the results in Chapter 4 made the errors plain one is capable of overlooking even in the presence of counter-evidence from theory if comprehensible feedback from the algorithms is missing.

The core principle and its relevancy to the speech processing community is discussed in Subsection 7.2.1. Then, the method is formalized in Subsection 7.2.2 by proposing a concrete workflow before it is exercised on a real world example in Subsection 7.2.3.

7.2.1 Problem Refinement

The aim of this chapter is to propose a method that helps making reasons for failure in complex (compositions of) speech processing algorithms graspable by humans. Grasping contains a certain extent of intuition. If an issue is intuitively clear, human creativity may generate hypotheses [Cosmides and Tooby 1996]. Thus, stated informally, *seeking intuition* is the core of this chapter's approach. Obviously, most researchers strive for intuition in order to make discoveries. But how can intuition be achieved?

For researchers in the field of computer vision it is particularly easy to gain intuitive understanding using visualization, since their objects (and, often, results) of analysis are original visual objects. Arguably, this makes the visual domain a good choice to transform data into in order to grasp their meaning. The same is true for the data mining area, where visualization is often applied to comprehend neighborhood relationships, a task that humans naturally associate with visual representations [Keim 2002]. However, the success of visualization methods and the corresponding overreliance of researchers on them can also be a hindering factor in other areas of research, because visualization is not in itself the only mediator of intuition. It is one of the possible transformations applicable to the data in order to find a representation for which humans are experts in perceiving meaning due to their natural abilities.

For example, in speech processing, the original domain of the input data is the auditory perception. There are still many applications for visualization in speech processing, but representing the speech signal's most prominent features as an image (the single popular technique here is the spectrogram) does not result in more intuition, but creates a higher-dimensional signal that needs an expert interpreter to make use of its many merits [Rose 2002]. In the worst case, mere visualization transforms the data into an unnatural domain, thereby implicitly reducing the range of understandable or discoverable features to what the transformation can and cannot do. If the way of visualization is not suitable for a given problem, researchers

Chapter 7. Perceptually Motivated Algorithm Design

may—devoid of knowing alternative ways—refrain from seeking intuition altogether, thereby risking to miss discoveries.

Mere visualization is not enough to let intuition emerge. For this purpose, algorithmic sub-results need to be recast to the specific perceptual domain in which humans are experts in intuitively grasping the context, the character and the reasons of the issue at hand. This subsumes visualization, but broadens the view to other possible transformations like resynthesis ("audibilization") by expecting insight not from an image alone, but from the unison of a domain suitable for the data *and* natural human grasping. Other methods to achieve intuition are needed, and particularly in speech processing there is a need for new developments, as Hill [2007] remarks: the area currently misses a culture of perceptually motivated research, partly induced by missing methodologies and tools.

The contribution of this chapter is threefold: first, it *motivates* the use of intuitive methods in the design of speech processing algorithms by presenting arguments and a successful example. Second, it *facilitates* the use of intuitive methods beyond visualization by proposing a methodology and workflow. This includes prerequisites and steps to follow on the way to hypothesizing solutions to the questions raised in the introduction. Third, it *enables* the use of intuitive methods by making available accompanying tools for multimodal intuitive analysis on the web.

7.2.2 The Proposed Methodology and Workflow

The following methodology is proposed to strive for intuition about the reasons of unexpected algorithmic outcomes: the starting point is an *existing algorithm* (or a process consisting of several algorithms) along with a certain *problem*, i.e., a question to- or aspect of interest in the algorithm. The problem might be as general as an observed malfunctioning (for example, a change detection algorithm operating at an unacceptable error rate) or as concrete as needing a good parameter setting.

The initial step, as depicted in Figure 7.1, is to identify all important phases in the algorithm or process. These phases do have intermediate results as implicit outcomes (the *data*). Insight into the algorithmic phase is sought by perceptually observing its produced data, thereby feeling what has changed since the previous phase and whether the action has worked reasonably. Therefore, it is necessary to transform the sub-results into a *suitable domain*.

The suitable domain is a specific *gestalt* into which the data is transformed: for example, not just a sound (as an ambassador of the auditory domain), but male speech or single-tone music (as representatives of more a concrete, specific or holistic notion of domain); not just an image, but a histogram or a gray scale gradient map. The suitable domain is characterized by the following property: it represents the data through metaphors humans use so frequently

7.2. A Methodology for Speech Research & Development

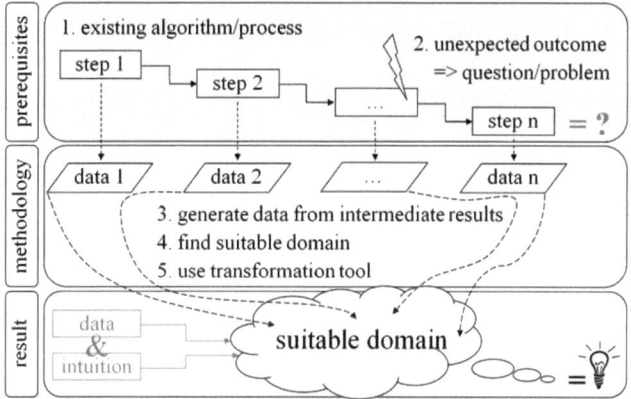

Figure 7.1: The proposed workflow.

in everyday life that they judge their meaning rather implicitly (intuitively) than explicitly (rationally). This makes the suitable domain dependent on the problem, the data and the observer. For instance, a certain problem might be to decide whether to continue a certain action. If the data can be transformed to the domain of traffic lights, a red light is intuitively judged by a human observer as not to continue the action. The red light is a strong metaphor in this context. Another example might be the problem of inferring a speakers gender. Wile this is difficult to investigate if the data is, e.g., in MFCC form, the issue is immediately clear without reflection as soon as the data is transformed back to the speech domain and the observer hears a low-pitched male voice. This instant awareness of either the answer to the initial problem, or other perplexing facts leading to new ways of thinking about the problem, is a frequent property of the presented approach.

Being aware of the need of- and subsequently finding a suitable domain for the transformation is the most important part of the workflow. It is in itself a creative process that cannot be fully automated. Still, with the following aids, it is easier to pursue this search than to generate hypotheses about the initial problem deafblindly: first, empirically, a suitable domain is often the one that corresponds naturally with the investigator's imagination of the data under the given problem. For example, one may think of feature distributions as mountain massifs (compare Figure 7.2 and Section 3.2). Second, if the data represents an object of the physical world rather than some abstract intermediate result, the domain of this physical counterpart gives useful insights about a suitable domain for the transformation—possibly, the transformation consists of undoing previous transformations, as resynthesis does in speech processing. For instance, a statistical voice model can be imagined as something that really sounds like a voice

Chapter 7. Perceptually Motivated Algorithm Design

(a) Analogy between a 2D probability density and a mountain chain.

(b) Plan for a 1000m tall mountain on the former Berlin Tempelhof air field.

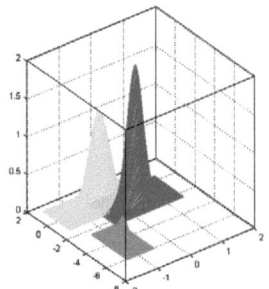

(c) Analogy of a 3D PDF to the mountain on the left.

Figure 7.2: Imagining some probability distributions (the axis' scaling does not matter here) as a mountain massifs. The imagination suggests a helpful transformation (display, in this case).

without being comprehensible, as has been exemplified in the last chapter.

After a suitable domain is identified, the last step is to find or design a *tool* that carries out the transformation. Tools for this purpose will not be completely generic. However, a set of tools for several purposes and modalities is presented in the next section. It comprises software to make most common speech features and -models audible and new tools to visualize Gaussian mixture-based models. Additional software is to be found on the accompanying website as given below.

Stepping through this workflow leads to a vivid representation in a suitable domain, allowing an experience of the inner workings of the algorithm under consideration. This provides a breeding ground for hypotheses about their failure in the given context. Revisiting the above-mentioned examples, if the mountain massif is too spiky, this may indicate changing the smoothness parameters of the distribution estimation technique, as is commonly understood. If the resynthesized voice model sounds not at all like a voice, this provokes further inquiries about possibly missing features in the data. The prerequisite for the methodology to work is

7.2. A Methodology for Speech Research & Development

that there is a representation of the data that corresponds with intuition. Fortunately, many patterns in speech processing have a natural origin and many pattern recognition problems a corresponding real world task they refer to.

The methodology described provides a framework for discovering reasons and possible solutions for problems in existing algorithms. This is useful for researchers when working on, adapting or extending present algorithms as well as for practitioners in debugging complex systems. But the practical relevance goes further: intuitive insight into state-of-the-art methods also makes their possible flaws and oversimplifications obvious. This can inspire completely new algorithms in an explorative way, thereby becoming a method of algorithm design rather than pure analysis. A third application is teaching: making algorithmic steps perceivable adds intuition and practical experience to theoretical understanding, conveying a keen sense for applications.

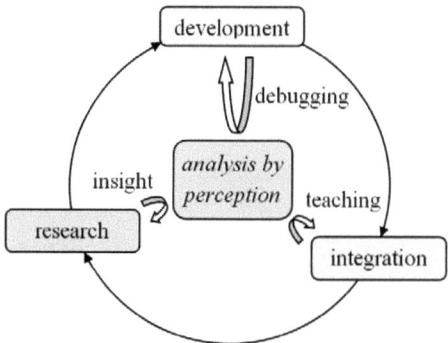

Figure 7.3: The "life cycle" of algorithm design using the proposed approach.

Consider the algorithm research and development life cycle depicted in Figure 7.3: algorithms are developed, than integrated within an existing system, then research has to be done in order to improve the algorithms and tackle a problem of increased difficulty. Perceptual analysis as just proposed helps to approach the specific problems at each stage: development is supported by debugging; integration, i.e., giving the algorithm away into the hands of a greater team of developers or users, is assisted via faster and deeper understanding through vivid acquisition. Research is enabled by providing insight into difficult matters in order to provoke new thoughts.

7.2.3 A Case Study

Next, the proposed methodology is applied step by step to the problem of speaker clustering. The focus here is on *how* the results have been achieved in order to exemplify the workflow, not

−133−

Chapter 7. Perceptually Motivated Algorithm Design

on the results themselves; they have been presented in the last chapter. Recounting the central question, it was the aim of Chapter 6 to show—in the presence of techniques that have once been built for speaker identification and now seem not expressive enough for the more difficult task of speaker clustering—which important aspect the techniques miss to represent.

To pursue this question and to start with the workflow, the *algorithm* under consideration is defined: the complete processing chain of speaker clustering. The chain can be roughly partitioned into feature extraction, model building and clustering. Because the success of the last phase depends largely on the quality of the voice models, it is omitted from further analysis, keeping the phases of MFCC feature extraction and GMM model building.

Next, the *problem* needs containment. The speaker clustering chain is large enough for improvements at the wrong point not being able to propagate until its end. Thus, first, the bottleneck needs to be found in the two identified phases. Then, second, a qualitative statement on what exactly is missing at this bottleneck is sought. Several other problem definitions are possible, like how each stage can be improved individually, but that would miss the point of the initial question. It is important to find a precise, manageable problem definition that captures the subconscious curiosity that initially lead to the research problem. In this case, this has been the dissatisfaction with current approaches per se instead of the search for small improvements.

The *data*, i.e., the intermediate results of the two phases, are two representations of a voice: the feature extraction yields a matrix of MFCC feature vectors, and the model building process yields the parameter vectors of a GMM that represent the statistical properties of the vector set and, hopefully, of the voice. This suggests a *suitable domain* for the transformation: if what is contained in the features and models could be listened to, missing information may be easily identified. This idea is simple, yet, it requires a new approach to audio resynthesis in order to be realizable, so it is far from being simplistic.

Using this information, the needed resynthesis methods are developed and a respective *tool* (`WebVoice`, see Section 7.3.2) is designed to perform the necessary operations. Listening yields a somewhat surprising result: resynthesized GMM voice models sound extremely strange to human ears, due to the resulting audio frames being completely independent of each other. This does not allow the emergence of intonation and hence creates no sensation of listening to speech. While it is difficult to state what exactly has been expected from listening to GMMs, a result so far apart from having anything in common with a voice has been unexpected. The user study and proof-of-concept implementation presented earlier have confirmed the first suspicion: the missing time coherence information in the voice models is the desired bottleneck.

7.3 Tool Support

The last section introduced a general methodology to generate hypotheses about misbehaving algorithms in speech processing: the created workflow helps to ignite creativity in contexts where there is no prior experience on how to make certain choices. Experience may be lacking in several ways: in experimentation, a new context renders commonly used best practice rules useless. In education, the complexity of speech processing methods can be overwhelming to novices. Tools help by hinting at affected or troubled areas as well as by allowing exciting explorations.

This section introduces a set of tools in support of the proposed methodology. It is organized as follows: Subsection 7.3.1 first proposes a novel algorithmic framework to resynthesize intermediate speech processing results as one possible transformation to the data in the sense of the last section. The corresponding implementation as the `WebVoice` toolkit is then presented in Subsection 7.3.2. Subsection 7.3.3 finally introduces the `PlotGMM` tool as a software to visually inspect (Gaussian) mixture models.

As a result, a comprehensive archive of resynthesis- and visualization tools for most purposes in speech processing and beyond has been compiled on the web[1], together with source code, examples, tutorials and other resources.

7.3.1 Resynthesis

Quick and intuitive insight into speech and speaker related features and models can be achieved by *re*-synthesizing the intermediate results of the speech processing system: they represent acoustic events, so the human auditory system can aid thorough technical experimentation by giving a direct, sensible feedback on how specific choices affect the final outcome. This auditory feedback can then further be enhanced visually by looking at graphical representations of a resynthesized signal, together yielding a toolbox of multi-sensory perceptual analysis instruments. Possible visualizations of the signal itself are pitch tracks and speech flakes [Pickover 1986] besides the already introduced waveform views and spectrograms as well as their similarly flavored derivatives [Cooke et al. 1993].

Related Work

Resynthesis based on voice features aims at restoring formerly uttered speech. The used techniques are those from speech synthesis, but the aim is to revert a previous analysis process rather than synthesizing something purely artificial. This is reflected several times in the literature: Milner and Shao [2006] introduce a system designed for distributed automatic speech

---

[1] http://www.informatik.uni-marburg.de/~stadelmann/eidetic.html.

Chapter 7. Perceptually Motivated Algorithm Design

recognition over mobile networks that outputs the restored speech. Demuynck et al. [2004] also work in the ASR domain, but focus on the aspect of analyzing what preprocessed MFCCs do and do not represent in order to improve feature extraction. In this case, truthful exhibition of the information loss in each step is important. Ellis [2005] provides Matlab routines for MFCC- and perceptual linear prediction (PLP) feature inversion to advocate playful preoccupation with speech recognition techniques. Aucouturier [2009] uses resynthesis to gain insights into the differences of human- and machine perception of music.

In contrast to resynthesis that is tailored to ASR- or speech coding needs [Kleijn and Paliwal 1995], the aim of resynthesis in the proposed framework is to exhibit what each voice processing stage does with the signal. The important stages are feature extraction (including signal preprocessing) and modeling, with a focus on the most widespread techniques, namely MFCCs, LPCs and pitch as features, and GMMs and HMMs as models. The primary requirement for a resynthesized signal is to make audible what information is contained in models and feature vectors. Thus, instead of making the result more intelligible or natural, even to reverse the effect of some intermediate steps such as a preemphasis filter is omitted in the proposed algorithm in order to strive for high fidelity.

A New Resynthesis Framework

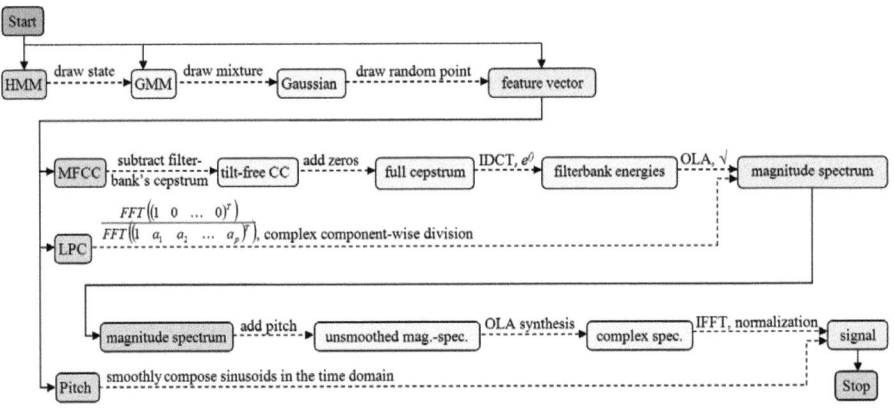

Figure 7.4: Flow diagram of the model inversion process.

The inversion process from a voice model back to audio is depicted in Figure 7.4. A GMM represents a probability distribution, so feature vectors following the distribution can be obtained via sampling from the model. This is a two-stage process: first, a mixture component with index m is chosen at random according to the distribution determined by the mixture

7.3. Tool Support

weights. This is accomplished by generating a uniformly distributed random number r in $[0, 1]$ and then summing up the mixture weights until the sum exceeds r; the mixture index m of the last added weight (of course, weights are ordered in the same way each time) subscripts the chosen mixture component. Second, a normal deviate is drawn from the mth mixture component via, e.g., the polar (Box-Muller) method [Knuth 1998]. Because the GMM was built from MFCC feature vectors, the resulting random vector is also a valid MFCC vector. If the GMM is just a state model inside a HMM, a zeroth stage has to be introduced that determines the GMM from which to sample according to the HMM's current state and state transition matrix. The state transition is randomized the same way a mixture component is chosen.

Depending on the actual feature type(s), the inversion process continues: converting a MFCC vector back to a waveform means to first cancel out the spectral tilt introduced by the (mel) filter bank. This is done by subtracting this filter bank's cepstrum in the cepstral domain. The circumsized cepstrum is then filled up with zeros and transformed back to the log filter bank domain by the inverse DCT, afterwards reversing the log() operation. This yields a vector of the size of the filterbank, which is expanded to spectrum size via an *overlap and add* (OLA) method [Verhelst 2000; Verhelst and Roelands 1993]. Taking the square root of each resulting component yields a standard magnitude spectrum. It lacks most of the pitch information that is removed by the heavy cepstral smoothing during feature extraction. More details on these steps can be found in the works of Ellis [2005] and Milner and Shao [2002, 2006].

A LPC vector is converted to a magnitude spectrum by first prefixing it with the zeroth coefficient (1.0) that has been discarded during feature extraction [Rabiner and Schafer 1978]. The new vector is then regarded as some signal and Fourier transformed to yield a complex spectrum via the FFT. Dividing the complex spectrum of an impulse [Smith 2003] by this spectrum yields the frequency response of the LPC filter [Rabiner and Juang 1993, ex. 3.4(c)][Stöcker 1995, p. 582].

Superimposing pitch (extracted via the RAPT algorithm [Talkin 1995] in the proposed system) on these MFCC or LPC spectra is done via the following scheme: the spectral envelope is amplified/de-amplified up to 25% according to the distance of each frequency bin to the next harmonic of F_0. Formally, letting $A = \{a_n | 1 \le n \le N\}$ be the magnitude spectrum of size N, this means for each component a_n of the spectrum to evaluate

$$\overline{a_n} = a_n \cdot \left[1 + \left(0.25 \cdot \sin\left(\frac{2\pi}{F_0} \cdot f_n + \frac{\pi}{2}\right)\right)\right] \quad (7.1)$$

where $\overline{a_n}$ is the new amplitude of the spectral component, f_n is the corresponding center frequency of the component and F_0 is the extracted pitch in Hertz, respectively. This introduces a repeated pattern of rise and descent and evokes a sensation of pitch. It works fine for MFCCs, but introduces considerable musical noise upon LPC spectra after phase reconstruction. How to deal with this has been exemplified by Goh et al. [1998], but is not further considered here.

The missing phase spectrum has to be estimated from the information present in the overlapping of frames. For this purpose, the iterative method introduced by Griffin and Lim [1984] is used. The process is stopped when the average (across frequency bins) absolute difference (error) between two successive iterations of the magnitude spectrum is less than 4% of the average magnitude in the current spectrum (or 100 iterations are reached, whatever happens first). The final signal is obtained by applying the inverse FFT to the complete sequence of complex spectra. It is normalized to have 30% of the maximum amplitude at its biggest peak. If pitch is the only extracted feature, the resynthesized signal is directly assembled in the time domain by a smooth composition of sinusoids at the frequency of F_0.

The presented approach differs in several aspects from existing approaches as the one of Demuynck et al. [2004], which it extends: by including the modeling stage and shifting the focus away from pure ASR methods, a more complete solution is offered. The novel way of reintroducing pitch into smoothed spectra is both methodically and computationally simple and effective.

7.3.2 WebVoice

To be useful for a wide range of users, a toolkit based on these resynthesis techniques has to be accessible, easy to use and needs to deliver quick results. Setting up the tool and learning to operate it must not introduce an additional barrier. This is offered within the `WebVoice` web service.

Initially, the resynthesis algorithm has been implemented within the `sclib` C++ class library for Windows- and Unix based systems. But a library has several drawbacks with respect to deployment, such as the need of a potential user to work with the source code, to adopt it to a specific platform, and to build a complex software package from scratch. This is certainly not beneficial for the application of a tool that is intended to *ease* work.

Service-Oriented Deployment

To wrap the resynthesis library up in a web service, accompanied by an automatic user interface (UI) generator, exhibits the needed properties. It makes using the tool as easy as browsing to the service's URI, using a plug-in for the Firefox web browser known as the "web service browser" [Heinzl et al. 2009a]. The browser plug-in is installed with a single click. Additionally, the *service-oriented architecture* (SOA) approach offers several advantages [Heinzl et al. 2009b]:

- Invocation is platform independent and does not need any installation.
- Software runs on the server side, using the computational power of the remote machine

7.3. Tool Support

(possibly a cluster).

- Source code does not need to be released (might be prohibited by organizational policies and licenses).
- Updates are directly available to everybody.

Figure 7.5: `WebVoice` in the web service browser.

Figure 7.5 shows the UI for one of `WebVoice`'s operations. It is automatically generated from the web service's WSDL (web service description language, an XML-like document accompanying the service and describing its interface) description. It offers drop-down boxes to select among the available methods and helps to input different data types for the parameters, e.g., to perform a file upload in the service invocation step. Data transfer is handled efficiently by the Flex-SwA framework [Heinzl et al. 2006] using a communication policy that allows to describe bulk data transfer protocols [Heinzl et al. 2008a].

After selecting an operation, loading up a (16 kHz, 16 bit, mono) RIFF WAVE file and possibly tailoring other parameters to a user's needs, the web service is invoked by simply clicking a button. When the computation on the server has finished, the result page opens with a MIME type-concordant representation of the result (a media player plays back the audio file in this case), offering to download it and also showing a textual representation and the SOAP message.

Chapter 7. Perceptually Motivated Algorithm Design

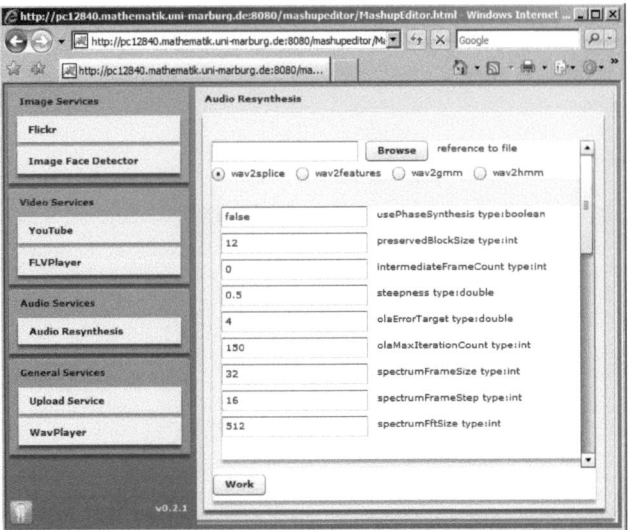

Figure 7.6: `WebVoice` in the mashup editor.

As an alternative to the Firefox add-on, a Flash-based rich internet application is also provided that works with a larger set of browsers, namely the service-enabled mashup editor "MIRO" [Heinzl et al. 2009c] able to invoke the `WebVoice` service. Figure 7.6 presents a screenshot of the mashup editor showing the UI of the `WebVoice` service.

The `WebVoice` endpoint (URI), the web service browser Firefox plug-in, and the mashup editor are all publicly available[2]. For the add-on to work correctly, Java version 1.6.0_04–1.6.0_07 is needed. The Java 7 preview versions (1.6.0_10 and newer) made changes to LiveConnect (which is used as the bridge from Firefox to Java [Mozilla Developer Center 2009]) such that the plug-in does not work correctly with these versions [Sun Developer Network 2010].

The Interface

Four methods are part of the web service and are offered to accomplish the goal of making the functionality and content of features and models audible. Each method's detailed description is shipped with `WebVoice` and contains explanations and sound default values for each parameter. Following is an overview:

- `wav2splice` offers to listen to a spliced version of the original signal. Splicing is the operation of randomizing the time order of subsequent non-overlapping blocks of the

---
[2]See http://mage.uni-marburg.de/ also for updates and further developments.

7.3. Tool Support

signal, where the block size can be specified. Listening to a spliced signal offers insights into the way pattern recognition systems handle data as a bag of frames [Aucouturier et al. 2007]. Sigmoidal interpolation between successive blocks can be switched on and controlled via some parameters to allow for smooth transitions. Additionally, the user can choose to hear or not to hear the effect of phase spectrum reestimation in order to discern the influence it has on the results of the following methods.

- wav2features goes one step further in the pattern recognition chain and offers to analyze various feature extraction methods: MFCCs and LPCs, both possibly accompanied by pitch, or pitch alone. The effects of virtually all possible parameters and the difference between the (combination of) techniques can be observed.

- wav2gmm provides GMM inversion using all the features (and respective parameter settings) known from above. The user has control over all modeling parameters. The same is true for the wav2hmm method that contributes the same service for continuous density HMMs of any internal structure.

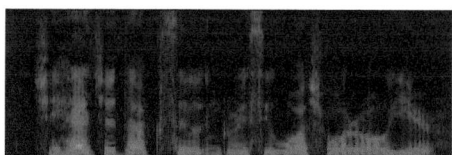

(a) Spectrogram of the original signal.

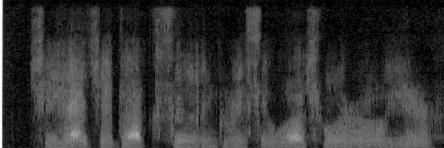

(b) Spectrogram of the resynthesized features.

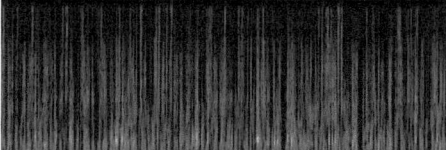

(c) Spectrogram of the resynthesized GMM.

Figure 7.7: Spectrogram comparison for the sentence "she had your dark suite in greasy wash water all year" uttered by a female speaker.

Chapter 7. Perceptually Motivated Algorithm Design

Figure 7.7(a) shows the spectrogram of a 3 seconds long sentence from the TIMIT database recorded under noise-free studio conditions and sampled at 16 kHz. When resynthesized using wav2features and a standard parameterization (i.e., MFCCs and pitch), the speech is still intelligible and the voice discernible from other resynthesized voices. It has, however, lost much of its natural appearance. The corresponding spectrogram is depicted in Figure 7.7(b). This is how MFCCs sound like.

The same signal resynthesized from a GMM (again using standard parameters and MFCC+pitch features) is depicted as a spectrogram in Figure 7.7(c). Here, the individual frames are completely independent of each other, although they strictly obey the original speaker's frequency distribution. This results in a sound that is not perceived as a voice by human listeners, although it still contains features for voice comparison. Apart from listening to this signal, its long term spectral analysis can reveal interesting details about the model at hand—i.e., what frequency characteristics are captured by the distribution.

7.3.3 PlotGMM

PlotGMM is a tool for visualizing GMMs using the "mountain massif" analogy presented earlier. The GMM is part of virtually all current implementations of speech processing systems, be it stand-alone for speaker recognition or as a state model in a speech-recognizing HMM. Having a process that helps to better understand what the model has "learned" can thus be beneficial. For example, is the number of mixture components reasonable for the distribution? Since one naturally thinks of statistical distributions as low-dimensional histograms (compare Figure 7.2(a)), this is best done by visualizing the model.

There are different methods to plot the underlying density of a data set, like U-Maps [Ultsch 2003b,c], kernel density plots or *multi-dimensional scaling* (MDS) [Bishop 2006]. Plotting a single Gaussian density function (even in many dimensions, if the covariance is assumed to be diagonal, as is mostly the case in speech processing) is also straightforward using tools like Matlab. However, all these approaches display the data (or their "true" distribution), not the trained GMM. To analyze what has been learned, an approach is taken here that is closer to the actual model.

A multi-mixture, multivariate Gaussian mixture model can be plotted just by using its parameters in order to to give an intuitive understanding of the model's spread and fit. The purpose hereby is to conduct a goodness-of-fit analysis of the model instead of the data, although this may, for instance, include a visual comparison with density plots of the data as produced, for example, by MDS. The shape and position of the distribution are of interest; this is contrary to analyzing the modeled content, in which case resynthesis would be recommended to gain insight. Providing ready-to-use software to facilitate this process might be of profit to the

7.3. Tool Support

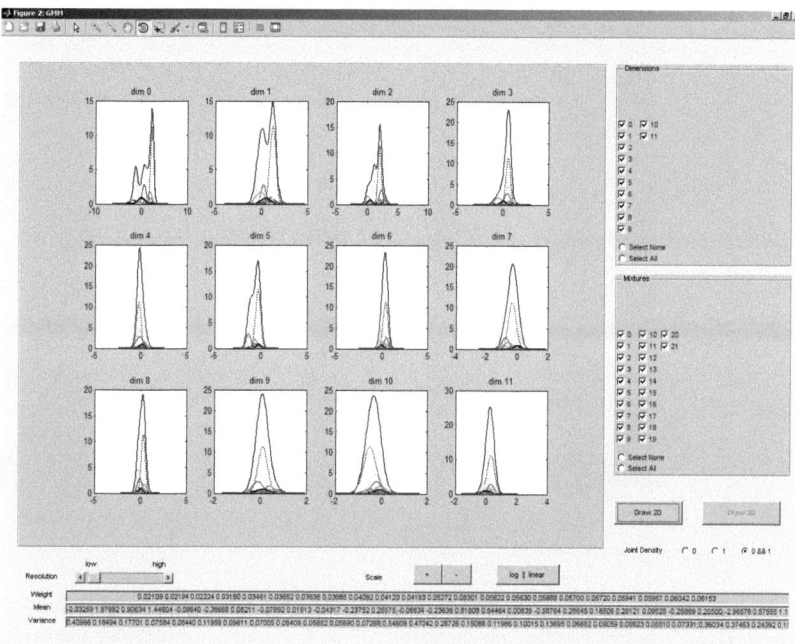

Figure 7.8: A 12-dimensional GMM with 22 mixtures. The joint density is drawn with the topmost solid blue line.

speech processing community as it was of profit for the results in Chapter 3.

PlotGMM is implemented as a set of Matlab routines accompanied by a Matlab-based graphical user interface (GUI) for visualizing the structure of a diagonal covariance GMM in 2D and 3D. Consider the screen shot depicted in Figure 7.8: it shows the GUI of plotGMM displaying a 12-dimensional real-world GMM having 22 mixtures and a diagonal covariance matrix. Each dimension is plotted individually, showing its overall joint density as well as the individual mixtures' contributions.

Located at the bottom of the window are the controls to edit the GMM's parameters and the appearance of the graphs. The resolution of the curves can be increased (at the expense of growing runtime), making their envelope smoother. Additionally, their sizes can be changed, subsequently scaling each mixture to the complete height as the plus/minus buttons are pressed. The scale can be toggled between linear and logarithmic, and the user can decide whether to see marginals and joint densities as in the figure, or either of them alone. The corresponding control is located at the right side of the window, directly below the buttons to redraw the selected mixtures and dimensions. If only two dimensions are marked, the "draw 3D" button

Chapter 7. Perceptually Motivated Algorithm Design

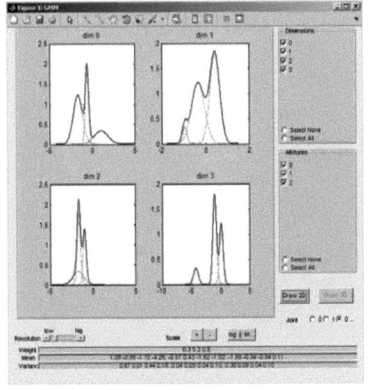 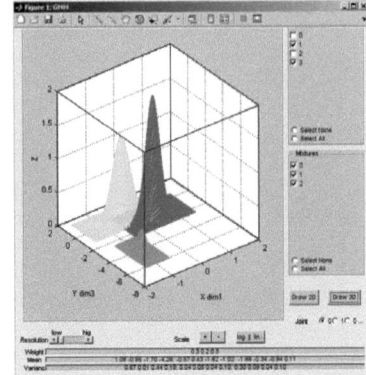

(a) Standard 2D plot.   (b) Plot of dimension one versus three in 3D.

Figure 7.9: A 4-dimensional GMM with 3 mixtures, plotted as univariate marginals and truly multivariate for selected dimensions.

gets enabled. The result is shown in Figure 7.9 for a simple synthetic GMM of 3 mixtures in 4 dimensions. Through the internal features of Matlab, the 3D plot can be zoomed, rotated and translated freely.

The plotGMM GUI has been created to reveal all modeled aspects in a GMM; at the same time, it is designed to comply with high usability demands, which has been tested in informal user studies. Via the Matlab compiler and runtime (Matlab compute runtime, MCR), it is able to be used stand-alone. The sclib is able to output model parameters directly in Matlab format in order to directly use its output as input to plotGMM.

7.4 Conclusions

In this chapter, a methodology has been presented to generate hypotheses about why algorithms in speech processing do not behave as expected. This human-in-the-loop approach strives for intuition into the problems by transforming algorithmic (sub-)results to a domain of perception where the human mind is considered to be an expert in conceiving the context and meaning of events, features and models naturally. This idea is best summarized by the phrase "eidetic design" as in "eidetic reduction" of phenomenology: it describes a method by which the researcher achieves intuition into the pure essence of an issue apart from what blurs its image [Encyclopædia Britannica 2009].

Using the workflow introduced in Section 7.2.2, eidetic design has practical applications in algorithm research and development, debugging and teaching. The methodology emerged from

7.4. Conclusions

the experience in researching and implementing speech processing systems as reported in this book and has shown its effectiveness several times. The methodical process has been exemplified by applying it step by step to the real world example of Chapter 6, leading to profound algorithmic improvements. More examples and resources are available on the accompanying website.

Furthermore, a corresponding software toolkit has been presented. The ease of use of the web service `WebVoice` and its playful character invites a user to a deeper engagement with the important topic of parameter tuning and method selection. This will likely shorten the time needed to become familiar with the supported pattern recognition techniques, and it will probably enhance the range of tasks to which they can readily be applied. The second tool, `PlotGMM`, has already shown it effectiveness in analyzing a GMMs learning status and pointing to valuable improvements in the course of Chapter 3. Both tools are available to the public.

Since eidetic design depends on such tools that impart the inner workings of an algorithm, future work will include developing new tools for other speech processing problems. Additionally, the flexible composition of techniques for resynthesis is an area of concern. The current implementations allow fast and easy testing of what the majority of users may need. But to offer even more flexibility in the light of tasks yet to be developed, it is beneficial to be able to plug modules together in the way a software library could be used—but with the usability of a graphical user interface and with the benefits of web service technology. For this purpose, the mashup editor is currently being extended to make the complete `sclib` accessible. Furthermore, it is planned to apply the method of eidetic design to other fields, such as general multimedia analysis applications. Finally, promising first results on computer security-related algorithms are in sight.

"You can't trust code that you did not totally create yourself."

Kenneth Lane Thompson (1943–)

8

Implementation and Integration

8.1 Introduction

The speech processing community has produced a number of high quality open source tools for research and development purposes. The most comprehensive multi-purpose software is probably the `Hidden Markov Model Toolkit` (HTK) that provides feature extraction- and modeling capabilities aimed at speech recognition [Young et al. 2005]. The Carnegie Mellon University's `Sphinx` system even comprises a complete large vocabulary speech recognizer [Deléglise et al. 2005], and the Speech@FIT laboratory offers a phoneme recognizer based on long temporal context [Schwarz 2009].

There are many more tools available for more specific problems, like, e.g., finding *matching pursuit* bases via `MPTK` [Krstulovic and Gribonval 2006], doing nonlinear time series analysis through the `TISEAN` package [Hegger et al. 1999] or time and pitch scaling with `SoundTouch` [Parviainen 2006], or performing *non-negative matrix factorization* using `LS-NMF` [Wang et al. 2006a]. Each mentioned tool is very valuable and recommendable if fitting to the task at hand. However, a capacious toolkit for voice (i.e., speaker) recognition is absent, except for the relatively small library `svlib` provided by He [1997] and the `SHOUT` toolkit finally aimed at speech recognition [Huijbregts 2008].

In this chapter, the `sclib` library developed during the work on this book is introduced as

Chapter 8. Implementation and Integration

a toolkit for speaker recognition in order to fill this vacancy[1]. Besides, it has been developed as the primary test bed for the algorithms presented in this book. Section 8.2 describes the design, content and capabilities of the library itself. Then, Section 8.3 broadens this scope by presenting software engineering concepts to integrate the library within service-oriented architectures. The `sclib` served as a motivating example in the development of the related ideas. Additionally, the section introduces the multimedia (video) analysis workbench `Videana`, which delegates all audio-related tasks to its subproject `sclib`.

Parts of the work presented in this chapter have been published in the following papers: [Ewerth et al. 2007b], [Heinzl et al. 2009a], [Heinzl et al. 2009b], [Seiler et al. 2009] and [Juhnke et al. 2009].

8.2 The sclib Class Library

The `sclib` has been implemented as a C++ class library in extension of He's speaker verification library `svlib`, to which it links. Its primary goal is reflected in its name: being a library for *s*peaker *c*lassification (or clustering). To build the `sclib` on top of the `svlib`, the latter one had to be altered and enhanced in several minor points, e.g. to make the binary i/o routines used to serialize all classes consistent across 32/64 bit architectures or to provide unified error codes as return values of base classes in order to maintain extensibility. Some code anomalies have been corrected, too, and Table 8.1 refers to this enhanced version of the `svlib` as it gives some statistics concerning the complexity of both libraries in terms of lines of code (LOC).

Project	Code [LOC]	Comment [LOC]	Blank [LOC]	Total [LOC]
svlib (enhanced)	9293	6248	2826	17488
sclib	67532	28772	13137	104116

Table 8.1: Comparison of the `svlib` and `sclib` libraries in terms of lines of code.

C++ has been chosen as the implementation language—apart from the rather tight coupling with the `svlib`, which is implemented in C++, too—in order to facilitate easy integration with other speech processing tools, where C/C++ (and Matlab) are predominantly used. The software is developed using Microsoft Visual Studio (currently version 2008) under Windows, but care is taken that it compiles and builds as well using `automake`, `autoconf` and `gcc` (version 4.4.3) under Unix-based systems, too.

The rest of this section is organized as follows: Subsection 8.2.1 reports on the library's content, and Subsection 8.2.2 briefly explains some of the underlying design principles. Subsection 8.2.3 gives an overview of possible workflows within the library.

---
[1]The `sclib` library is available upon request via email at stadelmann@informatik.uni-marburg.de.

8.2.1 Content

The sclib supports the complete pattern recognition process for speech analysis as introduced in Section 2.6.

Signal Analysis

One strand of the class hierarchy with roots in the svlib is responsible for loading sound signals stored in several forms: RIFF WAVE uncompressed waveforms, the NIST SPHERE format (possibly compressed) as used in the NIST speaker recognition evaluations or within the TIMIT database, and finally MPG/MP2/MP3 and most other contemporary audio codecs via coupling with the ffmpeg libraries [Böhme 2004]. Additionally, loaded signals may be resampled to any desirable channel count and sample rate using the integrated services of libsamplerate [de Castro Lopo 2010].

On top of a loaded signal, algorithms have been implemented to do basic signal processing: signal windowing using Hamming-, Hanning-, Bartlett- or rectangular windows; Fourier-, Hilbert-Huang-, cosine- and wavelet transform and partly their inversions; computation and smoothing of spectra and cepstra; digital filters in their recursive-, convolutive- or FFT-based form of implementation; speech enhancement via the MixMax assumption; finally, signal synthesis from LPC- or power spectra as well as from pitch trains.

In order for these and other algorithms to work, a bunch of low-level additions to the C++ standard library has been implemented. They comprise packages of linear algebra subroutines to do matrix computations, math- and statistics-related functions as well as tools for string processing, memory allocation, list processing and i/o, to name the most prominent groups of components.

Feature Extraction

A comprehensive list of speaker related features can be extracted with sclib routines: starting in the time domain, STE and ZCR can be extracted as simple features, and pitch- and formant tracks are available through an adaptation of algorithms from the Snack sound toolkit [Sjölander 2004; Talkin 1995]. In the frequency domain, power- and magnitude spectra, filterbank energies, LPC coefficients, their residuals and resulting cepstra, LSPs (via an adaptation of Speex [Valin 2010] and MELP [Texas Instruments 1998] algorithms), and MFCCs are the most prominent features.

Some features are included to resemble related work, such as band periodicity, brightness and bandwidth, the noise frame ratio, spectrum flux, and sub-band power from the work of Lu et al. [2003]; the cepstral peak feature from Ahmadi and Spanias [1999]; or wavelet energy

Chapter 8. Implementation and Integration

distribution as introduced in the work of Jafer and Mahdi [2003]. Additionally, symmetrized dot patterns (also known as speech flakes [Dabkowski and Posiewnik 1998; Pickover 1986, 1990]) can be extracted and saved via the integrated libeasybmp [Macklin 2006].

For enhanced functionality, an interface is provided to link to Matlab routines that have been compiled using the Matlab compiler and distributed with help of the MCR; it is currently used to find sparse features [Yang et al. 2007] using the l1-magic library [Candès and Romberg 2005].

On top of these "basic" features, the sclib offers the opportunity to extract several "meta" features in the sense of Viola and Jones [2004]: a matrix of extracted feature vectors per frame can be regarded as a matrix of pixels in an image, and Haar wavelet-like filters can be freely defined to compute differences between regions in the matrix. This way, interesting time-frequency regions can be found if the base features are, for example, filterbank energies.

In addition to pure feature extraction, handling extracted features is supported via numerous methods. Amongst them are feature selection (e.g., via the branch-and-bound method from van der Heijden et al. [2004]) and other essential operations like feature i/o or computing MD5 checksums for efficient caching within the library via an implementation adapted from Neumann [2007]. Features can also be converted, e.g., to other frame rates or other domains, and a comprehensive set of statistical functions is available to standardize and normalize features, do discriminant analyses, compute and add several moments or find outliers in the data.

Modeling

The sclib contains implementations of the majority of all ever used voice modeling methods. The most important subgroup within this list is formed by the mixture models: GMMs with diagonal covariances and possibly adapted from an UBM, GMMs with full covariances (via an adaptation of the algorithm by Baggenstoss [2002] that is able to dynamically add and remove mixtures), the AMU and MixMax model from Chapter 4 and finally HMMs.

Additionally, several other methods are available: simple models like a VQ approach, a single-Gaussian (but full covariance) model and the quasi-GMM from Lu and Zhang [2002]. More sophisticated methods are a non-parametric model based on Pareto density estimation [Ultsch 2002, 2003a], a model based on auto-associative neural networks [Yegnanarayana and Kishore 2002; Yegnanarayana et al. 2001] implemented using FAAN [Nissen 2005], and the time model from Chapter 6 based on an adaptation of the one-class SVM implementation of libsvm [Chang and Lin 2001].

These basic models may be subject to aggregating- or "meta" models. They group the available data into several clusters and employ the basic model to represent each cluster separately. One such model is the DD-GMM from Chapter 3, grouping the data per dimension.

Another one groups the data explicitly per underlying acoustic class in order to only compare equal phonemes.

To find good models, several model selection criteria from the literature have been implemented: the BIC, the WCD and the ICR as introduced in Section 2.6.4. They are also useful as termination criteria for a clustering process.

Classification

Models and classifiers are strictly separated within the `sclib` in terms of classes, but they nevertheless interact very closely: some models are used to build classifiers, e.g., the GMM is used to compute likelihoods inside the maximum likelihood classifier. Then, taking the example of the SVM classifier implemented via an adaptation of the `libsvm` [Chang and Lin 2001], parts of its algorithms are used to build the time model.

In addition to ML and SVM classification, the `sclib` library includes *decision stumps* and *nearest neighbor* (NN) classification. All four basic classifiers can be stacked to produce meta classifiers using implementations of classification trees and several versions of Adaboost. The latter ones incorporate confidence-rated predictions [Schapire and Singer 1999] and cost matrices for imbalanced training data [Suna et al. 2007], thus being blends of `AdaBoost.M1`, `AdaC2` and `Real AdaBoost.MH` from the literature.

Also strongly related to the classifiers are the implemented distance measures. Besides GLR and CLR as introduced in Section 2.6.4, the EMD, BMS, Euclidean, Mahalanobis, Bhattacharyya and Kullback-Leibler distance from Section 5.2 as well as the divergence shape distance [Campbell 1997] are available. Additionally, the SVM arc distance [Desobry et al. 2005a] has been implemented to compare one-class SVMs based on their internal representation as the EMD compares GMMs.

Segmentation

Using signal processing, feature extraction, model building and classification (together with the auxiliary methods working in between) as building blocks, several mid-level audio processing methods have been implemented. A big group of them can be summarized as being segmentation algorithms.

There are several algorithms for silence detection [Li et al. 2004; Lu et al. 2003], for the segregation of voiced an unvoiced speech [Ahmadi and Spanias 1999; Jafer and Mahdi 2003; Li et al. 2004; Shah et al. 2004; Sjölander 2004], for speaker change detection [Cettolo et al. 2005; Kotti et al. 2008a; Lu and Zhang 2002] and for audio type classification [Lu et al. 2003], all based on and extending work from the referenced literature.

Finally, voice recognition can be regarded as a last segmentation step via implemented algo-

Chapter 8. Implementation and Integration

rithms for speaker identification and clustering. All segmentation algorithms have corresponding scoring classes that compute the common figures of merit automatically given that ground truth data is available. Virtually all metrics found in the literature are available, whether it is for detection-, identification- or supervised/unsupervised classification tasks. A fragmentary excerpt can be found in Section 6.2.3.

8.2.2 Design Principles

The algorithmic implementations in the `sclib` are built around the concept of a "corpus": a set of audio data (in the most simple case a single file), possibly accompanied by ground truth, that needs to be processed.

The corpus object is responsible for providing an interface to the audio samples. It is able to respond to queries like "give me the signal between seconds 3.78 and 4.21". It loads the signal and the accompanying ground truth in the background and keeps them synchronized by providing conversions between different time scales like frames (referring to the specific frame rate parameters of a certain feature), milliseconds or samples. Additionally, it stores the algorithmic results. For instance, such a result might be the detected speaker change point between frames 3 789 and 3 790 in scene two of a certain sports video sound track.

The corpus object also provides an interface to retrieve certain parts of the data set, or filter parts of an extracted feature matrix, based on the algorithmic results or corresponding ground truth. This works across file borders if the corpus is constructed from a collection of files (e.g., within the `TIMIT` database). Overall, the corpus object can be viewed as a proprietary just-in-time database for audio data, storing and managing all available information during the time of processing. It offers persistence, i/o, retrieval and watches consistency, and it is internally filled with meta data by the algorithms in the `sclib`.

These algorithms all need proper parametrization in a flexible way. For this purpose there exists a singleton object called the "tweakable parameters" (or "tweak" for short). It is able to read configurations from `ini` files once and provides their values throughout the library. There is no hard coded parameter anywhere within the `sclib`, but there are currently 584 parameters for 52 distinct algorithms managed by the tweakable parameters object.

The tweak object holds all of the parameters, but for the sake of loose coupling and hence enhanced flexibility of the algorithms, they expect each parameter to be separately given when called, rather than being provided with the complete tweakable parameters object from which they might pick up "their" parameters by themselves. This design facilitates easy integration of the algorithms within other environments, but introduces a hurdle for the developer that is going to use the algorithms: function calls comprising more than 20 arguments are not rare. In contrast, a completely unified interface to each group of related algorithms (like, e.g., the feature extractors) is desirable for usability purposes.

This discrepancy is met within the `sclib` by providing an additional layer of abstraction for the groups of signal loading-, feature extraction-, modeling-, classification- and segmentation algorithms: the handler objects. Each group has a handler with a simple "give me feature/model/classifier x" interface. The handler takes care for the instantiation and proper parametrization of the desired object in a factory sense, returning the object itself or the result of the invocation of one of its methods. The handler also administers the knowledge about its group of algorithms, so that it can answer questions like "which features are needed by segmentation algorithm y". Additionally, it holds the auxiliary methods helpful in the context of this group's algorithms, like, for example, feature selection algorithms in the case of the feature handler.

8.2.3 Workflows

All code within the `sclib` has been implemented to be very flexible. Great care has been taken to not only tailor it to the specific needs at hand. Instead, its content should be usable as building blocks that can be plugged together in more ways as initially thought of, taking an emergent design approach [Bain 2008]. This enables a user to create audio processing applications within minutes: For instance, data is loaded via the corpus object, features are extracted using the feature handler, then passed on to some segmentation algorithm via its handler and the result written to a file using the i/o capabilities of the corpus object and the information in its now filled data base.

Several of such workflows have been deposited in a large object called "main tasks". It is basically a collection of C++ "scripts" built in order to run experiments as the ones reported on in previous chapters. They can be invoked using a very small program that loads the library, parses command line arguments, instantiates the main tasks object and calls one of its methods. Besides giving reference about the concrete implementation of the experiments leading to the previously presented results, these scripts may serve as a comprehensive base of examples for prospective new users of the `sclib`.

8.3 Integration

The work on this book and the `sclib` library is conducted in the context of two flanking projects: on the one hand, research on software-supported scientific media analysis, to which the `sclib` contributes the audio analysis part. On the other hand, work towards a scalable, service-oriented architecture that facilitates time-consuming multimedia analysis and consumption. This is achieved by providing compute power on the web for demanding algorithms as presented

Chapter 8. Implementation and Integration

in the previous chapters, and at the same time offering convenient usability for potential end users.

This section provides a brief overview of the work that was either enhanced or inspired by `sclib` algorithms and workflows. First, Subsection 8.3.1 introduces the scientific media analysis workbench `Videana` and its connection to the Grid. Then, Subsection 8.3.2 shows how native code can be automatically wrapped up for use within other programming languages and paradigms, as a preprocessing step for the service-oriented architecture introduced in Subsection 8.3.3.

8.3.1 Videana and the Grid

The Java-based software toolkit `Videana` is aimed at providing computer assisted methods to support the scholarly analysis of audio-visual material, in particular images and videos. Its focus is on disburdening media scholars from typically very time-consuming manual annotation tasks. Additionally, the software supports efficient search- and retrieval operations in large media databases and on the semantic web.

`Videana` currently supports the following tasks via automatic video content analysis: shot boundary detection, text detection and recognition (video OCR), estimation of camera motion and shot size, face detection, object- and semantic concept detection, dominant color extraction, audio segmentation, speaker clustering, and finally video summarization. Based on a plug-in approach, any type of analysis algorithm can be updated, exchanged or removed easily. The graphical user interface of `Videana` allows users to play back videos and to access particular video frames. Furthermore, the GUI allows users to manually correct erroneous analysis results. The produced meta data is saved via the "Multimedia Data Description Interface" of MPEG-7 [Martinez et al. 2002] into XML files that facilitate interoperability with other applications.

Figure 8.1 shows the main window of `Videana`. On the left side, there is a window for playing a video. There are two time lines shown at the bottom which visualize the analysis results for the temporal segmentation of the video into shots as well as for face detections. Additional time lines appear as analysis results get available. The vertical lines in the "Cuts" time line represent cuts (abrupt shot changes), and the colored areas in the time line "Faces" mark the sequences where a frontal face appears. On the right side, the temporal segmentation is presented in another way: single shots are represented by three frames (beginning, middle, and end frame of a shot). By a mouse click on an icon, the related video frame is directly accessible.

In order to facilitate batch analysis runs that would otherwise run for month (or worse) on a single computer, `Videana` comprises a connection to the Grid [Foster and Kesselman 2003]: Grid computing allows for a unified access to heterogeneous, distributed compute- and data

8.3. Integration

Figure 8.1: The main window of Videana.

resources. Besides empowering the computationally complex audio-visual analysis jobs, the Grid component of Videana is designed to provide seamless integration of Grid resources into the GUI with high usability.

The Grid component builds upon Omnivore [Heidt et al. 2008]. Omnivore is a meta job scheduler that is able to address dedicated high performance clusters as well as peer-to-peer nets (P2P) of desktop machines with spare compute power via forwarding of jobs to local schedulers. It is integrated within the leading Grid environment, Globus toolkit 4 (GT4) [Globus Alliance 2010]. The created net is able to resize dynamically and monitors itself, repairing appearing defects automatically on the fly.

Each Videana distribution contains a client that interacts with Omnivore. The interface can be activated with a single click in a configuration window, which also handles the creation of a proxy certificate for the user. The only prerequisite is a valid Grid certificate that attests the user's credentials. Afterwards, the user can decide for each job if it shall run locally or be distributed unto the Grid. The choice to distribute a job can also be made automatically depending on the file size of the analysis object and the corresponding anticipated run time.

8.3.2 Code Wrapping

When assembling a system to perform a certain complex task, it is reasonable to rely on existing and proven external code that performs certain sub tasks. This code is often implemented in

Chapter 8. Implementation and Integration

another programming language or for another platform, such that the saved implementation time is bought at the expense of writing wrapper code. This can cause problems, mainly due to programmers being inexperienced with either side of the gap. Additionally, the juncture between the existing code (or "native code") and a platform like a service-oriented architecture very often leads to code fragments which are inherently recurring. Wrapper code in the language of the target platform has to be developed for every single bit of native code. Furthermore, this has to be done for all subdomains and all platforms.

To address these problems, the legacy code description language (LCDL) has been developed which is capable of wrapping different types of native code automatically to several levels of abstraction. One of the main features and advantages of this approach is its extensibility. Neither its set of data types nor the binding are subject to any restrictions: both can be extended with a plug-in mechanism.

A typical use case for the LCDL arises when new algorithms from the `sclib`, implemented in C++, need to be coupled with the Java-based user interfaces or made available as prototypes for other researchers on the web: legacy code wrapping for a certain binding becomes necessary. Consider the concrete example of audio resynthesis presented in Section 7.3.2. While the previous chapter focused on the signal processing aspects of the problem as well as on how the code, exposed as a web service, can be accompanied with an easy-to-use client for prospective users, the focus here is on the prior step of wrapping up the application as a web service. For this purpose, a small C++ program called `screc` is created that accesses different workflows within `sclib`'s main tasks object.

The first step is the modeling of the LCDL information. This can be done using a basic LCDL editor realized within the Eclipse workbench. All information is entered here. A basic validation can also be performed in order to check if all needed elements and attributes are set. The corresponding XML file is shown in Listing 8.1.

```
 1  <lcdl:Service xmlns:lcdl="http://fb12.de/lcdl/1.1" name="screc">
      <operations name="screc">
 3      <output>
          <source xsi:type="lcdl:StdOutSource"/>
 5        <type xsi:type="lcdl:ElementReturn" name="returnValue"
              type="{http://www.w3.org/2001/XMLSchema}string"/>
 7      </output>
        <inputs xsi:type="lcdl:FileInput"
 9          name="audioFile" mode="in"
            type="{http://www.w3.org/2001/XMLSchema}any" />
11      <inputs xsi:type="lcdl:ElementInput"
            name="preEmphasizeFactor" mode="in"
13          type="{http://www.w3.org/2001/XMLSchema}double" />
        <inputs xsi:type="lcdl:StaticInput"
15          name="method" mode="in" value="21"
            type="{http://www.w3.org/2001/XMLSchema}int" />
17      <execute xsi:type="lcdl:Binary">
          <parameters name="audioFile"/>
```

8.3. Integration

```
19      <parameters name="method"/>
        <parameters prefix="-featureMfcc.preEmphasizeFactor"
21         name="preEmphasizeFactor" infix="="/>
        </execute>
23    </operations>
      <bindings xsi:type="lcdl:JavaProxy" packageName="de.fb12.sclib"/>
25  </lcdl:Service>
```

Listing 8.1: LCDL model (namespaces are omitted for reasons of readability).

The particular method under consideration (method=21 in line 15, referring to the 21st workflow in the main tasks object) takes as additional parameter the filename of an audio file, for which a GMM of standard speech features is built. Virtually any parameter of the feature extraction could be controlled via the tweak object receiving named input from command line parsing, but for brevity only the featureMfcc.preEmphasis parameter is taken as an example here—it controls the high frequency boost prior to further signal processing, which is clearly audible in the result. The name of the resulting file is written to stdout by the program. This information is captured and returned by the LCDL framework as a string.

```
1  package de.fb12.sclib;
   import de.fb12.lcdl.runtime.java.LcdlAnnotation;
3
   @LcdlAnnotation(model="screc")
5  public interface ISCrec {
     public java.lang.String screc(
7        java.io.File audioFile,
         java.lang.Double preEmphasizeFactor);
9  }
```

Listing 8.2: Generated Java interface.

Listing 8.2 shows the Java interface generated with the LCDL framework from the XML description in Listing 8.1. To use the native code in a Java program, Listing 8.3 shows how the LCDL factory is utilized to get an instance of the screc service (line 5). To invoke a method from the generated interface, a simple Java method call is necessary (line 7).

```
1  // ...
   File audioFile = new File("input.wav");
3  double preEmphasize = 0.97;

5  ISCrec screcService = (ISCrec)LcdlFactory.getInstance(ISCrec.class);

7  String filename = screcService.screc(audioFile, preEmphasize);
   // ...
```

Listing 8.3: Usage of the generated interface.

The Java-wrapped sclib method can now be further processed via LCDL using another binding to be put, for example, into a web service without any particular knowledge concerning SOAs on the side of the programmer.

8.3.3 A Service-Oriented Architecture for Multimedia Analysis

Today one comes across a SOA quite often because it offers a standardized way to invoke services and to exchange data. This allows for an easy way for establishing a distributed application which can take benefit of the computing- or storage power of a remote machine. Furthermore, a SOA provides a platform and a programming language which are independent of the software environment. In a SOA based on web- and Grid service technology (SOAP) one can benefit from quite a large number of standards which cope with security, data management, stateful resources et cetera.

Since multimedia analysis deals with computationally intensive tasks, it is reasonable to divide the analysis as a whole into several steps, such that single analysis steps can be distributed to different nodes. The paradigm of a SOA promises that these computationally intensive tasks can be exposed as services and effectively combined to new applications, thus speeding up the development of applications. For the combination of these services (called orchestration), it is reasonable to use the business process execution language for web services (BPEL) [Andrews et al. 2003], the de facto standard for workflows in the industry, to allow (corporate) users to integrate multimedia services into their existing service portfolio.

However, since all service data pass the BPEL engine, the application of BPEL to data-intensive applications from the multimedia domain is not very efficient. Furthermore, the development of web services is still difficult and time-consuming, and in practice it is almost impossible for ordinary end users. To obtain a broader user basis, it is necessary to simplify the use of web- and Grid services. Also, in order to provide a timely execution, a distributed infrastructure for multimedia processing should be easily scalable.

An approach to address these issues using already presented as well as new tools is the following sketch of a service-orientated architecture for multimedia applications. Figure 8.2 gives an overview of how these tools are arranged to interact on different layers in order to achieve the targeted goals.

Analysis capabilities are contributed by **Videana** and its libraries. Especially the encapsulation within the `sclib` facilitates the desired property of fine-grained workflow creation. In order for the `sclib` to be integrated into this framework, another signal loader class has been implemented that can read samples directly from a Java stream administered by the Flex-SwA framework [Heinzl et al. 2006] through the Java native interface (JNI). Flex-SwA enables the modeling of data flows in BPEL. In this way, an efficient and flexible data transfer is possible in BPEL workflows for multimedia applications.

In addition, several tools are offered to ease the development and usage of web services: the web and grid service browser [Heinzl et al. 2008b] and the mashup editor [Heinzl et al. 2009c] have been mentioned already in Section 7.3.2 and automatically generate user interfaces for

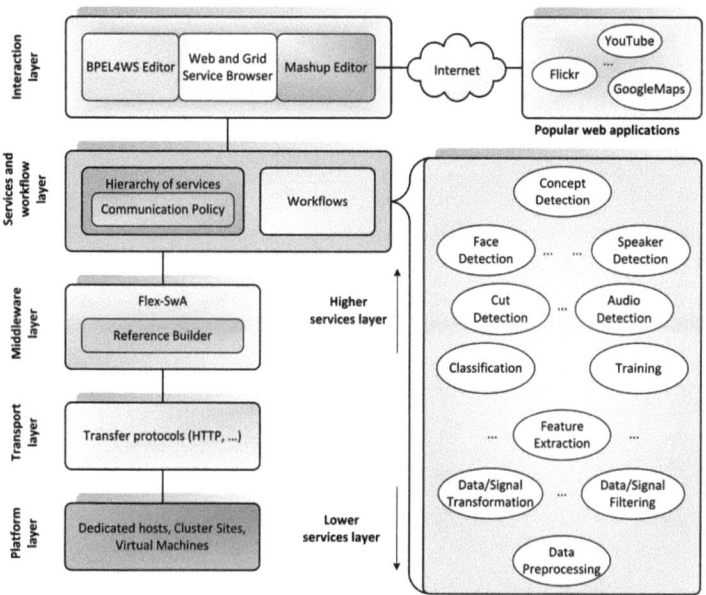

Figure 8.2: A layer model for the multimedia analysis framework.

services. The visual Grid orchestrator [Dörnemann et al. 2007, 2009] creates new services from existing ones, allowing for easy workflow creation. Scalability is achieved by the possibility to dynamically allocate resources from a computational cloud, such as the Amazon elastic compute cloud (EC2). Finally, communication policies [Heinzl et al. 2008a], embedded in a service's WSDL document, can be used to describe the protocol requirements of services in order to support real-time, streaming or file transfer requirements.

8.4 Conclusions

This chapter has introduced the sclib as a flexible and available library for audio analysis, especially speaker recognition. The library contains a comprehensive list of algorithms to facilitate the complete pattern recognition process for speaker recognition and beyond. Yet, it is classified as having "beta" status due to its origin as a research algorithm testbed: while several parts of the library are well tested and contain stable implementations of state- of-the-art algorithms, other parts remain subject to further development.

Subsequently, the work surrounding sclib's development has been briefly described: first, the scientific media analysis workbench Videana has been introduced that comprises the sclib

Chapter 8. Implementation and Integration

for audio analysis. Both pieces of software in a way drove each other's development. `Videana` contains a real-world, usable interface to Grid computing in order to ease the workload induced by the execution of time-consuming algorithms on big data sets. The other presented approaches all head in this direction of making Grid- and web services easily usable by (a) wrapping legacy code automatically as a service (LCDL), relieving (b) the bottleneck of data transfers in service workflows (Flex-SwA), creating (c) clients and user interfaces for services automatically (web and grid service browser, mashup editor), facilitating (d) workflow creation with graphical user interfaces (visual Grid orchestrator) and enforcing (e) user demands with policies. The `sclib` served as an use case and proof of concept example for several of these tools.

Future work lies within releasing a stable version of the `sclib` and in improving the setup and cooperation of the presented Grid- and service tools to move them beyond research tool status as well.

"A good video can make all the difference."

Brian Harold May (1947–)

9

Application to Video Content Analysis and Retrieval

9.1 Introduction

Automatic video content analysis has been researched for the past 15 years along with the advent of "multimedia" computers. The more data of rich content but weak structure got available and actually consumed and stored as a mass phenomenon, the more the necessity to find automatic ways of processing this new kind of information got obvious. Today, induced by the changes the web culture brings to contemporary life, this need has gained even more urgency: the availability of (nearly) everything (nearly) everywhere anytime changes the way video content analysis has to be approached, for example, in the handling of plenty of unreliable meta data—but it also strengthens its claim of importance [Zhang 2009].

As has been reminiscent already in the last chapter, the work presented in this book has contributed to distributed video analysis by providing audio analysis algorithms and fostering a multimodal approach. In this chapter, two instances of the created multimodal analysis scheme are highlighted. Section 9.2 presents a semantic video content analysis system that facilitates psychological research on the impact of violent computer games on proband's neural activities. Section 9.3 then describes video retrieval results within the annual TRECVid challenge. A discussion of the use and impact of audio analysis methods in these settings is given in Section

Chapter 9. Application to Video Content Analysis and Retrieval

9.4 before Section 9.5 concludes the chapter with a summary and outlook to future work.

Parts of the work presented in this chapter have been published in the following papers: [Ewerth et al. 2006], [Mühling et al. 2007a] and [Mühling et al. 2007b, 2008, 2009].

9.2 Semantic Video Analysis in Psychological Research

In this section, an automatic semantic video analysis system is presented to support interdisciplinary research efforts in the field of psychology and media science. The psychological research question studied is whether and how playing violent content in computer games may induce aggression.

Subsection 9.2.1 reports on the background of the study, including the experimental setup of the psychological approach and a description of the applied video content analysis system. Subsection 9.2.2 enlarges on the developed audio analysis methods before the results are given in Subsection 9.2.3.

9.2.1 Background

Computer games play a very important role in today's entertainment media. Yet, the number of computer games containing serious violence increases. There is an extensive ongoing debate about the question whether playing violent games causes aggressive cognitions, aggressive affects or aggressive behavior, in particular with respect to teens and young adults.

Weber et al. [2006] conducted a neurophysiologically grounded study on video game playing in which functional magnetic resonance imaging (fMRI) scans were taken during gaming. They demonstrated that a specific neurological mechanism is activated when playing a first-person-shooter game. The experimental design presented by Weber et al. is based on the definition of certain game states that can be correlated with the fMRI scans while a proband plays the game "Tactical Ops: Assault on Terror".

Originally, human annotators were required to index 120 hours of game content according to the current game state, which is obviously a very time-consuming task. Automatic video content analysis may help to reduce human annotation efforts to a minimum, thereby enabling a greater data basis to be used that is annotated on objective criteria only. The following game states, exemplified in Figure 9.1, are distinguished automatically:

Inactive: the player's avatar is dead or the game has not started yet.

Preparation: the avatar is buying equipment in the beginning of a new round.

Search/Explore/Danger: the player explores the virtual world and searches for hostages, enemies and weapons.

9.2. Semantic Video Analysis in Psychological Research

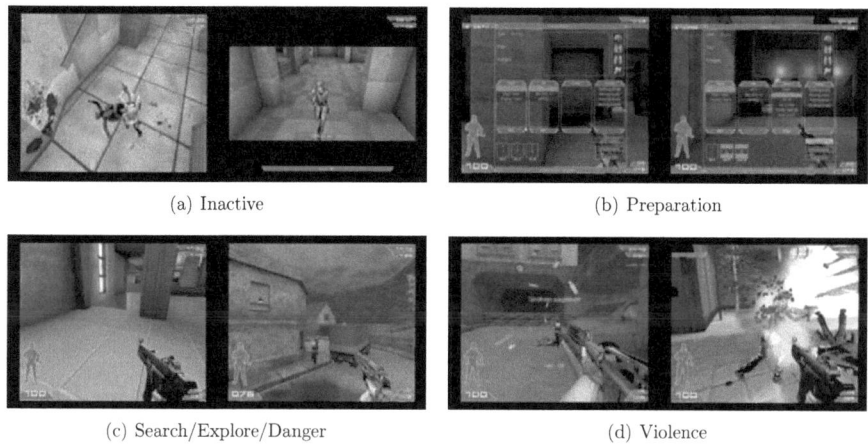

(a) Inactive (b) Preparation

(c) Search/Explore/Danger (d) Violence

Figure 9.1: Example frames of game states and assigned semantic categories.

Violence: the player's avatar is fighting and/or injured.

The proposed multimodal analysis system is designed to keep human annotation efforts at a minimum by using only one manually labeled training video of 12 minutes of length. It is based on the Videana workbench presented in the last chapter and thus aimed at staying true to a generic content analysis approach, refraining from exploiting domain-specific characteristics of the training data. The following features are extracted on a regular basis from each video: low-level video features (color moments, texture features), mid-level video features (analysis results for camera motion estimation as well as text- and face detection) and audio low- and mid-level features (to be presented below).

Early fusion is applied on these features to arrive at a combined feature set. It is fed into probability-emitting SVM classifiers to train models for each category versus the rest [Platt 1999]. For each frame of an evaluation video, the probability scores for each concept are smoothed and aggregated in a reasonable temporal neighborhood to exploit the continuity in the video; then, a second-level SVM is trained getting the probabilities and time series information as features to perform the final classification.

A second system has been created in order to account for the demand of less training data: instead of exploiting the time series information, a semi-supervised learning approach is taken [Ewerth 2008]. It takes into account the unlabeled evaluation data already in the training process and improves itself iteratively using bootstrapping. This way, the available information from the labeled training data is adapted into the direction of the unlabeled evaluation data, thus releasing the training data from having to represent every possible situation from the

Chapter 9. Application to Video Content Analysis and Retrieval

evaluation data.

9.2.2 Audio Type Classification

The semantic content of computer games is present in all modalities of their recordings: fighting and killing, for example, is visible in the video domain by the presence of enemies, muzzle flash as well as blood and gore; it is also audible in the accompanying soundtrack by means of shots or explosive sounds as well as moans. The automatic content analysis system extracts a number of general audio low- and mid level features via the `sclib` to support the recognition of the semantic categories.

The following 8 low-level features are extracted from non-overlapping 25 ms frames and are fed directly into the analysis system: 8th order MFCCs to capture the broad envelope of the spectrum; ZCR to measure oscillation and intra-frame variation; STE to account for loudness; sub-band energy distribution as a representative of the loudness ratio for 4 successive frequency bands; brightness and bandwidth to measure the spectrum's frequency centroid and spread; spectrum flux to capture the inter-frame spectral variation; band periodicity to measure the periodicity of the 4 sub bands; finally, noise frame ratio to measure noisiness corresponding to a lack of periodicity.

Additionally to using these low-level features directly, they are fed into an *audio type classification* (ATC) algorithm to produce mid-level features. The Algorithm is based on the approach of Lu et al. [2003] and improves it by using *adaptive* silence detection, an extended classification tree that also accounts for action events, and a heuristic post processing scheme that labels short silence periods within speech as "pause" without cutting a speech segment. The ATC system produces mid-level features on a per-second basis in the form of acoustic class labels and related probabilities for silence, pure- and noisy speech, music, background and action sounds. The low-level features are therefore represented per second by their normalized means and variances and then concatenated to form one feature vector per second. Each feature vector is further processed by a hierarchical tree of SVMs, if it was not previously classified as silence by an adaptively thresholding classifier based on the work of Otsu [1979].

Figure 9.2 shows the classification tree. It is trained on more than 32 hours of audio: `TIMIT` data for clean speech; `NOIZEUS` [Hu and Loizou 2006] and broadcast speech data for noisy speech; pop- and instrumental music, various movie sound samples from broadcast material and free web resources for different types of background- and action "noise" [Stadelmann 2006]. All sounds have been converted to 16 bit, 8 kHz, mono channel uncompressed waveforms from their original source formats (MP3, AIFF, AU, ...) using Winamp 5.0 and the Nullsoft `discwriter` plug-in v2.11 before being subject to classifier training.

Five-fold cross-validation on a subset of 15 000 feature vectors has been used to find the

9.2. Semantic Video Analysis in Psychological Research

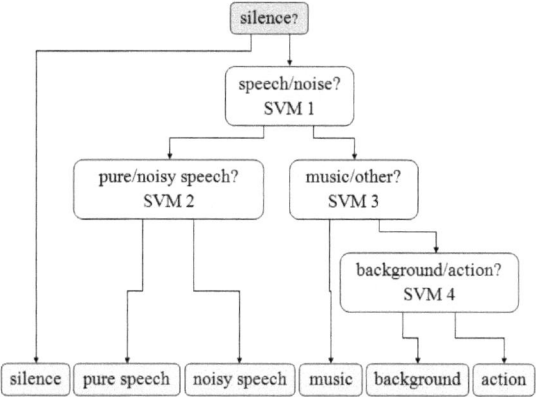

Figure 9.2: Scheme of the hierarchical audio type classifier.

best parameter settings for each of the four SVMs using an RBF kernel. The final acoustic class labels as depicted at the bottom of Figure 9.2 and their respective probabilities are fed into the automatic content (game state) analysis system as mid-level features to further guide the discovery of semantic patterns.

9.2.3 Results

The two systems—time-exploiting and semi-supervised—are evaluated on an evaluation corpus consisting of 4 game videos, each being approximately 6.5 minutes long and having a size of 352x288 pixels. The performance is assessed in terms of recall, precision and F_1: as usual in information retrieval, recall measures how many of the instances of a category are correctly classified ("found"), while precision measures how pure these classifications have been. F_1 is the harmonic mean of both.

System	Measure	Inactive [%]	Preparation [%]	Search [%]	Violence [%]
Time-exploiting	recall	0.916	0.831	0.926	0.567
	precision	0.941	0.877	0.885	0.684
	F_1	0.928	0.854	0.905	**0.620**
Semi-supervised	recall	0.920	0.922	0.949	0.553
	precision	0.976	0.960	0.900	0.660
	F_1	**0.948**	**0.941**	**0.924**	0.602

Table 9.1: Comparison of the two systems on the evaluation corpus.

Results in Table 9.1 show that the semi-supervised system clearly outperforms the simpler time-exploiting approach for most categories. Yet, the most important category for this study,

Chapter 9. Application to Video Content Analysis and Retrieval

violence, is best detected by the system that uses the temporal context of events. But noting that Weber et al. [2006] reported on 0.85% inter-coder reliability for their set of human annotators, both system's total recall values of 0.885% and 0.910%, respectively, seem very competitive. In fact, the study shows that automatic semantic video content analysis systems are applicable to interdisciplinary studies in the field of media and behavioral sciences.

9.3 The TRECVid Evaluations

TRECVid is an annual evaluation campaign organized by the US *national institute of standards and technology* (NIST) to record and advance the state of the art in automatic video retrieval methods. The challenge emerged as a track of the text retrieval conference (TREC) also organized by NIST and is an independent event since 2003. Different tasks like—in the year 2010—known-item/instance search, semantic indexing, copy detection and event detection are approached by teams from academia and industry on a common body of training- and evaluation data (collaboratively annotated to produce ground truth information). NIST provides standardized evaluation/scoring methods, making the teams' results comparable and TRECVid the primary benchmark of the community [Smeaton et al. 2006].

Subsection 9.3.1 introduces a system for the task of raw video footage summarization and retrieval. Subsection 9.3.2 reports on the approach to semantic concept detection, also known as high-level feature extraction.

9.3.1 Rushes Summarization and Retrieval

TRECVid'06 offered the task of "rushes summarization": vast amounts of raw, unedited (and thus highly repetitive) video footage (known as "rushes") should be made accessible to users (e.g., editors) via a retrieval interface employing summarization and easy browsing. The task has been approached using `Videana` and in particular the ATC algorithm from the last section as well as the speaker clustering system presented in Chapter 5.

The approach centers around the idea of sub-shot segmentation with respect to events like speech, silence, camera motion and face appearances. This takes into account that the user is only interested in those parts of the shots which contain non-redundant, interesting content. To produce the sub-shot segmentation, first, video cut detection is performed. Then, face sequences, camera motion- and audio features are employed at a temporal granularity if one second to segment these shots further into sub-shots. In particular, long sequences without any motion respectively long silent sequences are possible indicators for redundancy. A sub-shot is created whenever the binary classification result (e.g., a face appeared or not) for one of the mid-level features changes its value.

9.3. The TRECVid Evaluations

To remove redundant material within each rushes video, an unsupervised clustering approach is taken along with an appropriate visualization. The user can control which features are used for clustering and visualization. Based on the selected features, a distance matrix expressing the similarity of sub-shots is generated. Its visualization requires a mapping of the high-dimensional feature space to a two- or three-dimensional space. Multi-dimensional scaling [Mardia et al. 1979] has been used to generate this mapping, although Sammon's mapping [Sammon 1969] demonstrated equal performance in the experiments.

Before visualization can take place, the sub-shots are clustered using k-means, where the number k of clusters can be defined by the user, aided by reasonable defaults. Then, for each pair of clusters, the distance of their centers is computed to create the similarity matrix and MDS visualization. The clustering groups similar sub-shots together so that the user quickly gets an overview of the rushes material. By, e.g., zooming into one cluster, the user can browse through these clusters and thus search efficiently for interesting sub-shots.

(a) Complete video. (b) Zoom into lower left cluster.

Figure 9.3: MDS visualization of `franco85.mpg` using 3 clusters.

By first specifying a large number of clusters, which gives a general overview of a video's content, the user is able to efficiently and intuitively reduce the inherent redundancy. The likely over-segmentation can be handled in a second step by interactively decreasing the number of clusters to a visually more suitable number. An already refined example is shown Figure 9.3(a), where the initial number of clusters has been 4, showing two instances of the upper cluster. As can be seen from Figure 9.3(b), the sub-shot clusters offer a high degree of purity that is necessary for reliable summarization.

The performance of the retrieval component has been evaluated using the graphical user interface of **Videana**. It returns the top-50 retrieval list, for which the precision is computed as

Chapter 9. Application to Video Content Analysis and Retrieval

Feature	Top-50 precision [%]
Audio—music	58.00
Audio—silence	100.0
Audio—speech	94.00
Camera-motion—pan	72.00
Camera-motion—tilt	72.00
Camera-motion—zoom	42.00
$\#Faces = 1$	100.0

Table 9.2: Precision for individual features within the 50 top-ranked results using the complete rushes test material.

the performance index. The results for the best working individual features are given in Table 9.2. It is interesting to look at the false positives therein, i.e., at shots labeled to belong to a certain class although the ground truth states otherwise: for example, for music, 43% of the false positives include chirping of birds or blowing of a whistle, which is anyhow strongly related to the concept of music. Overall, the experiments show very good retrieval results for audio and face features: the proposed system demonstrated its potential for efficient exploration of rushes videos.

9.3.2 Semantic Concept Detection

To automatically search videos as effectively as text, it is necessary to deduce semantic meaning from the easily extracted low-level features. This is known as bridging the *semantic gap*. One approach to arrive at semantic meaning (or high-level features) is to define a finite set of relevant concepts and detect their individual presence or absence in each shot of a video. The set of extracted concepts can subsequently be queried like a set of words. In fact, if basic semantics-conveying units in a video can be detected as reliably as words can be stemmed [Porter 1980] in a text document, nothing hinders video-retrieval to be as powerful as current text retrieval methods. Additionally, the well-known methods from the text retrieval domain could then be applied. They operate on top of reliably detected dictionaries of (textual, but also audio-visual) words.

Low $MiAP < 5\%$	Neutral	High $MiAP > 15\%$
classroom, bridge, emergency vehicle, flower, bus, harbor, telephone	kitchen, boat/ship, airplane flying, two people, driver, cityscape, demonstration or protest, mountain	hand, nighttime, dog, street, singing

Table 9.3: List of semantic concepts to be detected at TRECVid'07, grouped by `Videana`'s ability to detect them.

TRECVid offers a task for semantic concept detection called "high-level feature detection" [Smeaton et al. 2009] (since 2010: "semantic indexing") in which the Videana-based multimodal video content analysis system has taken part several times. Table 9.3 shows the list of concepts to be detected in the year 2007.

The concepts are grouped together according to their detectability using the described system and the TRECVid evaluation metric of mean inferred average precision (MiAP). MiAP is the expected value of the probability that, given any relevant document from the ranked list of results, one finds an equally- or higher-ranked relevant document as well [Yilmaz and Aslam 2006]. The process of estimating this measure via sub-sampling allows NIST to evaluate many concepts for a growing group of participating teams with only limited counting resources.

The goal of the presented system is to learn models for the high-level semantic features based on extracted audio-visual low- and mid-level features similar to the ones described in Section 9.2.1. On the audio side, ATC results are combined with the outcome of voiced/unvoiced speech classification [Ahmadi and Spanias 1999] to produce 11 audio mid-level features (including an "undefined" error label and a combined "speech" feature comprising both pure- and noisy speech). They are then processed to solely describe the audio-content of a video shot by statistical values: mean, median, minimum, maximum, standard deviation, and skewness of the per-frame label probabilities are calculated. Furthermore, the percentage of the duration of each audio type label with respect to the shot length is calculated. Finally, these percentages and the distribution parameters of the probabilities are fed into the further SVM learning algorithm [Chang and Lin 2001] as the final audio mid-level features, resulting in a 77-dimensional audio feature vector that is again early-fused with the video features.

This baseline system, trained on the "sound and vision" training set from 2007, achieves 7.03% MiAP. The experiments reveal that the generalization capabilities of systems trained on broadcast news videos to the sound and vision data are limited. In total, the second best result for the high-level features "meeting" and "people marching" have been achieved among the TRECVid'07 participants, probably due to the employed face processing approach. For 10 out of the 20 evaluated high-level features, the system scored among the top seven submissions.

Several approaches have been taken to improve the baseline system. For example, transductive learning [Joachims 1999] or separate SVM models for color- and gray scale videos have been promising, but did neither yield higher scores nor improved generalization performance. Also, employing video context vectors, i.e., annotating each shot with the detection probabilities of the 101 Mediamill concepts [Snoek et al. 2006], has been evaluated, but did not improve the results. The same is true for using certain scale- and rotation-invariant interest point features (SURF) [Bay et al. 2008] in the video domain.

Additionally, adding audio low-level features did not improve the results: they have been composed to give a more general view of the audio content of a shot and to facilitate the recognition of, e.g., single sounds directly in the concept detection system. The set comprised 20 MFCCs with their first order derivatives, 10 LSPs and a measure of pitch. These 51 features were each summarized per shot in a histogram comprising 10 bins, resulting in a 510-dimensional audio low-level feature vector.

What does improve the results is to reduce the number of negative training instances by a simple sub-sampling method. A final MiAP of 8.27% has been achieved this way, compared to 5.91% of the baseline system on the 2008 data set. On the 2009 data set, a further improvement of the previous baseline from 8.88% to 9.53% MiAP has been achieved by using the following additions: specialized object detectors trained on separate public data sets for object classes like "airplane", "boat", "chair" and the like, supplemented with additional object-based features like position, frame coverage and -movement derived from object sequences.

These experiments reveal that the approaches exploiting object-based features algorithmically improve the overall high-level feature extraction results most significantly. Not only concepts that directly correspond to one of the detectable object classes profit from the additional object-based features, but almost all concepts profit from these features. Using direct object retrieval results, the second best result among all submitted runs for the concept "person riding a bicycle" has been achieved in 2009, and also "airplane flying" and "bus" were pushed under the top six teams.

9.4 Discussion

The good results of the presented multimodal video content analysis approach in various scenarios are promising and underline the validity of the algorithms implemented within the `sclib`. Especially the outstanding results for rushes summarization due to audio type classification demonstrate the impact of this kind of exploitation of the audio domain for semantic video analysis.

But other parts of the described results give rise to more critical thoughts: why did the "violence" category have the worst detection result among all concepts within video game content analysis? Has not a special "action" event detector been applied on the audio side to label, e.g., shootings and explosions? And what is the reason for the non-improvement of high-level feature detection using audio low-level features?

The reason might be the following: in both classifiers (i.e., within the mid-level feature-producing ATC system as well as in the final SVM classifier that shall detect the high-level features) a certain type of processing paradigm is applied. It suggests to extract all low-level feature vectors for a certain temporal span (i.e, one second, or a shot), then summarize them by concatenating their statistics to a single feature vector. All these feature vectors whose corresponding temporal span has been annotated with the presence of a certain high-level feature (e.g., "pure speech", or "boat") are then used to train a SVM for this concept.

In the case of MFCC low-level features, this means to describe one such temporal span with the mean (among other statistical quantities) spectral envelope of the span. Using the example of a shot from an action-filled scene, this will almost certainly be a blend of pushing music, transient sounds like gunfire and explosions and very emotional speech particles like screams. The average spectrum will no longer reveal the characteristics of any individual concept that is present throughout the span, but will have a high amplitude in almost all frequency bins, together with high variance.

This approach has clearly shown its potential in conjunction with video- and image-based features on news-like videos as well as for sounds of long continuity on the raw footage material. But it seems rather inappropriate for the more natural transient sounds occurring frequently in other domains. Learning from the high impact one of the presented improvements in the video domain had on the presented results in TRECVid'09, event-focused audio-object detectors might be a promising cure for the marked weakness: for example, an action classifier might help that does not work with averaging models (like GMMs or SVMs) as in speaker recognition, but with models accounting for the fine-grained temporal structure of the event like in speech recognition using, e.g., HMMs. The sclib offers all necessary algorithms to train such classifiers, yet, it takes some effort to develop and evaluate the corresponding models, their structure and parametrization.

In addition to ATC, the presented video analysis results have shed light on the applicability of speaker clustering to unconstrained data. Besides the improvements made to the state of the art in the last chapters with regard to handling short and noisy utterances, speaker clustering results played only a minor role within the video summarization system of Section 9.3.1. This is due to a rather low confidence in the produced final speaker labels. Since speaker clustering is still too unreliable to be used as a mid-level feature, a promising solution might be to incorporate more knowledge than just final decisions (e.g, ranked lists of probabilities for hypothesized speakers of each utterance) into the final multimodal classification system. The final system could then, based on other modalities and more context information, make a more informed decision.

9.5 Conclusions

This chapter has introduced the application of sclib algorithms to problems in automatic video content analysis and retrieval. In particular, an extended audio type classification algorithm has been presented and applied to two use cases within the Videana workbench: first, the suitability of the presented multimodal approach to labeling game videos with certain semantic classes has been shown. It has successfully been applied to interdisciplinary research in psychology in

Chapter 9. Application to Video Content Analysis and Retrieval

order to pursue the question whether playing violent computer games induces neural activities related to aggression.

Second, results in video summarization, browsing and semantic indexing have been presented. The multimodal approach is among the top 10 groups within the annual TRECVid evaluations for certain tasks. In particular, in the summarization of raw video footage the ATC results played an important role. Nevertheless, as has been discussed in the previous section, audio analysis with the aim of bridging the semantic gap in video retrieval has to be approached in a different way in order to unfold the complete potential of this modality. Additionally, the results presented in this chapter have shown that good algorithms for basic speaker recognition research do not automatically result in well applicable general audio analysis systems. To improve on the presented results, more effort has to be made in developing specialized audio object detectors using the algorithms already available in the `sclib`.

Thus, the most promising area for future research within audio-enriched video analysis is to overcome the approach of summarizing a complete shot with a single, averaged feature vector of low- and mid-level events. The direction is given by more event-based approaches like the ones of Jiang et al. [2009] who detect combined audio-visual atoms, and of Peng et al. [2009], who apply text-retrieval methods to a dictionary of audio words (that is, however, created in a way as has been discouraged in the last section).

*"Now this is not the end.
It is not even the beginning of the end.
But it is, perhaps, the end of the beginning."*
                    Winston Churchill (1874–1965)

10
Conclusions

10.1 Summary

In this book, several novel methods for voice modeling for automatic speaker recognition have been proposed.

Specifically, the *DD-GMM* has been introduced in Chapter 3 to address the problem of finding reliable models for short speech utterances. The DD-GMM yields more than 80% identification rate with less than 5.5 seconds of training- and 1.3 seconds of evaluation data and thus allows to recognize speakers in regions where baseline GMM approaches are not usable anymore. It is computationally inexpensive and easily integratable in common GMM-based systems, thereby able to profit from other short-utterance schemes as proposed in the literature.

The formulation of the *MixMax* model and its presentation in the literature have been corrected in Chapter 4. Extensive experiments and mathematical rigor have been used to provide arguments in favor of the model's inappropriateness for MFCC features. A solution has been proposed to the problem of explaining the good published results on singer recognition using MFCCs and MixMax models that reopens a branch of research in this area.

The robustness of the MixMax model against noise has been combined with a novel approach of comparing two such models solely based on their parameters in Chapter 5. The first-time use of the earth mover's distance for speaker clustering allows to accelerate the run-time of

Chapter 10. Conclusions

the system by a factor of 120 for a subset of the MPEG-7 video content set while yielding competitive recognition accuracy.

Challenging the still worse-than-human performance of the state-of-the-art in speaker clustering systems, an experimental setup has been proposed in Chapter 6 to answer the two important questions: (a) where in the processing chain of speaker clustering has an improvement to take place to maximally improve the final outcome? (b) How does this improvement look like qualitatively? The answer is that an account for the temporal succession of frames is crucially missing in the modeling stage that was still present in the ordered feature matrix after feature extraction. The *biomimetic approach* used to arrive at this conclusion implies that improving other parts of the processing chain will probably not show full potential until the issue of temporal modeling is addressed. A proof-of-concept implementation using context vectors and one-class SVMs has shown the validity of the results by improving the misclassification rate on a subset of the TIMIT corpus by 50%.

Based on the experience with the previously described algorithm design problems, the methodology of *eidetic design* has been proposed in Chapter 7 to generate hypotheses about why algorithms in speech processing do not behave as expected. It is a human-in-the-loop approach striving for intuition into the problems by transforming algorithmic (sub-)results to a domain of perception where the human mind is considered to be an expert in conceiving the context and meaning of events, features and models naturally. Eidetic design has practical applications in algorithm research and development, debugging and teaching. It has been successfully applied in the course of finding the DD-GMM as well as the time model of Chapter 6.

The sclib library has been developed in the course of this book and proposed as a capacious toolkit for automatic speaker recognition in Chapter 8. It is publicly available upon request and ready to use for expert users in their research projects. The library's usage for computationally expensive tasks is explicitly facilitated by providing interfaces to the world of Grid- and services computing that enhance its integration capabilities and usability. The respective tools have been developed in cooperation with other researchers.

The developed concepts, algorithms and implementations have been applied to problems from the domain of video content analysis and retrieval in the last chapter. A multimodal analysis algorithm has been developed and evaluated. It uses an audio type segmentation algorithm that employs several improvements over existing approaches. The complete multimodal approach has been successfully used to label game videos with semantic categories such as violence for psychological experiments, to summarize raw video footage and to detect several semantic concepts in the annual TRECVid evaluations. Especially the video summarization gained a lot of performance from the audio modality.

Overall, the state of the art in voice modeling and its application especially under adverse conditions has been advanced: this book constitutes an account of what is possible today in analyzing unrestricted video material with respect to voice. Some of the proposed methods are improvements to popular techniques that seem to have emerged quite straightforwardly in retrospect. Others have the potential to impact the direction of how voice processing research is conducted in the next years to come. The experiment showing how to unfold speaker clustering potential using time information belongs to this group of proposed methods, together with the integrated approach of algorithm design and development under the framework of eidetic design. The long-term objective of providing robust speaker diarization of contemporary mixed-reality movies for scientific media analysis, however, has not been reached, but approached.

10.2 Tactical Prospects

Several short term goals arise from the work presented in this book. Their realization depends merely on the investment of conceivable amounts of time in order to implement a promising extension, conduct a further experiment or evaluate other parameters and data.

For instance, testing the DD-GMM with other feature types, evaluating its performance using further data sets, and applying it as a classifier in other domains than speaker recognition seems promising. Then, to further address the speed issue in speaker clustering, a combination of the online- and hierarchical clustering schemes could be evaluated to take advantage of both their strengths.

The temporal modeling approach to speaker clustering bears several possibilities that could be studied to better understand the new feature and improve its exploitation: for instance, is the time succession of frames best grasped by concatenating several frames together, or are other data structures or summarizations better suited? What are good conditions and parameter settings for the one-class SVM model and how can they be found efficiently?

Another range of topics is clustered around the approach of eidetic design. The presented toolbox can be extended to address more design problems in speech processing and beyond. To make them usable, the mashup editor GUI is currently extended to provide access to the whole sclib in a plug-in fashion that allows to compose new workflows from these basic building blocks. To this end, it is also helpful to release a stable version of the library and improve the installation process and interoperability of the presented Grid- and service tools.

Finally, the sclib contains a lot of algorithms whose combined effect on speaker recognition performance has not been evaluated yet. Connecting some of these dead ends to capacious systems might yield the one or the other additional finding.

Chapter 10. Conclusions

10.3 Strategic Prospects

The following areas of future work define long term prospects with promising, but open ends. For example, the results concerning the MixMax model and its use within singer recognition research shed a whole new light on the state of the art in this area. As has been argued, one of the currently best working systems is not the MixMax & MFCC system, but a quite simple GMM baseline. To explore more sophisticated methods for singing voice modeling within popular music offers room for improvement. The direction of where to find such improvement can thereby be freely selected.

As has been reminiscent in the fundamentals chapter as well as in the explanation of fast and robust speaker clustering methods in Chapter 5, several commonly used techniques for speaker clustering on constrained data do not straightforwardly generalize to other data conditions: for example, the observed failure of the commonly used termination criteria for the clustering process deserves treatment. The same is true for speaker change detection algorithms under these new conditions. Furthermore, there is still room for greater noise robustness, to be achieved maybe by more auditory-like processing in artificial systems, through the application of blind source separation techniques or via speech enhancement.

More generally speaking, voice modeling might need a shift towards analyzing outstanding events rather than global averages in a speech stream as is done by humans. But how can this be achieved? How can the entire temporal context, the complete voice be considered holistically, just as in the popular forensic phonetic method of analyzing spectrograms in a Gestalt-based manner? The area of automatic speaker recognition still needs a breakthrough that pushes the performance an order of magnitude further, as is currently recognized by several authors referenced in the body of this work.

Two further topics show promising research paths apart from concrete voice modeling methods: first, the method of eidetic design could be applied to other fields, such as general multimedia analysis applications and computer security-related algorithms. Also, its usage in teaching abstract concepts is under consideration.

Second, audio-enriched video analysis shows a potential for improvement in overcoming the approach of summarizing a complete shot with a single, averaged feature vector of low- and mid-level events. Approaches that work more (outstanding) event-based, employ a tighter coupling of the modalities and exploit the results of specialized detectors have shown promising performance recently and are likely to indicate the road ahead.

10.4 Epilogue

After numerous ideas, 177 pages, 83 equations, 29 figures, 17 tables, several proposals, 10 chapters, and at least 3 listings, one question abides: *And, does it work?*

Yes.

It improves the scientific state of the art.

It contributes several algorithms that do things up to twice as good as has been possible before (at least if you regard halving the error as doubling the performance).

Two ideas may even substantially change the way speaker recognition will be approached in the future.

And under certain circumstances, it really works well. These circumstances can now be a bit more worse than before. And it works faster now.

But no.

Voice-based indexing of movies is still far-off. The speech and voice retrieval-based video recorder interface is still science fiction. We have to watch *Terminator 2* by ourselves to find Arnie saying *Hasta la vista, baby.*

Anyhow this is a good idea that I could pursue with some recreation...

Machines taking over control—very funny!

Appendices

"The modern king has become a vermiform appendix—useless when quiet, when obtrusive in danger of removal."

Austin O'Malley (1760–1854)

A
Additional Material for the Human Speaker Grouping Study

A.1 Introduction

This appendix contains additional material for the human speaker grouping study presented in Chapter 6. It is organized as follows: Section A.2 contains the instructions used as the sole information on the experiment for participants (additionally, the probands had the opportunity to choose a version in German language). Section A.3 presents the assessment sheet used by the participants to note their results. Finally, Section A.4 gives the detailed results of all individual participants.

A.2 Experimental Instructions: Speaker Grouping

Please read these instructions carefully until the end and resolve issues of understanding—then start and finish the experiment at a stretch.

Abstract:

The goal is to group sets of audio recordings: each group shall contain recordings of only one speaker. At the same time, all recordings of this speaker have to be in the same group.

Appendix A. Additional Material for the Human Speaker Grouping Study

Background:

This is part of a scientific investigation on how humans recognize voices. For this reason, 3 datasets with preprocessed recordings of different speakers will be analyzed. You are invited to participate in this investigation. To do so, you need no more skills than your intuitive ability to distinguish voices. The collected results of many participants will be analyzed anonymously and used in a scientific publication. Not your personal performance is what counts, but to draw conclusions on human abilities per se. So, please solve the tasks carefully, but also do not overstress yourself.

Data:

There are 3 data sets. Each one consists of 14 consecutively numbered audio recordings (01.wav–14.wav) of approximately 40 seconds length. The content of each recording is speech (or something like speech, although the likeness might not be heard directly). The recordings have been padded with silence. The data may be found on the supplementary medium (USB flash memory or CD) in the directory sg_experiment.

Additional material needed:

Pencil, eraser, stopwatch, assessment sheet, computer with headphones and software for playback.

Procedure:

The **experiment is carried out in 3 runs**: In run 1 data set 1 is analyzed, in run 2 data set 2 is analyzed, in run 3 data set 3 is analyzed. **This ordering is obligatory**. After writing your name, age and sex onto the assessment sheet, **each run is organized the same way**. This is how one run is carried out: The **stopwatch is started** at the beginning. The run is finished if

- you cannot (the way you see it) improve the result

- the **maximum time of 30 minutes** has passed

After each run the time it took you to do the grouping is written on the assessment sheet. In the meanwhile, you may listen to the 14 recordings of the current run

- in any order

- as often as you want

- complete or in parts

A.2. Experimental Instructions: Speaker Grouping

The goal is **to group together those recordings that have been spoken by the same "voice"**. You choose the number of groups you use according to your estimation of the overall number of speakers in this data set. Grouping is carried out by connecting the numbers of recordings on the assessment sheet with lines (as shown in Figure A.1).

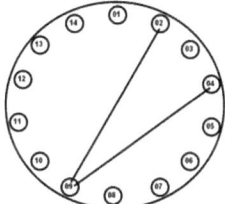

Figure A.1: A grouping of recordings 2, 4 and 9.

You can revise your decisions by erasing lines on the assessment sheet (if the figure of the current run is totally wasted, a backup figure on the last page of the assessment sheet can be used instead). The **decision to group recordings together must be taken solely based on the acoustical similarity of the voices** (all other "cues" or similarities are just randomness). Particularly, of no use is

- the graphical order of numbers (and lines) on the assessment sheet

- similarities of any kind to a prior run

- the content of a recording (language, words, sentences, length, ...)

- additional features of the used playback software (frequency analysis, ...)

After grouping all recordings of the current run, you should describe in 1–3 short sentences how you tried to solve the task and how you judge your own result.

Hint:
From run to run the recordings will have more in common with "normal" speech. Meanwhile, you should engage with the sound. This means not to focus on maybe unfamiliar patterns that all recordings of a run have in common, but on the more subtle differences, like the ones used when, for example, distinguishing two low-pitched male voices.

Appendix A. Additional Material for the Human Speaker Grouping Study

A.3 Assessment Sheet

Auswertungsbogen / assessment sheet

Name: ____________________
Alter / age: ________________
Geschlecht / sex: ___________

Datensatz / set: 1
Benötigte Zeit / used time: ____________

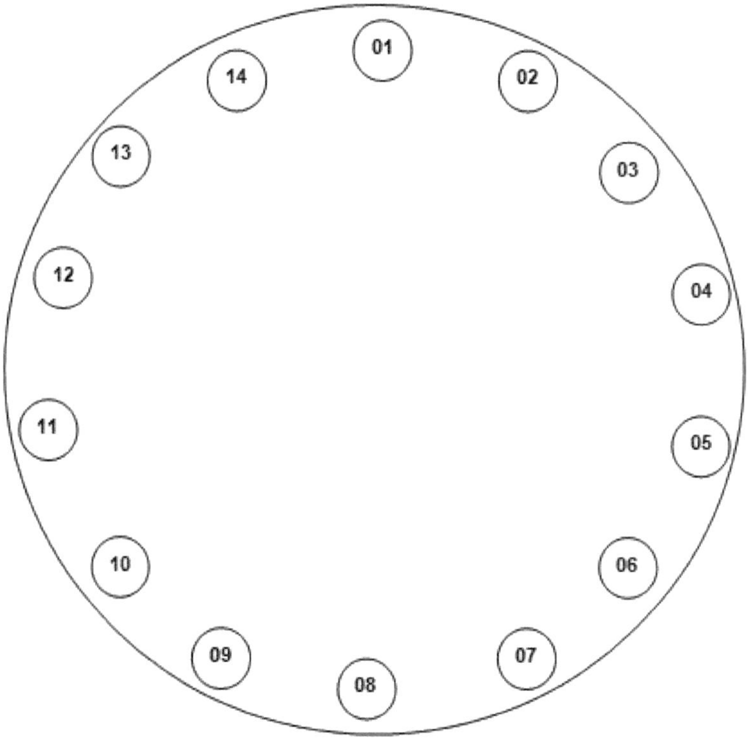

Lösungsmethode / used way to solve the task: ______________________________

Appendix A. Additional Material for the Human Speaker Grouping Study

Datensatz / set: 2
Benötigte Zeit / used time: _____

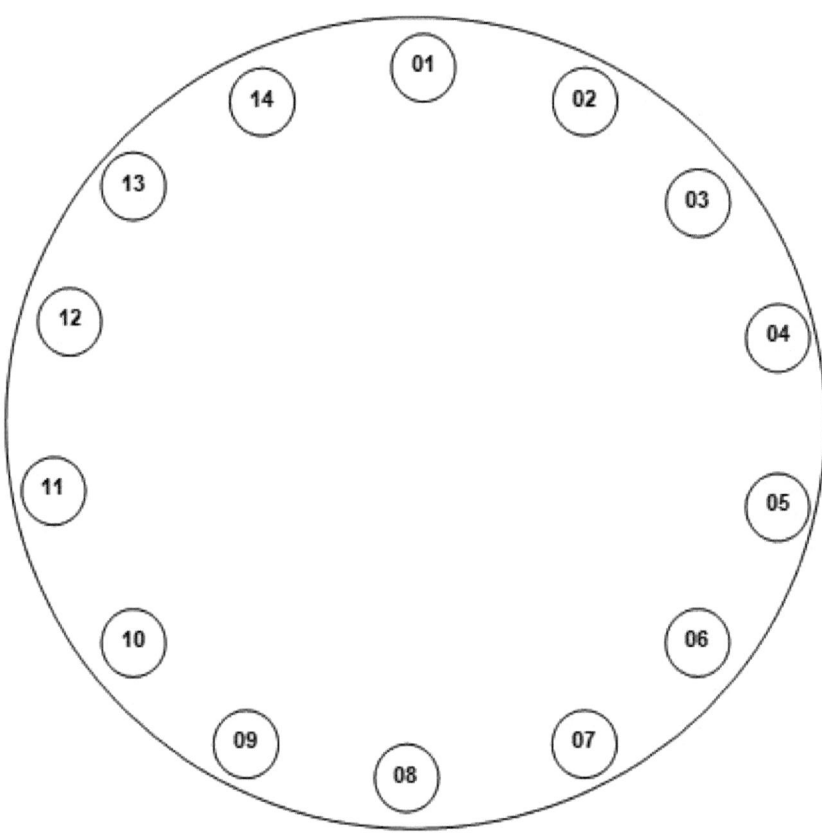

Lösungsmethode / used way to solve the task: _____
_____
_____
_____
_____

A.3. Assessment Sheet

Datensatz / set: 3
Benötigte Zeit / used time: _____

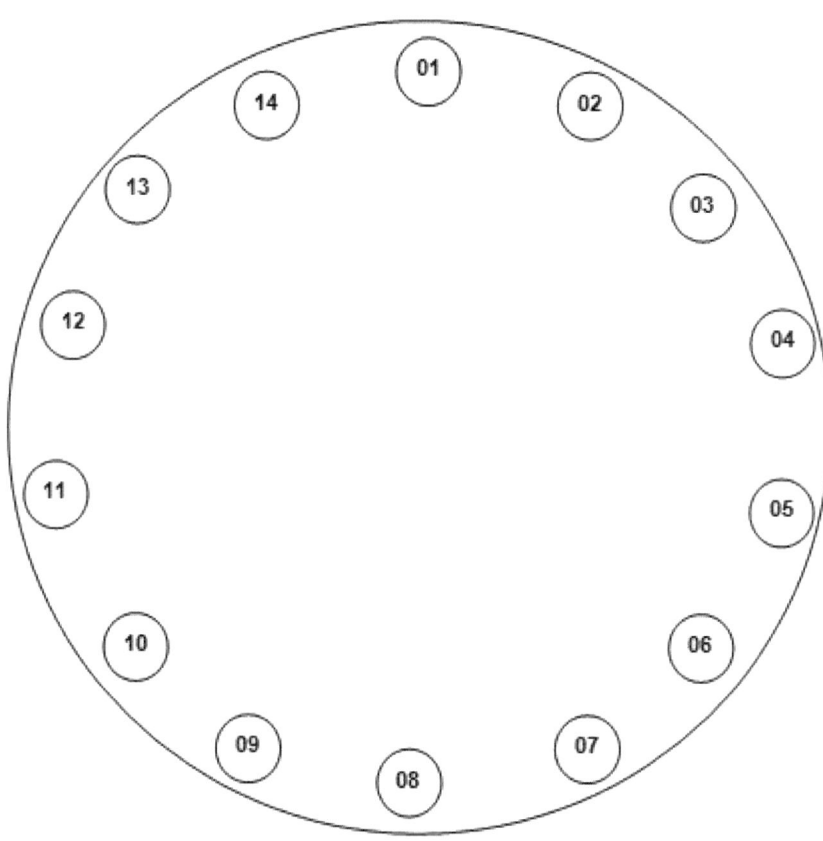

Lösungsmethode / used way to solve the task: _____
_____
_____
_____
_____
_____

Appendix A. Additional Material for the Human Speaker Grouping Study

Datensatz / set: _____ (nur falls nötig / use if necessary)
Benötigte Zeit / used time: _____

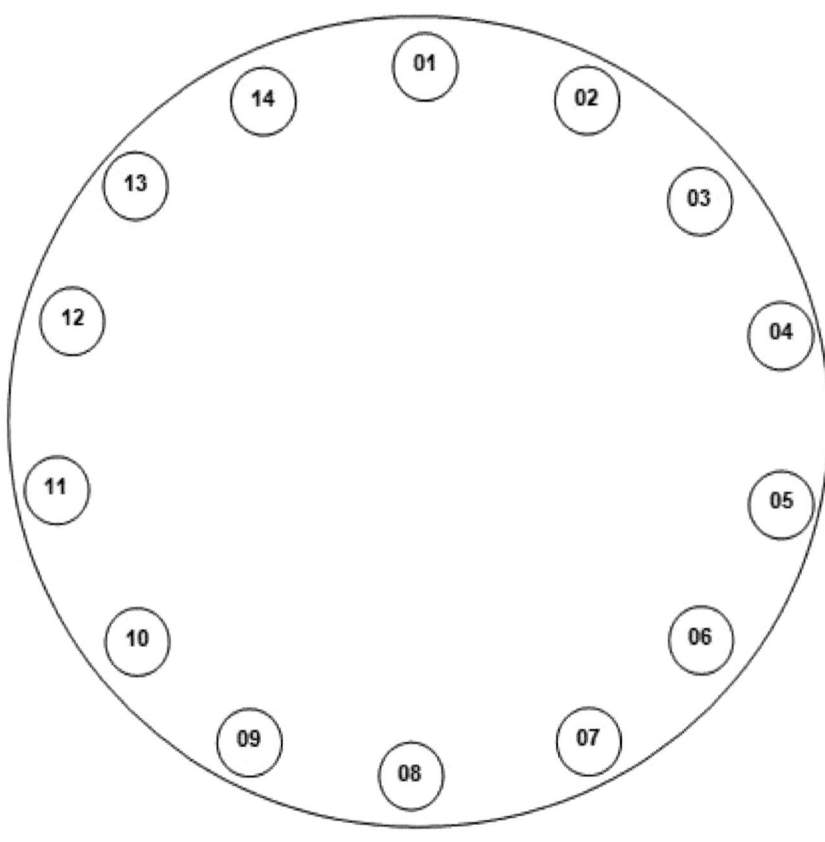

Lösungsmethode / used way to solve the task: _____
_____
_____
_____
_____

A.4 Individual Participant's Results

The following Tables A.1–A.3 contain individual probands' results for clustering the speakers in datasets 1–3. Each Table contains an "ID" column that identifies the proband (or indicates mean, variance and standard deviation of the rows before) while preserving privacy. Then, some additional personal information like "age" and "sex" is given, followed by statistical summarizations on how the probands did perform clustering: the time taken to perform the task, the number of created clusters, the number of directly correctly drawn lines, the number of correctly drawn lines if considering transitivity, and the overall number of lines drawn. The next 7 columns give the probability of individual speakers from the dataset to be grouped together correctly. For example, for a given proband, it is 1.0 if the pair of utterances of this speaker got connected, and 0.0 otherwise. Note the different order of speaker columns in each table due to the different arrangement of the utterances on the assessment sheet. The remaining columns give figures of merit as explained in Section 6.2.3. They assess the performance of each proband for the given dataset and have been computed on a per-utterance basis rather than based on samples to give equal weight to each misclassified utterance regardless of its length.

Appendix A. Additional Material for the Human Speaker Grouping Study

ID	Age [J]	Sex	Time [m]	Clusters [#]	Correct w/o trans. [#]	Correct [#]	Connections [#]	p(FJEMO) [0,1]	p(MJSWO) [0,1]	p(MREBO) [0,1]	p(MDABO) [0,1]	p(FAKSO) [0,1]	p(FELCO) [0,1]	p(FDACI) [0,1]	rec_O [0,1]	prec_O [0,1]	MR [0,1]	acp [0,1]	asp [0,1]	purity [0,1]	γ $\vee$	I_{BBN} $\wedge$	DER [0,1]
kdm	30	m	16	4	1	3	10	0	0	1	1	1	0	0	0.3571	0.3571	0.6429	0.3857	0.7143	0.5249	23	1.90	0.3658
mhm	21	m	30	4	4	4	9	1	0	1	0	0	1	1	0.5	0.5	0.5	0.4381	0.7857	0.5867	18	2.63	0.3329
mfm	29	m	18.03	7	4	2	7	1	0	0	0	0	1	0	0.5714	0.5714	0.4286	0.619	0.6429	0.6308	11	5.17	0.3187
rsf	24	f	20	4	2	1	10	1	0	1	0	0	0	0	0.5714	0.5714	0.4286	0.4524	0.7857	0.5962	17	2.83	0.3047
rsm	26	m	30	9	2	4	5	1	0	0	0	1	0	0	0.5714	0.7143	0.4286	0.6786	0.5714	0.6227	13	5.00	0.4234
tsm	31	m	20	4	1	4	10	0	0	0	0	0	0	0	0.5	0.5	0.5	0.4524	0.7857	0.5962	17	2.83	0.3185
csm	30	m	10	5	3	3	9	1	0	1	0	1	1	0	0.5714	0.5714	0.4286	0.5048	0.7143	0.6005	18	3.57	0.2631
ejm	26	m	5	8	1	1	6	0	0	0	0	0	0	0	0.5	0.5	0.5	0.6429	0.5714	0.6061	13	5.00	0.3057
abf	33	f	30	12	1	2	9	0	0	1	1	0	1	0	0.5714	0.5714	0.4286	0.9286	0.5714	0.7284	7	7.00	0.2013
mmm	31	m	20	5	2	2	9	0	0	1	1	0	1	0	0.3571	0.9286	0.6429	0.4214	0.6429	0.5205	21	2.40	0.4583
cbf	26	f	30	5	2	2	8	0	0	0	0	1	0	0	0.3571	0.3571	0.6429	0.4286	0.6429	0.5249	18	2.50	0.4364
rem	36	m	10	6	0	2	5	0	0	0	0	0	1	1	0.5714	0.5714	0.4286	0.5952	0.7143	0.6512	12	4.83	0.3395
hnf	25	f	16.917	9	3	1	10	1	0	1	1	0	0	0	0.5	0.6429	0.5	0.7143	0.5714	0.6389	11	5.50	0.4239
hmm	28	m	18.083	4	1	3	4	0	0	1	0	0	0	1	0.4286	0.4286	0.5714	0.3929	0.7143	0.5297	33	2.00	0.4903
dsm	28	m	23	8	2	2	6	1	0	1	0	1	1	1	0.5714	0.4286	0.4286	0.6905	0.6429	0.6662	11	5.67	0.291
dbf	41	f	20	4	3	3	10	0	0	1	0	0	0	0	0.4286	0.4286	0.5714	0.4048	0.7148	0.5377	19	2.17	0.3393
rhm	64	m	30	9	2	3	5	0	1	1	1	1	1	1	0.7143	0.8571	0.2857	0.8333	0.7143	0.7715	7	7.17	0.1501
asf	31	f	20	3	3	7	12	1	0	1	1	1	1	1	0.4286	0.4286	0.5714	0.4286	1	0.6547	40	2.50	0.4443
azm	27	m	30	6	3	4	8	1	0	1	0	0	1	1	0.6429	0.6429	0.3571	0.6429	0.7857	0.7107	10	5.50	0.2249
hkm	27	m	22	5	7	7	11	1	1	1	1	1	1	1	0.7143	0.7143	0.2857	0.7143	1	0.8452	8	6.50	0.1943
μ	30.7		20.952	6.05	2.2	3	8.05	0.45	0.25	0.7	0.4	0.25	0.55	0.4	0.5214	0.5679	0.4786	0.5685	0.7143	0.6272	16.35	4.133	0.3313
σ^2	80.642		55.419	5.73	2.4	2.95	6.37	0.26	0.2	0.22	0.25	0.2	0.26	0.25	0.0113	0.025	0.0113	0.0255	0.015	0.0075	70.03	3.151	0.0090
σ	8.9801		7.4444	2.39	1.5	1.72	2.52	0.51	0.44	0.47	0.5	0.44	0.51	0.5	0.1065	0.158	0.1065	0.1595	0.1226	0.0868	8.368	1.775	0.0950

Table A.1: Individual results on dataset 1 (resynthesized models).

A.4. Individual Participant's Results

ID	Age [J]	Sex	Time [m]	Clusters [#]	Correct w/o trans. [#]	Correct [#]	Connections [#]	p(FJEMO) [0..1]	p(MJSWO) [0..1]	p(MREBO) [0..1]	p(MDAB0) [0..1]	p(FAKSO) [0..1]	p(FELCO) [0..1]	p(FDACI) [0..1]	rec$_o$ [0..1]	prec$_o$ [0..1]	MR [0..1]	acp [0..1]	asp [0..1]	purity [0..1]	$\gamma_<$	$l_{BBN}_>$	DER [0..1]
kdm	30	m	12	6	1	1	8	0	0	0	0	0	1	0	0.5	0.5	0.5	0.5	0.5714	0.5345	22	3.5	0.3432
mhm	21	m	30	7	7	7	7	1	1	1	1	1	1	1	1	1	0	1	1	1	0	10.5	0
mfm	29	m	10.5	5	1	2	9	0	0	1	0	1	1	1	0.5	0.5	0.5	0.4405	0.6429	0.5463	18	3	0.4408
rsf	24	f	14	5	2	2	9	0	0	1	1	1	1	0	0.5	0.5	0.0714	0.9048	0.6429	0.5321	17	2.667	0.35
rsm	26	m	25	7	6	6	7	1	0	0	0	1	0	1	0.929	0.9286	0.2857	0.9048	0.9286	0.9166	3	9.167	0.0230
tsm	31	m	19	5	4	4	7	1	1	1	1	0	0	0	0.7143	0.7143	0.2857	0.7619	0.7857	0.7737	3	7.167	0.2994
csm	30	m	10	7	3	4	9	0	1	1	0	1	1	0	0.6429	0.6429	0.3571	0.5714	0.7857	0.6701	14	4.5	0.2275
ejm	26	m	4	5	2	2	6	0	0	0	1	1	0	0	0.3571	0.4286	0.6429	0.6905	0.6429	0.6662	11	5.667	0.2988
abf	33	f	30	8	7	7	7	1	1	1	1	1	1	1	1	1	0	1	1	1	0	10.5	0
mmm	31	m	24	7	1	2	8	0	1	0	0	1	0	0	0.5714	0.5714	0.5	0.5408	0.6429	0.5896	25	4.071	0.4636
cbf	26	f	30	7	2	2	6	1	0	1	1	1	0	1	0.6429	0.6429	0.4286	0.619	0.6429	0.6308	11	5.167	0.2453
rem	36	m	13	5	4	4	8	1	1	0	1	1	0	0	0.6429	0.7857	0.3571	0.5595	0.7857	0.663	13	4.333	0.3019
hnf	25	f	12.93	8	3	3	9	0	0	0	0	1	1	1	0.7143	0.7857	0.2857	0.7619	0.7143	0.7377	8	6.667	0.1944
hnm	28	m	14.25	6	2	2	6	1	0	1	1	1	1	1	0.4286	0.4286	0.5714	0.5119	0.6429	0.5737	16	3.667	0.3329
dsm	28	m	20	7	1	2	8	0	0	0	0	1	0	0	0.7143	0.7143	0.2857	0.6667	0.7143	0.6901	11	5.833	0.2679
dbf	41	f	22	6	3	5	7	1	1	1	1	1	1	1	0.4286	0.4286	0.5714	0.4643	0.5714	0.5151	17	3	0.3695
rhm	64	m	8	6	0	1	8	0	0	0	0	1	0	0	0.5714	0.5	0.4286	0.619	0.5714	0.5948	13	4.667	0.3978
asf	31	f	12	4	1	1	6	1	1	1	1	1	1	1	0.5714	0.5714	0.4286	0.5374	0.9286	0.7064	21	4.024	0.3765
azm	27	m	22	8	5	6	10	0	1	1	0	1	1	0	0.7857	0.8571	0.2143	0.8333	0.7857	0.8092	6	7.667	0.1354
hkm	27	m	14	4	3	3	11	0	1	1	1	1	1	0	0.4286	0.4286	0.5714	0.3976	0.7143	0.5329	21	2.067	0.4468
μ	30.7		17.33	6.35	2.95	3.3	7.75	0.4	0.25	0.6	0.35	0.7	0.6	0.4	**0.6179**	**0.6322**	**0.3821**	0.6422	0.7357	0.6841	12.7	5.392	**0.2757**
σ^2	80.64		59.48	1.71	4.16	3.69	1.99	0.25	0.2	0.25	0.24	0.22	0.25	0.25	**0.0377**	**0.0372**	**0.0377**	0.0331	0.0189	0.0226	51.48	6.276	**0.0203**
σ	8.98		7.712	1.31	2.04	1.92	1.41	0.5	0.44	0.5	0.49	0.47	0.5	0.5	**0.1943**	**0.1929**	**0.1943**	0.1818	0.1373	0.1504	7.175	2.505	**0.1426**

Table A.2: Individual results on dataset 2 (resynthesized features).

Appendix A. Additional Material for the Human Speaker Grouping Study

ID	Age [J]	Sex	Time [m]	# Clusters	# Correct w/o trans.	# Correct	# Connections	p(FJEMO) [0..1]	p(MJSWO) [0..1]	p(MREBO) [0..1]	p(MDABO) [0..1]	p(FAKSO) [0..1]	p(FELCO) [0..1]	p(FDACI) [0..1]	rec_o [0..1]	prec_o [0..1]	MR [0..1]	acp [0..1]	asp [0..1]	purity [0..1]	γ<	γ>	I_BBN	DER [0..1]
kdm	30	m	5	8	5	5	6	1	1	0	0	1	1	1	0.8571	0.9286	0.1429	0.9286	0.8571	0.8921	3	9	0.1377
mhm	21	m	7	7	7	7	7	1	1	1	1	1	1	1	1	1	0	1	1	1	0	10.5	0
mfm	29	m	7	7	5	5	7	1	1	0	0	1	1	1	0.8571	0.8571	0.1429	0.8571	0.8571	0.8571	4	8.5	0.04424
rsf	24	f	5	7	7	7	7	1	1	1	1	1	1	1	1	1	0	1	1	1	0	10.5	0
rsm	26	m	4	7	7	7	7	1	1	1	1	1	1	1	1	1	0	1	1	1	0	10.5	0
tsm	31	m	8.5	7	7	7	7	1	1	1	1	1	1	1	1	1	0	1	1	1	0	10.5	0
csm	30	m	10	7	7	7	7	1	1	1	1	1	1	1	1	1	0	1	1	1	0	10.5	0
ejm	26	m	7	8	6	6	6	1	0	1	0	1	1	1	0.9286	1	0.07143	1	0.9286	0.9636	1	10	0.02304
abf	33	f	15	7	7	7	7	1	1	1	1	1	1	1	1	1	0	1	1	1	0	10.5	0
mmm	31	m	14	6	6	6	6	1	1	1	1	1	1	1	0.8571	0.8571	0.1429	0.8571	1	0.9258	4	8.5	0.1159
cbf	26	f	20	7	7	7	7	1	1	1	1	1	1	1	1	1	0	1	1	1	0	10.5	0
ren	36	m	10	7	7	7	7	1	1	1	1	1	1	1	1	1	0	1	1	1	0	10.5	0
hnf	25	f	4.23	7	7	7	7	1	1	1	1	1	1	1	1	1	0	1	1	1	0	10.5	0
hmm	28	m	4.23	7	7	7	7	1	1	1	1	1	1	1	1	1	0	1	1	1	0	10.5	0
dsm	28	m	7	7	7	7	7	1	1	1	1	1	1	1	1	1	0	1	1	1	0	10.5	0
dbf	41	f	18	10	3	3	4	0	0	0	0	0	1	1	0.7143	0.9286	0.2857	0.9048	0.7143	0.8039	6	7.667	0.1548
rhm	64	m	18	7	7	7	7	1	1	1	1	1	1	1	1	1	0	1	1	1	0	10.5	0
asf	31	f	5	7	7	7	7	1	1	1	1	1	1	1	1	1	0	1	1	1	0	10.5	0
azm	27	m	5	7	7	7	7	1	1	1	1	1	1	1	1	1	0	1	1	1	0	10.5	0
hkm	27	m	5	7	7	7	7	1	1	1	1	1	1	1	1	1	0	1	1	1	0	10.5	0
μ	30.7		8.95	7.2	6.5	6.55	6.75	0.95	0.95	0.85	0.85	0.95	1	1	**0.9607**	**0.9786**	**0.0393**	0.9774	0.9679	0.9721	0.9	10.06	**0.0238**
σ²	80.6		27	0.59	1.1	1.1	0.51	0.05	0.05	0.13	0.13	0.05	0	0	**0.0062**	**0.0022**	**0.0061**	0.0024	0.0056	0.0033	3.25	0.77	**0.0025**
σ	8.98		5.19	0.77	1.1	1.05	0.72	0.22	0.22	0.37	0.37	0.22	0	0	**0.0785**	**0.0469**	**0.0785**	0.0485	0.075	0.057	1.8	0.877	**0.0500**

Table A.3: Individual results on dataset 3 (original speech).

−192−

Lists and Registers

List of Figures

2.1	Human speech production.	28
2.2	The human auditory system.	30
2.3	Waveform of the phrase "she had", spoken by a female voice.	34
2.4	Spectrum from the near-end vowel part of the phrase "she had".	36
2.5	Corresponding wideband spectrogram of the phrase "she had".	37
2.6	Overview of the pattern recognition process.	47
2.7	PDE plots of the detectability of speaker change points in different data sets.	63
2.8	A self-similarity matrix of the first 7 speakers of the `TIMIT` test set.	64
3.1	A 32-mixture GMM of 19-dimensional MFCCs.	71
3.2	Speaker identification rate versus removed percentage of training- and evaluation data.	73
3.3	Speaker identification rate versus changing data availability conditions.	74
3.4	Effect of utterance length on the number of model parameters.	75
3.5	Effect of utterance length on computing time.	76
4.1	Feature envelope comparison between FBEs and MFCCs.	83
4.2	Log-likelihood scores for all misidentified test utterances from `MPEG7`.	92
7.1	The proposed workflow.	131
7.2	Imagining some probability distributions as a mountain massifs.	132
7.3	The "life cycle" of algorithm design using the proposed approach.	133
7.4	Flow diagram of the model inversion process.	136
7.5	`WebVoice` in the web service browser.	139
7.6	`WebVoice` in the mashup editor.	140
7.7	Spectrogram comparison.	141
7.8	A 12-dimensional GMM with 22 mixtures.	143
7.9	A 4-dimensional GMM with 3 mixtures.	144

List of Figures

8.1	The main window of `Videana`.	155
8.2	A layer model for the multimedia analysis framework.	159
9.1	Example frames of game states and assigned semantic categories.	163
9.2	Scheme of the hierarchical audio type classifier.	165
9.3	MDS visualization of `franco85.mpg` using 3 clusters.	167
A.1	A grouping of recordings 2, 4 and 9.	183

Picture Credits

Figure 2.1 has been adapted from Fant [1960] and from Eulenberg and Wood [2010].

Figure 2.2 has been adapted from Moore [1987].

Elements of Figure 2.6 are due to the following sources:

- Robert Kulik, Bess Phillips and Rick Scott, http://www.floom.com/media/waveform_lotos.gif, visited 18. March 2010.

- Bert Speelpenning, http://bertspeelpenning.files.wordpress.com/2010/01/an-inverse-jpg, visited 18. March 2010.

- Journal of Neuroengineering and Rehabilitation, http://www.jneuroengrehab.com/content/figures/1743-0003-2-22-4-1.jpg, visited 18. March 2010.

- Karthi Umapathy, http://www.ee.ryerson.ca/~courses/ele888/ele_888_pat_class.gif, visited 18. March 2010.

- Jacob Morgan, http://www.jmorganmarketing.com/wp-content/uploads/2009/02/identit jpg, visited 18. March 2010.

Elements of Figure 7.2 are due to the following sources:

- David Simmer II, http://www.blogography.com/photos24/ForbiddenMountain.jpg, visited 18. March 2010.

- Jakob Tigges and Maltes Kroes, http://www.eikongraphia.com/images/tempelhof_mountain/Jakob_Tigges_-_Mountain_at_Tempelhof_1_S.jpg, visited 18. March 2010.

List of Tables

4.1	Singer/speaker identification rate on all three databases.	87
4.2	Raw identification results for all 3 databases in a contingency table.	88
4.3	Singer/speaker identification rates for AMU variants and baselines using MFCC features on all three databases.	89
4.4	Identification scatter matrix for the "GMM (32/8, per frame)" model on MPEG7 data.	93
4.5	Identification scatter matrix for the AMU model on MPEG7 data.	93
5.1	Overview of the used corpus.	102
5.2	Experimental results on the jornaldanoite1 video.	104
6.1	Comparison of human- and random clustering (a).	113
6.2	Comparison of human- and random clustering (b).	114
6.3	Performance of human- and random clustering in terms of different figures of merit.	116
6.4	Performance of human- and random clustering in terms of more figures of merit.	116
6.5	Popularity of human-used features.	117
6.6	Experimental results.	124
8.1	Comparison of the svlib and sclib libraries in terms of lines of code.	148
9.1	Comparison of the two systems on the evaluation corpus.	165
9.2	Precision for individual features within the 50 top-ranked results using the complete rushes test material.	168
9.3	List of semantic concepts to be detected at TRECVid'07.	168
A.1	Individual results on dataset 1 (resynthesized models).	190
A.2	Individual results on dataset 2 (resynthesized features).	191
A.3	Individual results on dataset 3 (original speech).	192

List of Listings

8.1 LCDL model (namespaces are omitted for reasons of readability). 156
8.2 Generated Java interface. 157
8.3 Usage of the generated interface. 157

Bibliography

A. G. Adami. Modeling Prosodic Differences for Speaker Recognition. *Speech Communication*, 49:277–291, 2007.

M. Afify, O. Siohan, and C.-H. Lee. Minimax Classification with Parametric Neighborhoods for Noisy Speech Recognition. In *Proceedings of the 7th European Conference on Speech Communication and Technology (Eurospeech'01)*, pages 2355–2358, Aalborg, Denmark, September 2001. ISCA.

C. C. Aggarwal. A Framework for Classification and Segmentation of Massive Audio Data Streams. In *Proceedings of the 13th ACM SIGKDD International Conference on Knowledge Discovery and Data Mining (KDD'07)*, pages 1013–1017, San Jose, CA, USA, August 2007. ACM.

Agnitio S.L. BATVOX: The Leading Tool for Forensics Speaker Recognition. Online web resource, 2008. URL http://www.agnitio.es/ingles/batvox.php. Visited 16. March 2010.

S. Ahmadi and A. S. Spanias. Cepstrum-Based Pitch Detection Using a New Statistical V/UV Classification Algorithm. *IEEE Transactions on Speech and Audio Processing*, 7(3):333–228, May 1999.

J. Ajmera and C. Wooters. A Robust Speaker Clustering Algorithm. In *IEEE Workshop on Automatic Speech Recognition and Understanding (ASRU'03)*, pages 411–416, St. Thomas, U.S. Virgin Islands, USA, November 2003. IEEE.

M. Al-Akaidi. *Fractal Speech Processing*. Cambridge University Press, 2004.

L. D. Alsteris and K. K. Paliwal. Short-Time Phase Spectrum in Speech Processing: A Review and Some Experimental Results. *Digital Signal Processing*, 17:578–616, 2007.

T. Andrews, F. Curbera, H. Dholakia, Y. Goland, J. Klein, F. Leymann, K. Liu, D. Roller, D. Smith, S. Thatte, I. Trickovic, and S. Weerawarana. *Business Process Execution Language for Web Services Version 1.1*. Microsoft, IBM, Siebel, BEA and SAP, 1.1 edition, 2003. URL http://download.boulder.ibm.com/ibmdl/pub/software/dw/specs/ws-bpel/ws-bpel.pdf. Visted 18. March 2010.

X. Anguera Miró. *Robust Speaker Diarization for Meetings*. PhD thesis, Universitat Politècnica de Catalunya, Bercelona, Spain, October 2006.

X. Anguera Miró, C. Wooters, B. Peskin, and M. Aguiló. Robust Speaker Segmentation for Meetings: The ICSI-SRI Spring 2005 Diarization System. In *Proceedings of the 2nd International Workshop on Machine Learning for Multimodal Interaction (MLMI'05)*, pages 402–414, Edinburgh, UK, July 2005. Springer.

A. Arauzo-Azofra, J. M. Benitez, and J. L. Castro. Consistency Measures for Feature Selection. *Journal of Intelligent Information Systems*, 30(3):273–292, June 2008.

R. Auckentaler, M. Carey, and H. lloyd Thomas. Score Normalization for Text-Independent Speaker Verification Systems. *Digital Signal Procesing*, 10(1–3):42–54, 2000.

J.-J. Aucouturier. A Day in the Life of a Gaussian Mixture Model: Informing Music Pattern Recognition with Psychological Experiments. *Journal of New Music Research*, submitted, 2009.

J.-J. Aucouturier and F. Pachet. Improving Timbre Similarity: How High is the Sky? *Journal of Negative Results in Speech and Audio Sciences*, 1(1), 2004.

J.-J. Aucouturier, B. Defreville, and F. Pachet. The Bag-of-Frames Approach to Audio Pattern Recognition: A Sufficient Model for Urban Soundscapes but not for Polyphonic Music. *Journal of the Acoustic Society of America*, 122:881–891, 2007.

P. M. Baggenstoss. Statistical modeling using Gaussian mixtures and HMMs with MATLAB. Technical Report TM 03-128, Naval Undersea Warfare Center, Newport, January 2002.

S. L. Bain. *Emergent Design: The Evolutionary Nature of Professional Software Development*. Addison-Wesley, 2008.

H. Banno, J. Lu, S. Nakamura, K. Shikano, and H. Kawahara. Efficient Representation of Short-Time Phase Based on Group Delay. In *Proceedings of the 23rd IEEE International Conference on Acoustics, Speech, and Signal Processing (ICASSP'98)*, pages 861–864, Seattle, WA, USA, May 1998. IEEE.

Y. Bar-Cohen. *Biomimetics: Biologically Inspired Technologies*. CRC Press, Boca Raton, FL, USA, 2006.

S. Baumann. *Artifcial Listening Systems: Modellierung und Approximation der Individuellen Perzeption von Musikähnlichkeit*. PhD thesis, Technical University of Kaiserslautern, Germany, 2005.

H. Bay, A. Ess, T. Tuytelaars, and L. V. Goo. SURF: Speeded Up Robust Features. *Computer Vision and Image Understanding*, 110(3):346–359, 2008.

T. Bayes. An Essay Towards Solving a Problem in the Doctrine of Chances. *Philosophical Transactions of the Royal Society of London*, 53:370–418, December 1763. By the late Rev. Mr. Bayes, communicated by Mr. Price, in a letter to John Canton, M. A. and F. R. S.

H. S. Beigi, S. H. Maes, and J. S. Sorensen. A Distance Measure Between Collections of Distributions and its Application to Speaker Recognition. In *Proceedings of the 23rd IEEE International Conference on Acoustics, Speech, and Signal Processing (ICASSP'98)*, volume 2, pages 753–756, Seattle, WA, USA, May 1998. IEEE.

J. Benesty, M. M. Sondhi, and Y. Huang, editors. *Springer Handbook of Speech Processing*. Springer, Berlin, Heidelberg, Germany, 2008.

C. M. Bishop. *Pattern Recognition and Machine Learning*. Springer, New York, NY, USA, 2006.

M. Böhme. Using libavformat and libavcodec. Online web resource, 18. February 2004. URL http://www.inb.uni-luebeck.de/~boehme/using_libavcodec.html. Visited 19. February 2010.

J.-F. Bonastre, F. Bimbot, L.-J. Boë, J. P. Campbell, D. A. Reynolds, and I. Magrin-Chagnolleau. Person Authentication by Voice: A Need for Caution. In *Proceedings of the 8th European Conference on Speech Communication and Technology (Eurospeech'03)*, pages 33–36, Geneva, Switzerland, September 2003. ISCA.

S. E. Bou-Ghazale and J. H. L. Hansen. A Comparative Study of Traditional and Newly Proposed Features for Recognition of Speech Under Stress. *IEEE Transactions on Speech and Audio Processing*, 8:429–442, 2000.

D. Burshtein and S. Gannot. Speech Enhancement Using a Mixture-Maximum Model. *IEEE Transactions on Speech and Audio Processing*, 10:341–351, 2002.

F. Camastra and A. Vinciarelli. *Machine Learning for Audio, Image and Video Analysis—Theory and Applications*. Springer, Berlin, Germany, 2008.

Bibliography

J. P. Campbell. Speaker Recognition: A Tutorial. *Proceedings of the IEEE*, 85:1437–1462, 1997.

W. M. Campbell, J. P. Campbell, D. A. Reynolds, D. A. Jones, and T. R. Leek. Phonetic Speaker Recognition with Support Vector Machines. *Advances in Neural Processing Systems*, 16:1377–1384, 2004.

W. M. Campbell, D. E. Sturim, D. A. Reynolds, and A. Solomonoff. SVM Based Speaker Verification using a GMM Supervector Kernel and NAP Variability Compensation. In *Proceedings of the 31st IEEE International Conference on Acoustics, Speech, and Signal Processing (ICASSP'06)*, volume 1, pages 97–100, Toulouse, France, April 2006. IEEE.

E. Candès and J. Romberg. l_1-*magic: Recovery of Sparse Signals via Convex Programming*. Caltech, October 2005. URL http://www.acm.caltech.edu/l1magic. Visited 18. March 2010.

E. J. Candès. Compressive Sampling. In *Proceedings of the Intetnational Congress of Mathematicians*, volume 3, pages 1433–1452, Madrid, Spain, 2006.

M. Cettolo, M. Vescovi, and R. Rizzi. Evaluation of BIC-based Algorithms for Audio Segmentation. *Computer Speech and Language*, 19:147–170, 2005.

C.-C. Chang and C.-J. Lin. *LIBSVM: A Library for Support Vector Machines*. National Taiwan University, Taipei 106, Taiwan, 2001. URL http://www.csie.ntu.edu.tw/~cjlin/libsvm.

Y.-H. Chao, W.-H. Tsai, and H.-M. Wang. Improving GMM-UBM Speaker Verification Using Discriminative Feedback Adaptation. *Computer Speech and Language*, 23:376–368, 2009.

S. S. Chen and P. S. Gopalakrishnan. Clustering via the Bayesian Information Criterion with Applications in Speech Recognition. In *Proceedings of the 23rd IEEE International Conference on Acoustics, Speech, and Signal Processing (ICASSP'98)*, volume 2, pages 645–648, Seattle, WA, USA, May 1998a. IEEE.

S. S. Chen and P. S. Gopalakrishnan. Speaker, Environment and Channel Change Detection and Clustering via the Bayesian Information Criterion. In *Proceedings of the DARPA Broadcast News Transcription and Understanding Workshop*, February 1998b.

Z.-H. Chen, Y.-F. Liao, and Y.-T. Juang. Prosody Modeling and Eigen-Prosody Analysis for Robust Speaker Recognition. In *Proceedings of the 30th IEEE International Conference on Acoustics, Speech, and Signal Processing (ICASSP'05)*, volume 1, pages 185–188, Philadelphia, PA, USA, March 2005. IEEE.

R. Chengalvarayan and L. Deng. Speech Trajectory Discrimination Using the Minimum Classification Error Learning. *IEEE Transactions on Speech and Audio Processing*, 6(6), 1998.

M. Cherubini, R. de Oliveira, and N. Oliver. Understanding Near-Duplicate Videos: A User-Centric Approach. In *Proceedings of the ACM International Conference on Multimedia (ACMMM'09)*, pages 35–44, Beijing, China, October 2009. ACM. Best paper candidate.

T. Chi, P. Ru, and S. A. Shamma. Multiresolution Spectrotemporal Analysis of Complex Sounds. *Journal of the Acoustical Society of America*, 118(2):887–906, 2005.

D. G. Childers, D. P. Skinner, and R. C. Kemerait. The Cepstrum: A Guide to Processing. *Proceedings of the IEEE*, 65(10):1428–1443, October 1977.

M. Cooke, S. Beet, and M. Crawford, editors. *Visual Representations of Speech Signals*. John Wiley & Sons, New York, NY, USA, 1993.

J. W. Cooley and J. W. Tukey. An Algorithm for the Machine Calculation of Comples Fourier Series. *Mathematics of Computation*, 19(90):297–301, 1965.

L. Cosmides and J. Tooby. Are Humans Good Intuitive Statisticians After All? Rethinking Some Conclusions from the Literature on Judgment under Uncertainty. *Cognition*, 58:1–73, 1996.

G. Cybenko. Approximation by Superpositions of a Sigmoidal Function. *Mathematics of Control, Signals, and Systems*, 2:303–314, 1989.

J. Dabkowski and A. Posiewnik. On Some Method of Analysing Time Series. *Acta Physica Plonica B*, 29(6):1791–1794, 1998.

S. B. Davis and P. Mermelstein. Comparison of Parametric Representations for Monosyllabic Word Recognition in Continuously Spoken Sentences. *IEEE Transactions on Acoustics, Speech and Signal Processing*, 28:357–366, 1980.

E. de Castro Lopo. Secret Rabbit Code. Online web resource, 2010. URL http://www.mega-nerd.com/SRC/index.html. Visited 22. February 2010.

P. Delacourt and C. J. Wellekens. DISTBIC: A Speaker-Based Segmentation for Audio Data Indexing. *Speech Comminucation*, 32:111–126, 2000.

P. Deléglise, Y. Estève, S. Meignier, and T. Merlin. The LIUM Speech Transcription System: A CMU Sphinx III-based System for French Broadcast News. In *Proceedings of the 9th European Conference on Speech Communication and Technology (Interspeech'05–Eurospeech)*, Lisbon,

Bibliography

Portugal, September 2005. ISCA. URL http://cmusphinx.sourceforge.net/. Visited 18. March 2010.

V. Dellwo, M. Huckvale, and M. Ashby. How is Individuality Expressed in Voice? An Introduction to Speech Production and Description for Speaker Classification. In C. Müller, editor, *Speaker Classification I*, Lecture Notes in Artificial Intelligence, chapter 1, pages 1–20. Springer, 2007.

A. Dempster, N. Laird, and D. Rubin. Maximum Likelihood From Incomplete Data Via the EM Algorithm. *Journal of the Royal Statistical Society, Series B*, 39:1–38, 1977.

K. Demuynck, O. Garcia, and D. Van Compernolle. Synthesizing Speech from Speech Recognition Parameters. In *Proceedings of the 8th International Conference on Spoken Language Processing (ICSLP Interspeech'04)*, volume 2, pages 945–948, Jeju Island, Korea, October 2004. ISCA.

A. N. Deoras and M. Hasegawa-Johnson. A Factorial HMM Approach to Simultaneous Recognition of Isolated Digits Spoken by Multiple Talkers on One Audio Channel. In *Proceedings of the 29th IEEE International Conference on Acoustics, Speech, and Signal Processing (ICASSP'04)*, volume 1, pages 861–864, Montreal, QC, Canada, May 2004. IEEE.

F. Desobry, M. Davy, and C. Doncarli. An Online Kernel Change Detection Algorithm. *IEEE Transactions on Signal Processing*, 53(8), 2005a.

F. Desobry, M. Davy, and W. J. Fitzgerald. A Class of Kernels for Sets of Vectors. In *Proceedings of the 13th European Symposium on Artificial Neural Networks (ESANN'05)*, pages 461–466, Bruges, Belgium, April 2005b. MIT Press.

N. Dhananjaya and B. Yegnanarayana. Speaker Change Detection in Casual Conversations Using Excitation Source Features. *Speech Communication*, 50:153–161, 2008.

T. Dörnemann, T. Friese, S. Herdt, E. Juhnke, and B. Freisleben. Grid Work Flow Modelling Using Grid-Specific BPEL Extensions. In *Proceedings of German eScience Conference (GES'07)*, pages 1–8, Baden-Baden, Germany, May 2007.

T. Dörnemann, M. Mathes, R. Schwarzkopf, E. Juhnke, and B. Freisleben. DAVO: A Domain-Adaptable, Visual BPEL4WS Orchestrator. In *Proceedings of the 23rd IEEE International Conference on Advanced Information Networking and Applications (AINA '09)*, pages 121–128, Bradford, UK, May 2009. IEEE.

A. Doucet and X. Wang. Monte Carlo Methods for Signal Processing—A Review in the Statistical Signal Processing Context. *IEEE Signal Processing Magazine*, pages 152–170, November 2005.

A. Drygajlo. Forensic Automatic Speaker Recognition. *IEEE Signal Processing Magazine*, 24(2):132–135, March 2007.

D. P. W. Ellis. PLP and RASTA (and MFCC, and inversion) in Matlab. Online web resource, 2005. URL http://www.ee.columbia.edu/~dpwe/resources/matlab/rastamat/. Visited 19. February 2010.

Encyclopædia Britannica. eidetic reduction. Online web resource, 2009. URL http://www.britannica.com/EBchecked/topic/180957/eidetic-reduction. Visited 19. February 2010.

Y. Ephraim, H. Lev-Ari, and W. J. J. Roberts. A Brief Survey of Speech Enhancement. In *The Electronic Handbook*. CRC Press, April 2005.

A. Erell and D. Burshtein. Noise Adaptation of HMM Speech Recognition Systems Using Tied-Mixtures in the Spectral Domain. *IEEE Transactions on Speech and Audio Processing*, 5(1): 72–74, January 1997.

A. Erell and M. Weintraub. Filterbank-Energy Estimation Using Mixture and Markov Models for Recognition of Noisy Speech. *IEEE Transactions on Speech and Audio Processing*, 1(1): 68–76, January 1993.

M. Ester and J. Sander. *Knowledge Discovery in Databases: Techniken und Anwendungen*. Springer, 2000.

J. Eulenberg and C. Wood. CSD 232—Descriptive Phonetics Spring Semester 2010. Online web resource, March 2010. URL https://www.msu.edu/course/asc/232/index.html. Visited 03. March 2010.

R. Ewerth. *Robust Video Content Analysis via Transductive Learning Methods*. PhD thesis, University of Marburg, Marburg, Germany, 2008.

R. Ewerth and B. Freisleben. Video Cut Detection Without Thresholds. In *Proceedings of the 11th Workshop on Signals, Systems and Image Processing (IWSSIP'04)*, pages 227–230, Poznan, Poland, September 2004. PTETiS.

R. Ewerth, C. Behringer, T. Kopp, M. Niebergall, T. Stadelmann, and B. Freisleben. University of Marburg at TRECVID 2005: Shot Boundary Detection and Camera Motion Estimation

Results. In *Proceedings of TREC Video Retrieval Evaluation Workshop (TRECVid'05)*. Available online, 2005. URL http://www-nlpir.nist.gov/projects/tvpubs/tv.pubs.org.htm.

R. Ewerth, M. Mühling, T. Stadelmann, E. Qeli, B. Agel, D. Seiler, and B. Freisleben. University of Marburg at TRECVID 2006: Shot Boundary Detection and Rushes Task Results. In *Proceedings of TREC Video Retrieval Evaluation Workshop (TRECVid'06)*. Available online, 2006. URL http://www-nlpir.nist.gov/projects/tvpubs/tv.pubs.org.htm.

R. Ewerth, M. Mühling, and B. Freisleben. Self-Supervised Learning of Face Appearances in TV Casts and Movies. *International Journal on Semantic Computing*, 1(2):185–204, 2007a.

R. Ewerth, M. Mühling, T. Stadelmann, J. Gllavata, M. Grauer, and B. Freisleben. Videana: A Software Toolkit for Scientific Film Studies. In *Proceedings of the International Workshop on Digital Tools in Film Studies*, pages 1–16, Siegen, Germany, 2007b. Transcript Verlag.

M. Faúndez-Zanuy and E. Monte-Moreno. State-of-the-Art in Speaker Recognition. *IEEE Aerospace and Electronic Systems Magazine*, 20:7–12, 2005.

M. Faúndez-Zanuy, G. Kubin, W. B. Kleijn, P. Maragos, S. McLaughlin, A. Esposito, A. Hussain, and J. Schoentgen. Nonlinear Speech Processing: Overview and Applications. *International Journal of Control and Intelligent Systems*, 30(2):1–10, 2002.

G. Fant. *Acoustic Theory of Speech Production*. Mouton & Co, The Hague, The Netherlands, 1960.

B. Fergani, M. Davy, and A. Houacine. Unsupervised Speaker Indexing Using One-Class Support Vector Machines. In *Proceedings of the 14th Eurpoean Signal Processing Conference (EUSIPCO'06)*, Florence, Italy, September 2006. Eurasip.

B. Fergani, M. Davy, and A. Houacine. Speaker Diarization using One-Class Support Vector Machines. *Speech Communication*, 50:355–365, 2008.

L. Ferrer, H. Bratt, V. R. R. Gadde, S. Kajarekar, E. Shriberg, K. Sönmez, A. Stolcke, and A. Venkataraman. Modeling Duration Patterns for Speaker Recognition. In *Proceedings of the 8th European Conference on Speech Communication and Technology (Eurospeech'03)*, pages 2017–2020, Geneva, Switzerland, September 2003. ISCA.

M. Fink, M. Cevell, and S. Baluja. Social- and Interactive-Television Applications Based on Real-Time Ambient-Audio Identification. In *Proceedings of the 4th European Interactive TV Conference (Euro-ITV'06)*, Athens, Greece, May 2006. Best paper award.

Bibliography

W. M. Fisher, G. R. Doddington, and K. M. Goudie-Marshall. The DARPA Speech Recognition Research Database: Specification and Status. In *Proceedings of the DARPA Speech Recognition Workshop*, pages SAIC–86/1546, Palo-Alto, CA, USA, February 1986. DARPA.

J. Foote. Visualizing Music and Audio Using Self-Similarity. In *Proceedings of the 7th ACM International Conference on Multimedia (ACMMM'99)*, pages 77–80, Orlando, FL, USA, October 1999. ACM.

J. Foote. Automatic Audio Segmentation Using a Measure of Audio Novelty. In *Proceedings of the IEEE International Conference on Multimedia and Expo (ICME'00)*, volume 1, pages 452–455, New York, NY, USA, July 2000. IEEE.

I. Foster and C. Kesselman. *The Grid 2: Blueprint for a New Computing Infrastructure*. Morgan Kaufmann, 2nd edition, December 2003.

Y. Freund and R. E. Schapire. A Decision-Theoretic Generalization of On-Line Learning and an Application to Boosting. *Journal of Computer and System Sciences*, 55(1):119–139, August 1997.

G. Friedland. Analytics for experts. *ACM SIGMM Records*, 1(1), March 2009.

G. Friedland, O. Vinyals, Y. Huang, and C. Müller. Prosodic and other Long-Term Features for Speaker Diarization. *IEEE Transactions on Speech and Audio Processing*, 17:985–993, 2009.

S. Furui. *Digital Speech Processing, Synthesis, and Recognition. Second Edition, Revised and Expanded*. Marcel Dekker, New York, Basel, 2001.

S. Furui. 50 Years of Progress in Speech and Speaker Recognition. In *Proceedings of the 10th International Conferences Speech and Computer (SPECOM'05)*, pages 1–9, Patras, Greece, October 2005.

S. Furui. 40 Years of Progress in Automatic Speaker Recognition. In *Proceedings of the 3rd International Conference on Advances in Biometrics (ICB'09)*, pages 1050–1059, Sassari, Italy, June 2009. IAPR/IEEE.

M. J. F. Gales. *Model-Based Techniques for Noise Robust Speech Recognition*. PhD thesis, Cambridge University, UK, 1996.

M. J. F. Gales and S. Young. An Improved Approach to the Hidden Markov Model Decomposition of Speech and Noise. In *Proceedings of the 17th IEEE International Conference on Acoustics, Speech, and Signal Processing (ICASSP'92)*, volume 1, pages 233–236, San Francisco, CA, USA, March 1992. IEEE.

Bibliography

M. J. F. Gales, D. Y. Kim, P. C. Woodland, H. Y. Chan, D. Mrva, R. Sinha, and S. E. Tranter. Progress in the CU-HTK Broadcast News Transcription System. *IEEE Transactions on Audio, Speech, and Language Processing*, 14(5):1513–1525, September 2006.

T. Ganchev, N. Fakotakis, and G. Kokkinakis. Comparative Evaluation of Various MFCC Implementations on the Speaker Verification Task. In *Proceedings of the 10th International Conference on Speech and Computer (SPECOM'05)*, pages 191–194, Patras, Greece, October 2005.

H. Gish, M.-H. Siu, and R. Rohlicek. Segregation of Speakers for Speech Recognition and Speaker Identification. In *Proceedings of the 16th IEEE International Conference on Acoustics, Speech, and Signal Processing (ICASSP'91)*, volume 2, pages 873–876, Toronto, Canada, May 1991. IEEE.

Globus Alliance. The Globus Toolkit Homepage. Online web resource, 2010. URL http://www.globus.org/toolkit/. Visited 23. February 2010.

B. Goertzel and C. Pennachin. *Artificial General Intelligence*. Springer, Berlin, Heidelberg, Germany, 2007.

Z. Goh, K.-C. Tan, , and B. T. G. Tan. Postprocessing Method for Suppressing Musical Noise Generated by Spectral Subtraction. *IEEE Transactions on Speech and Audio Processing*, 6: 287–292, 1998.

J. Goldberger and H. Aronowitz. A Distance Measure Between GMMs Based on the Unscented Transform and its Application to Speaker Recognition. In *Proceedings of the 9th European Conference on Speech Communication and Technology (Interspeech'05–Eurospeech)*, pages 1985–1989, Lisbon, Portugal, September 2005. ISCA.

K. Grauman and T. Darrell. Fast Contour Matching Using Approximate Earth Mover's Distance. In *Proceedings of the IEEE Computer Society Conference on Computer Vision and Pattern Recognition (CVPR'04)*, pages 220–227, Washington DC, USA, June 2004. IEEE.

D. W. Griffin and J. S. Lim. Signal Estimation from Modified Short-Time Fourier Transform. *IEEE Transactions on Acoustics, Speech, and Signal Processing*, 32:236–243, 1984.

V. Gupta, P. Kenny, P. Ouellet, G. Boulianne, and P. Dumouchel. Combining Gaussianized/Non-Gaussianized Features to Improve Speaker Diarization of Telephone Conversations. *IEEE Signal Processing Letters*, 14(12):1040–1043, 2007.

S. Guruprasad, N. Dhananjaya, and B. Yegnanarayana. AANN Model for Speaker Recognition Based on Difference Cepstrals. In *Proceedings of the International Joint Conference on Neural Networks (IJCNN'03)*, pages 692–697, Portland, OR, USA, July 2003. IEEE.

K. J. Han and S. S. Narayanan. A Robust Stopping Criterion for Agglomerative Hierarchical Clustering in a Speaker Diarization System. In *Proceedings of the 8th Interspeech'07—Eurospeech*, pages 1853–1856, Antwerpen, Belgium, August 2007. ISCA.

K. J. Han and S. S. Narayanan. Signature Cluster Model Selection for Incremental Gaussian Mixture Cluster Modeling in Agglomerative Hierarchical Speaker Clustering. In *Proceedings of the 10th Annual Conference of the International Speech Communication Association (Interspeech'09)*, Brighton, UK, September 2009. ISCA.

K. J. Han, S. Kim, and S. S. Narayanan. Strategies to Improve the Robustness of Agglomerative Hierarchical Clustering Under Data Source Variation for Speaker Diarization. *IEEE Transactions on Audio, Speech, and Language Processing*, 16:1590–1601, 2008.

M. Hasegawa-Johnson and A. Alwan. Speech Coding: Fundamentals and Applications. In J. Proakis, editor, *Wiley Encyclopedia of Telecommunications and Signal Processing*. Wiley, 2002.

A. Haubold and J. R. Kender. Accomodating Sample Size Effect on Similarity Measures in Speaker Clustering. In *Proceedings of the IEEE International Conference on Multimedia & Expo (ICME'08)*, pages 1525–1528, Hannover, Germany, June 2008. IEEE.

J. He. Jialong He's Speaker Recognition (Identification) Tool. Online web resource, 1997. URL http://www.speech.cs.cmu.edu/comp.speech/Section6/Verification/jialong.html. Visited 19. February 2010.

R. M. Hegde, H. A. Murthy, and G. V. R. Rao. Application of the Modified Group Delay Function to Speaker Identification and Discrimination. In *Proceedings of the 29th IEEE International Conference on Acoustics, Speech, and Signal Processing (ICASSP'04)*, volume I, pages 517–520, Montreal, QC, Canada, May 2004. IEEE.

R. Hegger, H. Kantz, and T. Schreiber. Practical Implementation of Nonlinear Time Series Methods: The TISEAN Package. *Chaos*, 9:413–435, 1999. URL http://www.mpipks-dresden.mpg.de/~tisean/. Visited 18. March 2010.

M. Heidt, T. Dörnemann, K. Dörnemann, and B. Freisleben. Omnivore: Integration of Grid Meta-Scheduling and Peer-to-Peer Technologies. In *Proceedings of the 8th IEEE International*

Bibliography

Symposium on Cluster Computing and the Grid (CCGrid'08), pages 316–323, Lyon, France, May 2008.

S. Heinzl, M. Mathes, T. Friese, M. Smith, and B. Freisleben. Flex-SwA: Flexible Exchange of Binary Data Based on SOAP Messages with Attachments. In *Proceedings of the IEEE International Conference on Web Services (ICWS'06)*, pages 3–10, Chicago, USA, September 2006. IEEE Press.

S. Heinzl, M. Mathes, and B. Freisleben. A Web Service Communication Policy for Describing Non-Standard Application Requirements. In *Proceedings of the IEEE/IPSJ Symposium on Applications and the Internet (Saint'08)*, pages 40–47, Turku, Finland, July 2008a. IEEE Computer Society Press.

S. Heinzl, M. Mathes, and B. Freisleben. The Grid Browser: Improving Usability in Service-Oriented Grids by Automatically Generating Clients and Handling Data Transfers. In *Proceedings of the 4th IEEE International Conference on eScience*, pages 269–276, Indianapolis, IN, USA, December 2008b. IEEE Press.

S. Heinzl, M. Mathes, T. Stadelmann, D. Seiler, M. Diegelmann, H. Dohmann, and B. Freisleben. The Web Service Browser: Automatic Client Generation and Efficient Data Transfer for Web Services. In *Proceedings of the 7th IEEE International Conference on Web Services (ICWS'09)*, pages 743–750, Los Angeles, CA, USA, July 2009a. IEEE Press.

S. Heinzl, D. Seiler, E. Juhnke, T. Stadelmann, R. Ewerth, M. Grauer, and B. Freisleben. A Scalable Service-Oriented Architecture for Multimedia Analysis, Synthesis, and Consumption. *International Journal of Web and Grid Services*, 5(3):219–260, 2009b. Inderscience Publishers.

S. Heinzl, D. Seiler, M. Unterberger, A. Nonenmacher, and B. Freisleben. MIRO: A Mashup Editor Leveraging Web, Grid and Cloud Services . In *Proceedings of the 11th International Conference on Information Integration and Web-based Applications & Services (iiWAS'09)*, pages 15–22, Kuala Lumpur, Malaysia, December 2009c. ACM and OCG.

D. R. Hill. Speaker Classification Concepts: Past, Present and Future. In C. Müller, editor, *Speaker Classification I – Fundamentals, Features, and Methods*, volume 4343 of *LNAI*, chapter 2, pages 21–46. Springer, 2007.

T. Hofmann. Probabilistic Latent Semantic Analysis. In *Proceedings of the 15th Annual Conference in Uncertainty in Artificial Intelligence (UAI'99)*, pages 289–296, Stockholm, Sweden, July 1999.

Bibliography

R. C. Holte. Very Simple Classification Rules Perform Well on Most Commonly Used Datasets. *Machine Learning*, 11:63–90, 1993.

Y. Hu and P. C. Loizou. Subjective Comparison of Speech Enhancement Algorithms. In *Proceedings of the 31st IEEE International Conference on Acoustics, Speech, and Signal Processing (ICASSP'06)*, volume 1, pages 153–156, Toulouse, France, May 2006. IEEE.

H. Huang and J. Pan. Speech Pitch Determination Based on Hilbert-Huang Transform. *Signal Processing*, 86:792–803, 2006.

N. E. Huang, Z. Shen, S. R. Long, M. C. Wu, H. H. Shih, Q. Zheng, N.-C. Yen, C. C. Tung, and H. H. Liu. The Empirical Mode Decomposition and the Hilbert Spectrum for Nonlinear and Non-Stationary Time Series Analysis. *Proceedings of the Royal Scoiety London A*, 454: 903–995, 1998.

M. A. H. Huijbregts. *Segmentation, Diarization and Speech Transcription: Surprise Data Unraveled*. PhD thesis, Universiteit Twente, Twente, The Netherlands, November 2008. URL http://wwwhome.cs.utwente.nl/~huijbreg/shout/index.html. Visited 18. March 2010.

A. N. Iyer, U. O. Ofoegbu, R. E. Yantorno, and B. Y. Smolenski. Speaker Distinguishing Distances: A Comparative Study. *International Journal of Speech Technology*, 10:95–107, 2007.

E. Jafer and A. E. Mahdi. A Wavelet-based Voiced/Unvoiced Classification Algorithm. In *Proceedings of the 4th EURASIP Conference Focused on Video/Image Processing and Multimedia Communications (EC-VIP-MC'03)*, volume 2, pages 667–672, 2003.

H. Jayanna and S. M. Prasanna. Multiple Frame Size and Rate Analysis for Speaker Recognition under Limited Data Condition. *IET Signal Processing*, 3(3):189–204, 2009.

M. Jessen and M. Jessen. Forensische Sprechererkennung und Tonträgerauswertung in Praxis und Forschung—Teil 2. *Die Kriminalpolizei*, 1:30–33, 2009.

W. Jiang, C. Cotton, S.-F. Chang, D. Ellis, and A. Loui. Short-Term Audio-Visual Atoms for Generic Video Concept Classification. In *Proceedings of the ACM International Conference on Multimedia (ACMMM'09)*, pages 5–14, Beijing, China, October 2009. ACM. Best paper candidate.

H. Jin, F. Kubala, and R. Schwartz. Automatic Speaker Clustering. In *Proceedings of the DARPA Speech Recognition Workshop*, pages 108–111, 1997.

Bibliography

K. Jingqiu, L. Yibing, M. Zhiyong, and Y. Keguo. Improved Algorithm of Correlation Dimension Estimation and its Application in Fault Diagnosis for Industrial Fan. In *Proceedings of the 25th Chinese Control Conference (CCC'06)*, pages 1291–1296, Harbin, Heilongjiang, China, August 2006.

T. Joachims. Transductive Inference for Text Classification using Support Vector Machines. In *Proceedings of the 16th International Conference on Machine Learning (ICML'99)*, pages 200–209, Bled, Slovenia, June 1999.

C. Joder, S. Essid, and G. Richard. Temporal Integration for Audio Classification With Application to Musical Instrument Classification. *IEEE Transactions on Audio, Speech, and Language Processing*, 17:174–186, 2009.

E. Juhnke, D. Seiler, T. Stadelmann, T. Dörnemann, and B. Freisleben. LCDL: An Extensible Framework for Wrapping Legacy Code. In *Proceedings of International Workshop on @WAS Emerging Research Projects, Applications and Services (ERPAS'09)*, pages 638–642, Kuala Lumpur, Malaysia, December 2009.

S. S. Kajarekar, N. Scheffer, M. Graciarena, E. Shriberg, A. Stolcke, L. Ferrer, and T. Bocklet. The SRI NIST 2008 Speaker Recognition Evaluation System. In *Proceedings of the 34th IEEE International Conference on Acoustics, Speech, and Signal Processing (ICASSP'09)*, pages 4205–4208, Taipei, Taiwan, April 2009. IEEE.

H. Kantz and T. Schreiber. *Nonlinear Time Series Analysis*. Cambridge University Press, Cambridge, UK, 2nd edition, 2004.

V. Kartik, D. Srikrishna Satish, and C. Chandra Sekhar. Speaker Change Detection using Support Vector Machines. In *Proceedings of ISCA Tutorial and Research Workshop on Non-Linear Speech Processing (NOLISP'05)*, pages 130–136, Barcelona, Spain, April 2005. ISCA.

P. A. Keating and C. Esposito. Linguistic Voice Quality. *UCLA Working Papers in Phonetics*, 105:85–91, 2007.

D. A. Keim. Information Visualization and Visual Data Mining. *IEEE Transactions on Visualization and Computer Graphics*, 7(1):100–107, January–March 2002.

E. Keogh, S. Lonardi, and C. A. Ratanamahatana. Towards Parameter-Free Data Mining. In *Proceedings of the 10th International Conference on Knowledge Discovery and Data Mining (KDD'04)*, pages 206–215, Seattle, USA, August 2004. ACM SIGKDD.

D.-S. Kim. On the Perceptually Irrelevant Phase Information in Sinusoidal Representation of Speech. *IEEE Transactions on Speech and Audio Processing*, 9(8):900–905, November 2001.

T. Kinnunen and H. Li. An Overview of Text-Independent Speaker Recognition: from Features to Supervectors. *Speech Communication*, 52:12–40, 2010. doi: 10.1016/j.specom.2009.08.009.

S. Kizhner, T. P. Flatley, N. E. Huang, K. Blank, and E. Conwell. On the Hilbert-Huang Transform Data Processing System Development. In *Proceedings of the IEEE Aerospace Conference (IEEEAC'04)*, pages 1961–1979, 2004.

D. H. Klatt. A Digital Filterbank For Spectral Matching. In *Proceedings of the 1st IEEE International Conference on Acoustics, Speech, and Signal Processing (ICASSP'76)*, pages 573–576, Philadelphia, PA, USA, April 1976. IEEE.

W. B. Kleijn and K. K. Paliwal. *Speech Coding and Synthesis*. Elsevier Science Inc., New York, NY, USA, 1995.

D. E. Knuth. *The Art of Computer Programming, Volume 2: Seminumerical Algorithms, Third Edition*. Addison Wesley, USA, 1998.

I. Kokkino and P. Maragos. Nonlinear Speech Analysis Using Models for Chaotic Systems. *IEEE Transactions on Speech and Audio Processing*, 13(6):1098–1109, November 2005.

M. Köppen. The Curse of Dimensionality. In *Proceedings of the 5th Online World Conference on Soft Computing in Industrial Applications (WSC5)*, Held on the internet, September 2000.

S. B. Kotsiantis, I. D. Zaharakis, and P. E. Pintelas. Machine Learning: A Review of Classification and Combining Techniques. *Arificial Intelligence Review*, 26(3):159–190, November 2006.

M. Kotti, E. Benetos, and C. Kotropoulos. Computationally Efficient and Robust BIC-Based Speaker Segmentation. *IEEE Transactions on Audio, Speech, and Language Processing*, 16:920–933, 2008a.

M. Kotti, V. Moschou, and C. Kotropoulos. Speaker Segmentation and Clustering. *Signal Processing*, 88:1091–1124, 2008b.

K. L. Kroeker. Face Recognition Breakthrough. *Communications of the ACM*, 52(8):18–19, August 2009.

S. Krstulovic and R. Gribonval. MPTK: Matching Pursuit Made Tractable. In *Proceedings of the 31st IEEE International Conference on Acoustics, Speech, and Signal Processing (ICASSP'06)*, volume 3, pages 496–499, Toulouse, France, May 2006. IEEE. URL http://mptk.irisa.fr/. Visited 18. March 2010.

Bibliography

S. Kuroiwa, Y. Umeda, S. Tsuge, and F. Ren. Nonparametric Speaker Recognition Method Using Earth Mover'sDistance. *IEICE Transactions on Information and Systems*, E89–D(3): 1074–1081, March 2006.

U. Küsters. Data Mining Methoden: Einordnung und Überblick. In H. Hippner, U. Küsters, M. Meyer, and K. Wilde, editors, *Handbuch Data Mining im Marketing, Knowledge Discovery in Marketing Databases*, pages 95–130. Vieweg, 2001.

P. Ladefoged. *Vowels and Consonants*. Blackwell Publishing, 2nd edition, 2005.

A. Larcher, J.-F. Bonastre, and J. S. D. Mason. Short Utterance-based Video Aided Speaker Recognition. In *Proceedings of the 10th IEEE Workshop on Multimedia Signal Processing (MMSP'08)*, pages 897–901, Cairns, Queensland, Australia, October 2008. IEEE.

LASG Forum. Explanations of Misconception in a Wavelet Analysis Paper by Torrence and Compo and in EMD-HHT Method by Huang. Online web resource, September 2004. URL http://bbs.lasg.ac.cn/bbs/thread-3380-1-1.html. Visited 05. March 2010.

E. Levina and P. Bickel. The Earth Mover's Distance is the Mallows Distance: Some Insights from Statistics. In *Proceedings of the 8th IEEE International Conference on Computer Vision (ICCV'01)*, volume 2, pages 251–256, Vancouver, BC, Canada, July 2001. IEEE.

Y. Li, S. S. Narayanan, and C.-C. J. Kuo. Content-Based Movie Analysis and Indexing Based on Audiovisual Cues. *IEEE Transactions on Circuits and Systems for Video Technology*, 14: 1073–1085, 2004.

B. Lindblom, R. Diehl, and C. Creeger. Do 'Dominant Frequencies' Explain the Listener's Response to Formant and Spectrum Shape Variations? *Speech Communication*, 2008. doi: 10.1016/j.specom.2008.12.003.

Y. Linde, A. Buzo, and R. M. Gray. An Algorithm for Vector Quantizer Design. *IEEE Transactions on Communications*, 28(1):84–95, 1980.

Linguistic Data Consortium. The DARPA TIMIT Acoustic-Phonetic Continuous Speech Corpus. Online web resource, 1990. URL http://www.ldc.upenn.edu/Catalog/readme_files/timit.readme.html. Visited 24. February 2010.

D. Liu and F. Kubala. Online Speaker Clustering. In *Proceedings of the 29th IEEE International Conference on Acoustics, Speech, and Signal Processing (ICASSP'04)*, volume 1, pages 333–336, Montreal, QC, Canada, May 2004. IEEE.

L. Liu and J. He. On the Use of Orthogonal GMM in Speaker Recognition. In *Proceedings of the 24th IEEE International Conference on Acoustics, Speech, and Signal Processing (ICASSP'99)*, volume 2, pages 845–848, Phoenix, AZ, USA, March 1999. IEEE.

B. T. Logan and A. J. Robinson. Enhancement and Recognition of Noisy Speech Within an Autoregressive Hidden Markov Model Framework Using Noise Estimates from the Noisy Signal. In *Proceedings of the 22nd IEEE International Conference on Acoustics, Speech, and Signal Processing (ICASSP'97)*, volume 2, pages 843–846, Munich, Germany, April 1997. IEEE.

B. T. Logan and A. Salomon. A Music Similarity Function Based On Signal Analysis. In *Proceedings of the IEEE International Conference on Multimedia and Expo (ICME'01)*, pages 190–193, Tokyo, Japan, August 2001. IEEE.

L. Lu and H.-J. Zhang. Real-Time Unsupervised Speaker Change Detection. In *Proceedings of the 16th International Conference on Pattern Recognition (ICPR'02)*, volume 2, pages 358–261, Quebec City, Canada, August 2002.

L. Lu and H.-J. Zhang. Unsupervised Speaker Segmentation and Tracking in Real-Time Audio Content Analysis. *Multimedia Systems*, 10:332–343, 2005.

L. Lu, H.-J. Zhang, and S. Z. Li. Content-Based Audio Classification and Segmentation by Using Support Vector Machines. *Multimedia Systems*, 8(6):482–492, April 2003.

P. Macklin. EasyBMP: Cross-Platform Windows Bitmap Library . Online weg resource, 2006. URL http://easybmp.sourceforge.net/. Visited 22. February 2010.

J. Makhoul, F. Kubala, T. Leek, D. Liu, L. Nguyen, R. Schwartz, and A. Srivastava. Speech and Language Technologies for Audio Indexing and Retrieval. *Proceedings of the IEEE*, 88: 1338–1353, 2000.

A. S. Malegaonkar, A. M. Ariyaeeinia, P. Sivakumaran, and S. G. Pillay. Discrimination Effectiveness of Speech Cepstral Features. *Lecture Notes in Computer Science*, 5372:91–99, 2008.

S. Mallat. *A Wavelet Tour of Signal Processing*. Academic Press, 2nd edition, 2001.

B. B. Mandelbrot. *The Fractal Geometry of Nature*. Henry Holt, updated edition, 2000.

K. V. Mardia, J. T. Kent, and J. M. Bibby. *Multivariate Analysis*. Academic Press, 1979.

J. M. Martinez, R. Koenen, and F. Pereira. MPEG-7: The Generic Multimedia Content Description Standard, Part 1. *IEEE MultiMedia*, 9(2):78–87, April–June 2002.

Bibliography

L. Mary and B. Yegnanarayana. Extraction and Representation of Prosodic Features. *Speech Communication*, 2008. doi: 10.1016/j.specom.2008.04.010.

I. V. McLoughlin. Line Spectral Pairs. *Signal Processing*, 88:448–467, 2008.

S. Meignier, D. Moraru, C. Fredouille, J.-F. Bonastre, and L. Besacier. Step-by-Step and Integrated Approaches in Broadcast News Speaker Diarization. *Computer Speech and Language*, 20:303–330, 2006.

B. A. Mellor and A. P. Varga. Noise Masking in a Transformed Domain. In *Proceedings of the 18th IEEE International Conference on Acoustics, Speech, and Signal Processing (ICASSP'93)*, volume 2, pages 87–90, Minneapolis, MN, USA, April 1993. IEEE.

T. Merlin, J.-F. Bonastre, and C. Fredouille. Non Directly Acoustic Process for Costless Speaker Recognition and Indexation. In *Proceedings of the International Workshop on Intelligent Communication Technologies and Applications, With Emphasis on Mobile Communications (COST 254)*, Neuchatel, Switzerland, May 1999.

B. Milner and X. Shao. Speech Reconstruction from Mel-Frequency Cepstral Coefficients using a Source-Filter Model. In *Proceedings of the 7th International Conference on Spoken Language Processing (ICSLP Interspeech'02)*, pages 2421–2424, Denver, CO, USA, September 2002. ISCA.

B. Milner and X. Shao. Clean Speech Reconstruction from MFCC Vectors and Fundamental Frequency using an Integrated Front-End. *Speech Communication*, 48:697–715, 2006.

T. M. Mitchell. *Machine Learning*. WCB/McGraw-Hill, USA, 1997.

B. C. J. Moore. World of the mind: hearing. Online web resource, 1987. URL http://www.answers.com/topic/hearing-7. Visited 03. March 2010.

B. C. J. Moore. *Psychology of Hearing, Fifth Edition*. Elsevier Academic Press, London, UK, 2004.

A. Morris, D. Wu, and J. Koreman. GMM based Clustering and Speaker Separability in the TIMIT Speech Database. Technical Report Saar-IP-08-08-2004, Saarland University, 2004.

V. Moschou, M. Kotti, E. Benetos, and C. Kotropoulos. Systematic Comparison of BIC-Based Speaker Segmentation Systems. In *Proceedings of th 9th International Workshop Multimedia Signal Processing (MMSP'07)*, Chania, Greece, October 2007.

Mozilla Developer Center. LiveConnect. Online web resource, 2009. URL https://developer.mozilla.org/en/LiveConnect. Visited 18. March 2010.

MPEG 7 Requirement Group. Description of MPEG 7 Content Set. *ISO/IEC JTC1/SC29/WG11/N2467*, 1998.

M. Mühling, R. Ewerth, T. Stadelmann, B. Freisleben, R. Weber, and K. Mathiak. Semantic Video Analysis for Psychological Research on Violence in Computer Games. In *Proceedings of the ACM International Conference on Image and Video Retrieval (CIVR'07)*, pages 611–618, Amsterdam, The Netherlands, July 2007a. ACM.

M. Mühling, R. Ewerth, T. Stadelmann, B. Shi, C. Zöfel, and B. Freisleben. University of Marburg at TRECVID 2007: Shot Boundary Detection and High-Level Feature Extraction. In *Proceedings of TREC Video Retrieval Evaluation Workshop (TRECVid'07)*. Available online, 2007b. URL http://www-nlpir.nist.gov/projects/tvpubs/tv.pubs.org.htm.

M. Mühling, R. Ewerth, T. Stadelmann, B. Shi, and B. Freisleben. University of Marburg at TRECVID 2008: High-Level Feature Extraction. In *Proceedings of TREC Video Retrieval Evaluation Workshop (TRECVid'08)*. Available online, 2008. URL http://www-nlpir.nist.gov/projects/tvpubs/tv.pubs.org.htm.

M. Mühling, R. Ewerth, T. Stadelmann, B. Shi, and B. Freisleben. University of Marburg at TRECVID 2009: High-Level Feature Extraction. In *Proceedings of TREC Video Retrieval Evaluation Workshop (TRECVid'09)*. Available online, 2009. URL http://www-nlpir.nist.gov/projects/tvpubs/tv.pubs.org.htm.

T. Munakata. *Fundamentals of the New Artificial Intelligence: Neural, Evolutionary, Fuzzy and More*. Springer, London, UK, 2nd edition, 2008.

R. Munkong and B.-H. Juang. Auditory Perception and Cognition. *IEEE Signal Prcessing Magazine*, pages 98–117, May 2008.

H. A. Murthy and V. Gadde. The Modified Group Delay Function and its Application to Phoneme Recognition. In *Proceedings of the 28th IEEE International Conference on Acoustics, Speech, and Signal Processing (ICASSP'03)*, volume 1, pages 68–71, Hong Kong, China, April 2003. IEEE.

A. Nádas, D. Nahamoo, and M. A. Picheny. Speech Recognition Using Noise-Adaptive Prototypes. *IEEE Transactions on Acoustics, Speech and Signal Processing*, 37:1495–1503, 1989.

B. Neumann. C++ Implementierung der MD5-Prüfsumme. Online web resource, 2007. URL http://www.ben-newman.de/com/MD5.php. Visited 23. February 2010.

Bibliography

R. J. Niederjohn and J. A. Heinen. Understanding Speech Corrupted by Noise. In *Proceedings of the IEEE International Conference on Industrial Technology (ICIT'96)*, pages P1–P5, Shanghai, 1996. IEEE.

M. Nishida and T. Kawahara. Speaker Indexing for News Articles, Debates and Drama in Broadcast TV Programs. In *Proceedings of the IEEE International Conference on Multimedia Computing and Systems (ICMCS'99)*, volume 2, pages 466–471, Los Alamitos, CA, USA, June 1999. IEEE.

S. Nissen. Neural Networks Made Simple. *Software 2.0*, 2:14–19, 2005. URL http://leenissen.dk/fann/. Visited 18. March 2010.

NIST/SEMATECH. e-Hanfbook of Statistical Methods. Online web resource, 2003. URL http://www.itl.nist.gov/div898/handbook/. Visited 10. March 2010.

H. Nyquist. Certain Topics in Telegraph Transmission Theory. *Proceedings of the IEEE*, 90(2): 280–305, February 2002. Reprint of classic paper from 1928.

A. V. Oppenheim and R. W. Schafer. From Frequency to Quefrency: A History of the Cepstrum. *IEE Signal Processing Magazine*, pages 95–106, September 2004.

N. Otsu. A Threshold Selection Method from Gray Level Histograms. *IEEE Transactions on Systems, Man and Cybernetics*, 9:62–66, March 1979.

F. Pachet and P. Roy. Exploring Billions of Audio Features. In *Proceedings of the 5th International Workshop on Conten-Based Multimedia Indexing (CBMI'07)*, pages 227–235, Bordeaux, France, June 2007. IEEE, Eurasip.

M. Pardo and G. Sberveglieri. Learning From Data: A Tutorial With Emphasis on Modern Pattern Recognition Methods. *IEEE Sensors Journal*, 2(3):203–217, 2002.

O. Parviainen. Time and Pitch Scaling in Audio Processing. *Software Developer's Journal*, 4, 2006. URL http://www.surina.net/soundtouch/. Visited 18. March 2010.

R. D. Patterson. Auditory Images: How Complex Sounds are Represented in the Auditory System. *Journal of the Acoustical Society of Japan*, 21(4):183–190, 2000.

Y. Peng, Z. Lu, and J. Xiao. Semantic Concept Annotation Based on Audio PLSA Model. In *Proceedings of the ACM International Conference on Multimedia (ACMMM'09)*, pages 841–845, Beijing, China, October 2009. ACM.

C. A. Pickover. On the Use of Symmetrized Dot Patterns for the Visual Characterization of Speech Waveforms and Other Sampled Data. *Journal of the Acoustic Society of America*, 80:955–960, 1986.

C. A. Pickover. *Computers, Pattern, Chaos, and Beauty: Graphics from an Unseen World.* St. Martin's Press, New York, NY, USA, 1990.

C. A. Pickover and A. Khorasani. Fractal Characterization of Speech Waveform Graphs. *Computers & Graphics*, 10(1):51–61, 1986.

J. W. Picone. Signal Modeling Techniques in Speech Recognition. *Proceedings of the IEEE*, 81 (9):1215–1247, September 1993.

J. C. Platt. Fast Training of Support Vector Machines Using Sequential Minimal Optimization. In B. Schölkopf, C. J. Burges, and A. J. Smola, editors, *Advances in Kernel Methods: Support Vector Learning*, pages 185–208. MIT Press, April 1999.

M. F. Porter. An Algorithm for Suffix Stemming. *Program*, 14(3):130–137, July 1980.

P. Prandoni and M. Vetterli. From Lagrange to Shannon... and Back: Another Look at Sampling. *IEEE Signal Processing Magazine*, pages 138–144, September 2009.

S. R. M. Prasanna, C. S. Gupta, and B. Yegnanarayana. Extraction of Speaker-Specific Excitation Information from Linear Prediction Residual of Speech. *Speech Communication*, 48: 1243–1261, 2006.

W. H. Press, B. P. Flannery, S. A. Teukolsky, and W. T. Vetterling. *Numerical Recipes in C.* Cambridge University Press, 1988.

M. Przybocki and A. Martin. NIST Speaker Recognition Evaluation Chronicles. In *Proceedings of the Speaker and Language Recognition Workshop (Odyssey'04)*, Toledo, Spain, May 2004. ISCA.

L. R. Rabiner. A Tutorial on Hidden Markov Models and Selected Applications in Speech Recognition. *Proceedings of the IEEE*, 77(2):257–286, 1989.

L. R. Rabiner and B.-H. Juang. *Fundamentals of Speech Recognition.* Prentice Hall, Upper Saddle River, NJ, USA, 1993.

L. R. Rabiner and R. W. Schafer. *Digital Processing of Speech Signals.* Prentice Hall, Englewood Cliffs, NJ, USA, 1978.

Bibliography

S. Rahman. Kristallographische Methoden zur Digitalen Stimmanalyse: Die Stimme als Realstruktur (Teil I). In *Proceedings of the 17th Annual Meeting of the German Association for Crystallography*, pages 100–101, Hannover, Germany, March 2009a. Oldenbourg Verlag.

S. Rahman. Kristallographische Methoden zur Digitalen Stimmanalyse: Die Stimme als Realstruktur (Teil II). In *Proceedings of the 17th Annual Meeting of the German Association for Crystallography*, pages 73–74, Hannover, Germany, March 2009b. Oldenbourg Verlag.

A. Ramsperger. *Strukturanalyse der Riboflavin Synthase aus* Methanococcus jannaschii. PhD thesis, Technischen Universität München, München, Germany, December 2005.

R. T. Rato, M. D. Ortigueira, and A. G. Batista. On the HHT, its Problems, and Some Solutions. *Mechanical Systems and Signal Processing*, 22(6):1374–1394, 2008.

D. A. Reynolds. Speaker Identification and Verification using Gaussian Mixture Speaker Models. *Speech Communication*, 17:91–108, 1995.

D. A. Reynolds and R. C. Rose. Robust Text-Independent Speaker Identification Using Gaussian Mixture Speaker Models. *IEEE Transactions on Speech and Audio Processing*, 3:72–83, 1995.

D. A. Reynolds and P. Torres-Carrasquillo. The MIT Lincoln Laboratory RT-04F Diarization Systems: Applications to Broadcast News and Telephone Conversations. In *Proceedings of the NIST Rich Transcription Workshop (RT'04)*. NIST, November 2004.

D. A. Reynolds and P. Torres-Carrasquillo. Approaches and Applications of Audio Diarization. In *Proceedings of the 30th IEEE International Conference on Acoustics, Speech, and Signal Processing (ICASSP'05)*, volume 5, pages 953–956, Philadelphia, PA, USA, March 2005. IEEE.

D. A. Reynolds, E. Singer, B. A. Carlson, G. C. O'Leary, J. J. McLaughlin, and M. A. Zissman. Blind Clustering of Speech Utterance Based on Speaker and Language Characteristics. In *Proceedings of the 5th International Conference on Spoken Languae Processing (ICSLP'98)*, pages 3193–3196, Sydney, Australia, November 1998. ISCA.

D. A. Reynolds, T. F. Quatieri, and R. B. Dunn. Speaker Verification Using Adapted Gaussian Mixture Models. *Digital Signal Processing*, 10:19–41, 2000.

D. A. Reynolds, W. Andrews, J. P. Campbell, J. Navratil, B. Peskin, A. G. Adami, Q. Jin, D. Klusacek, J. Abramson, R. Mihaescu, J. Godfrey, D. Jones, and B. Xiang. The SuperSID Project: Exploiting High-Level Information for High-Accuracy Speaker Recognition.

In *Proceedings of the 28th IEEE International Conference on Acoustics, Speech, and Signal Processing (ICASSP'03)*, volume 4, pages 784–787, Hong Kong, China, April 2003. IEEE.

D. A. Reynolds, W. M. Campbell, T. P. Gleason, C. B. Quillen, D. E. Sturim, P. A. Torres-Carrasquillo, and A. G. Adami. The 2004 MIT Lincoln Laboratory Speaker Recognition System. In *Proceedings of the 30th IEEE International Conference on Acoustics, Speech, and Signal Processing (ICASSP'05)*, volume 1, pages 177–180, Philadelphia, PA, USA, March 2005. IEEE.

R. Rifkin and A. Klautau. In Defense of One-Vs-All Classification. *Journal of Machine Learning Research*, 5:101–141, 2004.

G. Rigoll and S. Müller. Statistical Pattern Recognition Techniques for Multimodal Human Computer Interaction and Multimedia Information Processing. In *Proceedings of the International Workshop on Speech and Computer*, pages 60–69, Moscow, Russia, October 1999. Survey paper.

G. Rilling, P. Flandrin, and P. Gonçalvès. On Empirical Mode Decomposition and its Algorithms. In *Proceedings of the 6th IEEE/Eurasip Workshop on Nonlinear Signal and Image Processing (NSIP'03)*, Grado, Italy, June 2003.

P. Rose. *Forensic Speaker Identification*. Taylor & Francis, London and New York, 2002.

P. Rose. Technical Forensic Speaker Recognition: Evaluation, Types and Testing of Evidence. *Computer Speech and Language*, 20:159–191, 2006.

R. C. Rose, E. M. Hofstetter, and D. A. Reynolds. Integrated Models of Signal and Background with Application to Speaker Identification in Noise. *IEEE Transactions on Speech and Audio Processing*, 2:245–258, 1994.

Y. Rubner, L. Guibas, and C. Tomasi. The Earth Mover's Distance, Multi-Dimensional Scaling, and Color-Based Image Retrieval. In *Proceedings of the DARPA Image Understanding Workshop*, pages 661–668, New Orleans, MS, USA, May 1997. DARPA.

Y. Rubner, C. Tomasi, and L. J. Guibas. A Metric for Distributions with Applications to Image Databases. In *Proceedings of the 6th IEEE International Conference on Computer Vision (ICCV'98)*, pages 59–66, Bombay, India, January 1998. IEEE.

Y. Rubner, C. Tomasi, and L. J. Guibas. The Earth Mover's Distance as a Metric for Image Retrieval. *International Journal of Computer Vision*, 40:99–121, 2000.

H.-J. Sacht. *Bausteine für BASIC-Programme*. Humboldt-Taschenbuchverlag, 1988.

Bibliography

S. Salcedo-Sanz, A. Gallardo-Antolín, J. M. Leiva-Murillo, and C. Bousoño-Calzón. Offline Speaker Segmentation Using Genetic Algorithms and Mutual Information. *IEEE Transactions on Evolutionary Computation*, 10(2):175–186, 2006.

J. W. Sammon. A Nonlinear Mapping for Data Structure Analysis. *IEEE Transactions on Computers*, C-18(5):401–4009, May 1969.

L. Saul and M. Rahim. Markov Processes on Curves for Automatic Speech Recognition. In *Proceedings of the Conference on Advances in Neural Information Processing Systems II*, pages 751–757. MIT Press, 1998.

R. E. Schapire and Y. Singer. Improved Boosting Algorithms Using Confidence-rated Predictions. *Machine Learning*, 37(3):297–336, December 1999.

G. Schattauer. Fachmann für Kochsalz. *Focus*, 39:54–56, September 2007.

J. Schmidhuber. Driven by Compression Progress: A Simple Principle Explains Essential Aspects of Subjective Beauty, Novelty, Surprise, Interestingness, Attention, Curiosity, Creativity, Art, Science, Music, Jokes. In *Proceedings of the 12th International Conference on Knowledge-Based Intelligent Information and Engineering Systems*, volume 1 of *Lecture Notes in Artificial Intelligence 5177*, pages 11–45, Zagreb, Croatia, 2008. Springer.

B. Schölkopf and A. J. Smola. *Learning With Kernels*. Adaptive Computation and Machine Learning. MIT Press, Cambridge, Massachusetts, USA, 2002.

B. Schouten, M. Tistarelli, C. Garcia-Mateo, F. Deravi, and M. Meints. Nineteen Urgent Research Topics in Biometrics and Identity Management. *Lecture Notes in Computer Science*, 5372:228–235, 2008.

P. Schwarz. *Phoneme Recognition based on Long Temporal Context*. PhD thesis, Brno University of Technology, Czech Republic, 2009. URL http://speech.fit.vutbr.cz/en/software/phoneme-recognizer-based-long-temporal-context. Visited 18. March 2010.

R. Sedgewick. *Algorithms in C*. Computer Science. Addison Wesley, December 1990.

D. Seiler, R. Ewerth, S. Heinzl, T. Stadelmann, M. Mühling, B. Freisleben, and M. Grauer. Eine Service-Orientierte Grid-Infrastruktur zur Unterstützung Medienwissenschaftlicher Filmanalyse. In *Proceedings of the Workshop on Gemeinschaften in Neuen Medien (GeNeMe'09)*, pages 79–89, Dresden, Germany, September 2009.

C. C. Sekhar and M. Panaliswami. Classification of Multidimensional Trajectories for Acoustic Modeling Using Support Vector Machines. In *Proceedings of the International Conference on*

Intelligent Sensing and Information Processing (ICISIP'04), pages 153–158, Chennai, India, January 2004.

J. P. Seo, M. S. Kim, I. C. Baek, Y. H. Kwon, K. S. Lee, S. W. Chang, and S. I. Yang. Similar Speaker Recognition using Nonlinear Analysis. *Chaos, Solitons and Fractals*, 21(21):159–164, 2004.

J. K. Shah, A. N. Iyer, B. Y. Smolenski, and R. E. Yantorno. Robust Voiced/Unvoiced Classification using Novel Features and Gaussian Mixture Model. In *Proceedings of the 29th IEEE International Conference on Acoustics, Speech, and Signal Processing (ICASSP'04)*, Montreal, QC, Canada, May 2004. IEEE.

K. Sjölander. The Snack Sound Toolkit. Online web resource, 2004. URL http://www.speech.kth.se/snack/. Visited 22. February 2010.

S. S. Skiena. *The Algorithm Design Manual*. Springer, London, UK, 2nd edition, 2008.

A. F. Smeaton, P. Over, and W. Kraaij. Evaluation Campaigns and TRECVid. In *Proceedings of the 8th ACM International Workshop on Multimedia Information Retrieval (MIR'06)*, pages 321–330, Santa Barbara, CA, USA, October 2006. ACM.

A. F. Smeaton, P. Over, and W. Kraaij. High-Level Feature Detection from Video in TRECVid: a 5-Year Retrospective of Achievements. In A. Divakaran, editor, *Multimedia Content Analysis, Theory and Applications*, pages 151–174. Springer Verlag, Berlin, Germany, 2009.

S. W. Smith. *Digital Signal Processing—A Practical Guide for Engineers and Scientists*. Newnes, USA, 2003.

C. G. M. Snoek, M. Worring, J. C. van Gemert, J.-M. Geusebroek, and A. W. M. Smeulders. The Challenge Problem for Automated Detection of 101 Semantic Concepts in Multimedia. In *Proceedings of the ACM International Conference on Multimedia (ACMMM'06)*, pages 421–430, Sanat Barbara, CA, USA, October 2006. ACM.

M. K. Soenmez, L. Heck, M. Weintraub, and E. Shriberg. A Lognormal Tied Mixture Model of Pitch for Prosody-Based Speaker Recognition. In *Proceedings of the 5th European Conference on Speech Communication and Technology (Eurospeech'97)*, pages 1391–1394, Rhodes, Greece, September 1997. ISCA.

A. Solomonoff, A. Mielke, M. Schmidt, and H. Gish. Clustering Speakers by Their Voices. In *Proceedings of the 23rd IEEE International Conference on Acoustics, Speech, and Signal Processing (ICASSP'98)*, pages 757–760, Seattle, WA, USA, May 1998. IEEE.

Bibliography

N. Srinivasamurthy and S. Narayanan. Language-Adaptive Persian Speech Recognition. In *Proceedings of the 8th European Conference on Speech Communication and Technology (Eurospeech'03)*, pages 3137–3140, Geneva, Switzerland, September 2003. ISCA.

T. Stadelmann. Free Web Resources Contributing to the Movie Audio Classification Corpus. Online web resources, 2006. URL http://www.acoustica.com/sounds.htm;http: //www.alcljudprod.se/english/ljud.php;http://nature-downloads.naturesounds. ca/;http://www.ljudo.com/;http://www.meanrabbit.com/wavhtml/wavepage.htm; http://www.partnersinrhyme.com/;http://www.stonewashed.net/sfx.html;http: //www.soundhunter.com/. Visited 24. February 2010.

T. Stadelmann and B. Freisleben. Fast and Robust Speaker Clustering Using the Earth Mover's Distance and MixMax Models. In *Proceedings of the 31st IEEE International Conference on Acoustics, Speech, and Signal Processing (ICASSP'06)*, volume 1, pages 989–992, Toulouse, France, April 2006. IEEE.

T. Stadelmann and B. Freisleben. Unfolding Speaker Clustering Potential: A Biomimetic Approach. In *Proceedings of the ACM International Conference on Multimedia (ACMMM'09)*, pages 185–194, Beijing, China, October 2009. ACM.

T. Stadelmann and B. Freisleben. Dimension-Decoupled Gaussian Mixture Model for Short Utterance Speaker Recognition. In *Proceedings of the 20th International Conference on Pattern Recognition (ICPR'10)*, accepted for publication, Istanbul, Turkey, August 2010a. IAPR.

T. Stadelmann and B. Freisleben. On the MixMax Model and Cepstral Features for Noise-Robust Voice Recognition. Technical report, University of Marburg, Marburg, Germany, July 2010b.

T. Stadelmann, S. Heinzl, M. Unterberger, and B. Freisleben. WebVoice: A Toolkit for Perceptual Insights into Speech Processing. In *Proceedings of the 2nd International Congress on Image and Signal Processing (CISP'09)*, pages 4358–4362, Tianjin, China, October 2009.

T. Stadelmann, Y. Wang, M. Smith, R. Ewerth, and B. Freisleben. Rethinking Algorithm Development and Design in Speech Processing. In *Proceedings of the 20th International Conference on Pattern Recognition (ICPR'10)*, accepted for publication, Istanbul, Turkey, August 2010. IAPR.

H. Stöcker, editor. *Taschenbuch Mathematischer Formeln und Moderner Verfahren*. Verlag Harri Deutsch, Frankfurt am Main, Germany, 3rd revised and expanded edition, 1995.

D. E. Sturim, D. A. Reynolds, E. Singer, and J. P. Campbell. Speaker Indexing in Large Audio Databases using Anchor Models. In *Proceedings of the 26th IEEE International Conference on Acoustics, Speech, and Signal Processing (ICASSP'01)*, pages 429–432, Salt Lake City, UT, USA, May 2001. IEEE.

D. E. Sturim, W. M. Campbell, Z. N. Karam, D. A. Reynolds, and F. S. Richardson. The MIT Lincoln Laboratory 2008 Speaker Recognition System. In *Proceedings of the 10th Annual Conference of the International Speech Communication Association (Interspeech'09)*, Brighton, UK, September 2009. ISCA.

T. Su and J. G. Dy. In Search of Deterministic Methods for Initializing K-Means and Gaussian Mixture Clustering. *Intelligent Data Analysis*, 11:319–338, 2007.

Sun Developer Network. LiveConnect Support in the Next Generation Java™ Plug-In Technology Introduced in Java SE 6 update 10. Online web resource, 2010. URL http://java.sun.com/javase/6/webnotes/6u10/plugin2/liveconnect/index.html. Visited 18. March 2010.

Y. Suna, M. S. Kamel, A. K. C. Wong, and Y. Wang. Cost-Sensitive Boosting for Classification of Imbalanced Data. *Pattern Recognition*, 40(12):3358–3378, December 2007.

D. Talkin. A Robust Algorithm for Pitch Tracking (RAPT). In W. B. Klejin and K. K. Paliwal, editors, *Speech Coding and Synthesis*, chapter 3, pages 495–518. Elsevier Science, Amsterdam, NL, 1995.

D. M. J. Tax. *One-Class Classification—Concept-Learning in the Absence of Counter-Examples*. PhD thesis, Technische Universteit Delft, The Netherlands, 2001.

Texas Instruments. Specifications for the Analog to Digital Conversion of Voice by 2 400 Bit/Second Mixed Excitation Linear Prediction. Draft, May 1998.

K. Thearling, B. Becker, D. DeCoste, B. Mawby, M. Pilote, and D. Sommerfield. Visualizing Data Mining Models. In U. Fayyad, G. G. Grinstein, and A. Wierse, editors, *Information Visualization in Data Mining and Knowledge Discovery*, pages 205–222. Morgan Kaufmann Publishers, San Francisco, CA, USA, 2001.

T. Thiruvaran, E. Ambikairajah, and J. Epps. Group Delay Features for Speaker Recognition. In *Proceedings of the 6th International Conferences on Information, Communications and Signal Processing (ICICS'07)*, pages 1–5, Singapore, December 2007. IEEE.

C. Tomasi. Code for the Earth Movers Distance (EMD). Online web resource, 1998. URL http://www.cs.duke.edu/~tomasi/software/emd.htm. Visited 22. February 2010.

S. E. Tranter and D. A. Reynolds. An Overview of Automatic Speaker Diarization Systems. *IEEE Transactions on Audio, Speech, and Language Processing*, 14:1557–1565, 2006.

W.-H. Tsai and H.-M. Wang. A Query-by-Example Framework to Retrieve Music Documents by Singer. In *Proceedings of the IEEE International Conference on Multimedia and Expo (ICME'04)*, pages 1863–1866, Taipei, Taiwan, June 2004. IEEE.

W.-H. Tsai and H.-M. Wang. On the Extraction of Vocal-related Information to Facilitate the Management of Popular Music Collections. In *Proceedings of the Joint Conference on Digital Libraries (JCDL'05)*, pages 197–206, Denver, CO, USA, June 2005.

W.-H. Tsai and H.-M. Wang. Automatic Singer Recognition of Popular Music Recordings via Estimation and Modeling of Solo Voice Signals. *IEEE Transactions on Audio, Speech, and Language Processing*, 14:330–331, 2006.

W.-H. Tsai, D. Rodgers, and H.-M. Wang. Blind Clustering of Popular Music Recordings Based on Singer Voice Characteristics. *Computer Music Journal*, 28(3):68–78, 2004.

W.-H. Tsai, S.-S. Chen, and H.-M. Wang. Automatic Speaker Clustering using a Voice Characteristic Reference Space and Maximum Purity Estimation. *IEEE Transactions on Audio, Speech, and Language Processing*, 15:1461–1474, 2007.

Z. Tufekci, J. N. Gowdy, S. Gurbuz, and E. Patterson. Applied Mel-Frequency Wavelet Cofficients and Parallel Model Compensation for Noise-Robust Speech Recognition. *Speech Communication*, 48:1294–1307, 2006.

O. B. Tüzün, M. Demirekler, and K. B. Bakiboglu. Comparison of Parametric and Non-Parametric Representations of Speech for Recognition. In *Proceedings of the 7th Mediterranean Electrotechnical Conference (Melecon'94)*, volume 1, pages 65–68, Antalya, Turkey, April 1994.

R. Typke, P. Giannopoulos, R. C. Veltkamp, FransWiering, and R. van Oostrum. Using Transportation Distances for Measuring Melodic Similarity. In *Proceedings of the 4th International Conference on Music Information Retrieval (ISMIR'03)*, pages 107–114, Washington, D.C., USA, October 2003.

A. Ultsch. Proof of Pareto's 80/20 Law and Precise Limits for ABC-Analysis. Technical Report 02/c, Databionics Research Group, University of Marburg, Marburg, Germany, 2002.

A. Ultsch. Pareto Density Estimation: A Density Estimation for Knowledge Discovery. In *Innovations in Classification, Data Science, and Information Systems - Proceedings 27th*

Annual Conference of the German Classification Society (GfKL'03), pages 91–100. Springer, 2003a.

A. Ultsch. Maps for the Visualization of High Dimensional Data Spaces. In *Proceedings of the Workshop on Self Organizing Maps (WSOM'03)*, pages 225–230, Kitakyushu, Japan, September 2003b.

A. Ultsch. U^*-Matrix: a Tool to Visualize Clusters in High Dimensional Data. Technical Report 36, University of Marburg, Dept. of Computer Science, DataBionics Research Lab, 2003c.

J.-M. Valin. Speex: A Free Codec For Free Speech. Online web resource, 2010. URL http://www.speex.org/. Visited 22. February 2010.

F. van der Heijden, R. P. W. Duin, D. de Ridder, and D. M. J. Tax. *Classification, Parameter Estimation and State Estimation: An Engineering Approach using MATLAB®*. John Wiley & Sons, West Sussex, England, 2004.

D. A. van Leeuwen, A. F. Martin, M. A. Przybocki, and J. S. Bouten. NIST and NFI-TNO Evaluations of Automatic Speaker Recognition. *Computer Speech and Language*, 20:128–158, 2006.

C. J. K. van Rijsbergen. *Information Retrieval*. Butterworth-Heinemann, 2nd edition, 1979.

V. N. Vapnik. *Statistical Learning Theory*. Wiley, New York, 1998.

A. P. Varga and R. K. Moore. Hidden Markov Model Decomposition of Speech and Noise. In *Proceedings of the 15th IEEE International Conference on Acoustics, Speech, and Signal Processing (ICASSP'90)*, pages 845–848, Albuquerque, NM, USA, April 1990. IEEE.

R. Vergin and D. O'Shaughnessy. Pre-Emphasis and Speech Recognition. In *Proceedings of the IEEE Canadian Conference on Electrical and Computer Engineering (CCECE/CCGEI'95)*, volume 2, pages 1062–1065, Montréal, Canada, September 1995. IEEE.

W. Verhelst. Overlap-Add Methods for Time-Scaling of Speech. *Speech Communication*, 30(4): 207–221, April 2000.

W. Verhelst and M. Roelands. An Overlap-Add Technique on Waveform Similarity (WSOLA) For High Quality Time-Scale Modification of Speech. In *Proceedings of the 18th IEEE International Conference on Acoustics, Speech, and Signal Processing (ICASSP'93)*, volume 2, pages 554–557, Minneapolis, MN, USA, April 1993. IEEE.

Bibliography

P. Viola and M. J. Jones. Robust Real-Time Face Detection. *International Journal of Computer Vision*, 57(2):137–154, 2004.

M. Vlachos, G. Kollios, and D. Gunopulos. Discovering Similar Multidimensional Trajectories. In *Proceedings of the 18th International Conference on Data Engineering (ICDE'02)*, pages 673–684, San Jose, CA, USA, February 2002.

R. Vogt and S. Sridharan. Minimising Speaker Verification Utterance Length through Confidence Based Early Verification Decisions. *Lecture Notes in Computer Science*, 5558/2009: 454–463, 2009.

R. Vogt, C. J. Lustri, and S. Sridharan. Factor Analysis Modelling for Speaker Verification with Short Utterances. In *Proceedings of the Speaker and Language Recognition Workshop (Odyssey'08)*, Stellenbosch, South Africa, January 2008a. ISCA.

R. Vogt, S. Sridharan, and M. Mason. Making Confident Speaker Verification Decisions with Minimal Speech. In *Proceedings of the International Conference on Spoken Language Processing (ICSLP Interspeech'08)*, pages 1405–1408, Brisbane, Australia, September 2008b. ISCA.

G. Wang, A. V. Kossenkov, and M. F. Ochs. LS-NMF: A Modified Non-Negative Matrix Factorization Algorithm Utilizing Uncertainty Estimates. *BMC Bioinformatics*, 7(175), March 2006a. URL http://bioinformatics.fccc.edu/software/OpenSource/LS-NMF/lsnmf.shtml. Visited 18. March 2010.

W. Wang, X. Liv, and R. Zhang. Speech Detection Based on Hilbert-Huang Transform. In *Proceedings of the 1st International Multi-Symposium on Computer and Computational Sciences (IMSCCS'06)*, volume 1, pages 290–293, Hangzhou, Zhejiang, China, June 2006b.

R. Weber, U. Ritterfeld, and K. Mathiak. Does Playing Violent Video Games Induce Aggression? Empirical Evidence of a Functional Magnetic Resonance Imaging Study. *Media Psychology*, 8:39–60, 2006.

I. H. Witten and E. Frank. *Data Mining: Practical Machine Learning Tools and Techniques*. Morgan Kaufman Publishers, San Francisco, CA, USA, 2nd edition, 2005.

D. Wu. *Discriminative Preprocessing of Speech: Towards Improving Biometric Authentication*. PhD thesis, Saarland University, Germany, 2006.

D. Wu, J. Li, and H. Wu. α-Gaussian Mixture Modelling for Speaker Recognition. *Pattern Recognition Letters*, 2009. doi: 10.1016/j.patrec.2008.12.013.

A. Y. Yang, J. Wright, Y. Ma, and S. S. Sastry. Feature Selection in Face Recognition: A Sparse Representation Perspective. Technical Report UCB/EECS-2007-99, EECS Department, University of California, Berkeley, August 2007.

F. Yates. Contingency Table Involving Small Numbers and the χ^2 Test. *Journal of the Royal Statistical Society*, 1(2):217–235, 1934.

B. Yegnanarayana and S. P. Kishore. AANN: An Alternative to GMM for Pattern Recognition. *Neural Networks*, 15(3):459–469, April 2002.

B. Yegnanarayana, K. S. Reddy, and S. P. Kishore. Source and System Features for Speaker Recognition using AANN Models. In *Proceedings of the 26th IEEE International Conference on Acoustics, Speech, and Signal Processing (ICASSP'01)*, pages 409–413, Salt Lake City, UT, USA, May 2001. IEEE.

E. Yilmaz and J. A. Aslam. Estimating Average Precision with Incomplete and Imperfect Judgments. In *Proceedings of the 15th ACM International Conference on Information and Knowledge Management (CIKM'06)*, pages 102–111, Arlington, VA, USA, November 2006.

S. Young, G. Evermann, M. J. F. Gales, T. Hain, D. Kershaw, G. Moore, J. Odell, D. Ollason, D. Povey, V. Valtchev, and P. Woodland. *The HTK Book (for HTK Version 3.3)*. Cambridge University Engineering Department, Cambridge, UK, 2005. URL http://htk.eng.cam.ac.uk/. Visited 18. March 2010.

J. Yuan, H. Wang, L. Xiao, W. Zheng, J. Li, F. Lin, and B. Zhang. A Formal Study of Shot Boundary Detection. *IEEE Transactions on Circuits and Systems for Video Technology*, 17 (2):168–186, 2007.

H.-J. Zhang. Multimedia Content Analysis and Search: New Perspectives and Approaches. In *Proceedings of the ACM International Conference on Multimedia (ACMMM'09)*, page 1, Beijing, China, October 2009. ACM. Keynote talk.

S. Zhang, W. Hu, T. Wang, J. Liu, and Y. Zhang. Speaker Clustering Aided by Visual Dialogue Analysis. In *Proceedings of the 9th Pacific Rim Conference on Multimedia (PCM'08)*, volume 5353, pages 693–702, Tainan, Taiwan, December 2008. Springer.

S.-X. Zhang, M.-W. Mak, and H. M. Meng. Speaker Verification via High-Level Feature-Based Phonetic-Class Pronunciation Modeling. *IEEE Transactions on Computers*, 56(9):1189–1198, 2007.

Z. Zhao and H. Liu. Searching for Interacting Features. In *Proceedings of the 20th International Joint Conference on Artificial Intelligence (IJCAI'07)*, pages 1156–1161, Hyderabad, India, January 2007.

F. Zheng, G. Zhang, and Z. Song. Comparison of Different Implementations of MFCC. *Journal of Computer Science and Technology*, 16:582–589, 2001.

X. Zou, X. Li, and R. Zhang. Speech Enhancement Based on Hilbert-Huang Transform Theory. In *Proceedings of the 1st International Multi-Symposium on Computer and Computational Sciences (IMSCCS'06)*, volume 1, pages 208–213, Hangzhou, Zhejiang, China, June 2006.

Die VDM Verlagsservicegesellschaft sucht für wissenschaftliche Verlage abgeschlossene und herausragende

Dissertationen, Habilitationen, Diplomarbeiten, Master Theses, Magisterarbeiten usw.

für die kostenlose Publikation als Fachbuch.

Sie verfügen über eine Arbeit, die hohen inhaltlichen und formalen Ansprüchen genügt, und haben Interesse an einer honorarvergüteten Publikation?

Dann senden Sie bitte erste Informationen über sich und Ihre Arbeit per Email an *info@vdm-vsg.de*.

Sie erhalten kurzfristig unser Feedback!

VDM Verlagsservicegesellschaft mbH
Dudweiler Landstr. 99   Telefon +49 681 3720 174
D - 66123 Saarbrücken   Fax   +49 681 3720 1749
www.vdm-vsg.de

Die VDM Verlagsservicegesellschaft mbH vertritt

Printed by Books on Demand GmbH, Norderstedt / Germany